SHATTERED BUT UNBROKEN

SHATTERED BUT UNBROKEN
Voices of Triumph and Testimony

Edited by

Amelia van der Merwe
and Valerie Sinason

KARNAC

First published in 2016 by
Karnac Books Ltd
118 Finchley Road
London NW3 5HT

British Library Cataloguing in Publication Data

A C.I.P. for this book is available from the British Library

ISBN-13: 978-1-78220-349-0

Typeset by Medlar Publishing Solutions Pvt Ltd, India

Printed in Great Britain by TJ International Ltd, Padstow, Cornwall

www.karnacbooks.com

For Liam

CONTENTS

ACKNOWLEDGEMENTS   xi

ABOUT THE EDITORS AND CONTRIBUTORS   xiii

PROLOGUE
Anna and the missing memoir   xix

INTRODUCTION   xxi
Valerie Sinason and Amelia van der Merwe

PART I: VOICES

CHAPTER ONE
Remarks on the publication of detailed case studies   3
Richard P. Kluft

CHAPTER TWO
Commentary on life writing from survivors   11
Annalise, Wendy Hoffman, Alison Miller, Mary Bach-Loreaux,
Paula Bennett, Amelia van der Merwe, Kim Noble, and Joanna

PART II: TESTIMONIES

INTRODUCTION TO PART II   57
Valerie Sinason

CHAPTER THREE
History of trauma-related dissociation, with a focus
    on dissociative identity disorder   61
Onno van der Hart

CHAPTER FOUR
Cross-temporal and cross-cultural perspectives on dissociative
    disorders of identity   89
Eli Somer

CHAPTER FIVE
"Dissociating dissociation"—debates and controversies   111
Amelia van der Merwe

CHAPTER SIX
Variations in identity alteration—a qualitative study
    of experiences of psychiatric patients with dissociative
    identity disorder   133
Christa Krüger

CHAPTER SEVEN
Dissociative identity disorder, culture, and memory   163
Lina Hartocollis

CHAPTER EIGHT
The psychiatric comorbidity of dissociative identity disorder:
    an integrated look   181
Vedat Şar

CHAPTER NINE
Dissociative identity disorder and its saturation with shame   211
Phil Mollon

CHAPTER TEN
What's different about ritual abuse and mind control   221
Alison Miller

CHAPTER ELEVEN
Reflections on the treatment of dissociative identity disorder
    and dissociative disorder not otherwise specified—a closer
    look at selected issues   233
Richard P. Kluft

EPILOGUE   259
Amelia van der Merwe

INDEX   267

ACKNOWLEDGEMENTS

The editors would like to thank the following: Stellenbosch University, South Africa and the Mellon Foundation for their support, without which this book would not have been possible; the ethics and legal department at Stellenbosch University in particular for their interested and principled engagement in the conceptualisation of this book; Prof. Leslie Swartz, for his invaluable input and ideas, and support and guidance throughout the process of putting this book together; Karnac Books for its moral commitment to challenging subjects such as dissociative identity disorder; the RA/MC special interest group of the International Society for the Study of Trauma and Dissociation, and the European Society for Trauma and Dissociation for the important work that they do.

And finally, thank you to Anna for her courage and for the way she found her voice.

ABOUT THE EDITORS AND CONTRIBUTORS

Editors

Dr. Amelia van der Merwe has worked in the area of violence and its psychological consequences since 1999. Her research has focused on community violence, intimate partner violence, and ritual abuse and its effect on psychological outcomes. She has worked at the University of Cape Town (SA), The Policy Research Bureau (UK), the Human Sciences Research Council (SA) and the University of Stellenbosch (SA) in both research and teaching capacities. This is her fourth book, and she has written many book chapters and journal articles on the effects of violence and abuse, specifically on child and adolescent emotional and developmental outcomes. She is currently doing post-doctoral research at the University of Stellenbosch.

Valerie Sinason is a poet, writer, child psychotherapist, and adult psychoanalyst. She is a founder director of the Clinic for Dissociative Studies and president of the Institute for Psychotherapy. She is an honorary consultant psychotherapist at the University of Cape Town Child Guidance Clinic, and chair of trustees of the First People Centre, New Bethesda, South Africa. She is a patron of Dorset Action on Abuse (DAA). She co-edited *Psychoanalytic Psychotherapy after Child Abuse* (Karnac, 2008) and in 2012, she published *Trauma Dissociation and Multiplicity* (Routledge). She has published more than 100 papers and chapters, and fourteen books, including two poetry collections.

Contributors

Annalise is a survivor of ritual abuse, and has dissociative identity disorder.

Mary Bach-Loreaux is an American poet, artist and survivor whose work has been published in the UK (*Trauma, Dissociation and Multiplicity: Working on Identity and Selves* ed V. Sinason, Routledge, 2012), quoted anonymously in other websites and books in Europe, as well as published online in *Analysands Speak, The Psychoanalytic Experience* (ed Esther Altshul Helfgott, Ph.D. Editor), online on *FragLit,* Spring 2009 in the print journal, *Pine Mountain Sand and Gravel* and in their just-released anthology, *Quarried: Three Decades of Pine Mountain Sand & Gravel.* Mary has shown one-woman watercolors and fine arts photography in survivor shows in American cities. She provided the cover drawing (but not the design) for Kathleen Sullivan's book, *Unshackled: A Survivor's Story of Mind Control.*

Paula Bennett is a UK writer and survivor of ritual abuse. After years of work on the traumatic impact of ritual satanist abuse Paula Bennett (not her real name) decided to use her own lived experience to help others. One of the few survivors to speak to the press about the British serial abuser Jimmy Savile she always has aided police and parliamentarians. She has written various pieces on ritual abuse and is working on more.

Lina Hartocollis, PhD, is associate dean and director of the doctorate in clinical social work (DSW) programme at the University of Pennsylvania in Philadelphia. Her research and scholarly interests include cultural determinants of mental health diagnosis, clinical management of dissociative disorders, and doctoral education.

Wendy Hoffman is a survivor, a retired licensed clinical social worker whose practice specialised in treating the dissociated disorders, and a published writer. Her first major autobiographical book, *The Enslaved*

Queen, A Memoir about Electricity and Mind Control (Karnac, 2014) has now been followed by her second autobiographical book *White Witch in a Black Robe: A True Story About Criminal Mind Control* (Karnac, 2016). That same year, she also published a book of poetry, *Forceps: Poems about the Birth of the Self* (Karnac, 2016).

Joanna has dissociative identity disorder, writes poetry and prose and has been published in books on DID including *Trauma, Dissociation and Multiplicity: Working on Identity and Selves* (ed V. Sinason, Routledge, 2012).

Richard P. Kluft, M.D., PhD, practises psychiatry, psychoanalysis, and medical hypnosis in Bala Cynwyd, Pennsylvania. He is clinical professor of psychiatry at Temple University School of Medicine and faculty at the Psychoanalytic Center of Philadelphia. Author of over 250 scientific papers, reviews, and chapters, and editor of several books, mostly involving trauma and dissociation, he has presented widely. His contributions have brought him numerous honours and recognitions. His most recent text, *Shelter from the Storm*, explores innovative and safe approaches to the abreaction of trauma. Also a novelist, Dr. Kluft's *Good Shrink/Bad Shrink* (2014) explores the misuse of psychological science.

Christa Krüger is a professor in the department of psychiatry in the Faculty of Health Sciences at the University of Pretoria, South Africa, as well as a specialist psychiatrist and head of a clinical unit at Weskoppies Psychiatric Hospital in Pretoria. Her research covers clinical, psychosocial, neurophysiological, and cultural aspects of dissociation. She also serves as research supervisor to master's level and doctoral candidates. She serves as a director on the board and on several committees of the International Society for the Study of Trauma and Dissociation (ISSTD) and is a fellow of the ISSTD.

Alison Miller, PhD, is a practising clinical psychologist in Victoria, British Columbia, Canada. She has been working with survivors of organised abuse, including ritual abuse and mind control, for twenty-five years. She is the author of *Healing the Unimaginable: Treating Ritual Abuse and Mind Control* (for therapists) and *Becoming Yourself: Overcoming Mind Control and Ritual Abuse* (for survivors), both published by Karnac in 2012 and 2014. She is a fellow of the ISST-D, and is the Chair-Elect for 2017 of its special interest group on ritual abuse and mind control.

Phil Mollon, PhD, is a psychoanalyst, clinical psychologist, and energy psychotherapist in the UK. He is well known as a writer and speaker on topics including shame, trauma, dissociation, self-psychology, and EMDR—and has pioneered the development of psychoanalytic energy psychotherapy. He wrote the first British book on dissociation: *Multiple Voices, Multiple Selves: Working with Trauma, Violation, and Dissociation* (Wiley, 1998). With 40 years of clinical experience, in both the British NHS and private practice, he has explored many different approaches, always seeking better ways of helping those who are troubled with mental health problems. His work remains rooted in psychoanalysis, whilst also incorporating neurobiological, cognitive, and energetic perspectives. Most recently he has addressed problems of psychotherapy with ADHD and autistic spectrum in his book *The Disintegrating Self* (Karnac, 2015).

Kim Noble is a British mother and artist who has dissociative identity disorder. Fourteen of her alter personalities have now exhibited their art in over 55 solo and group exhibitions nationally and internationally. In 2005 she was the first artist in residence at Springfield university hospital. She appeared on Oprah Winfrey's celebratory farewell season and has spoken on various TV and radio programs. Her book *"All of me"* was published by Piatkus in 2011. She has written about DID in various books including *Attachment, Trauma and Multiplicity: Working with Dissociative Identity Disorder and Trauma,* and a foreword to Alison Miller's book *"Believing the Unbelievable"* (Karnac, 2014).

Vedat Şar, M.D., is a professor of psychiatry in Koç University School of Medicine (KUSOM), Istanbul, Turkey. He has published extensively on epidemiology, clinical exploration, and psychotherapy of clinical consequences of childhood trauma, complex PTSD, and dissociative disorders. Prof. Şar is currently president of the European Society for Traumatic Stress Studies, and is a former president of the International Society for the Study of Trauma and Dissociation. He has received numerous honours including David Caul, Morton Prince, Cornelia Wilbur, Pierre Janet, and lifetime achievement awards. He serves on the editorial boards of the *Journal of Trauma and Dissociation* and *European Journal of Psychotraumatology.*

Eli Somer is a clinical psychologist and clinical professor of psychology at the school of social work of the University of Haifa, Israel. He is former president of both the European Society for Trauma and Dissociation and the International Society for the Study of Trauma and Dissociation (ISSTD). Eli Somer is an ISSTD fellow and recipient of the organisation's Cornelia Wilbur and lifetime achievement awards. He is founder and scientific advisor of Trauma and Dissociation Israel and has more than 100 scientific publications in the field of trauma and dissociation to his name.

Onno van der Hart, PhD, is emeritus professor of psychopathology of chronic traumatisation at Utrecht University, the Netherlands, and a psychologist/psychotherapist in private practice. He specialises in the diagnostics and treatment of clients with complex trauma-related disorders, including the dissociative disorders, and his consultations, teaching and research are also in this area. He is a past president of the International Society for Traumatic Stress Studies.

Anna and the missing memoir

The inspiration and origin of this book was an African woman who has called herself Anna. Anna was a survivor of ritual abuse and her family are still alive and a danger to her. Anna told us about her life and wrote a haunting memoir. It had been our intention that this memoir be Part I of this book. We wanted to publish her memoir alongside the academic chapters in Part II, and now we cannot. During consultations with the legal department of the university where Anna has started her undergraduate degree, Anna became concerned that publishing her memoir would put her in danger. Co-editor Amelia checked with her own university, Stellenbosch, who agreed with Anna, so the book had to be reconceptualised. This first reconceptualised part of the book is dedicated to all those whose voice, like Anna's, has been silenced.

All our professional contributors, noted clinicians in this field whose work had provided solace and inspiration for Anna in Part II, have now been shown her silent testament. Together with the thinking of courageous survivors who have engaged with the issue of safety and speaking out in Part I, these two strands weave a banner of support.

As a way of reflecting on voices that are compromised, we include fragments, thoughts, and comments by a small range of survivors in the section that follows. We have tried to be representative in including an example of different choices made, being anonymous, using a pseud-onym, or using a real name. All have different views. There is no right or wrong in this. Each human being has to balance her own safety. Some feel safest in the full glare of public light and, not represented here, are those who have told a full and graphic story complete with names of abusers and details of abuse. Equally unrepresented are those who feel safest in their own silence. We hope the range of views here allows sur-vivors to consider their own options.

First we turn to the introduction to the volume, followed by a short commentary on some of the consequences of "coming out" with stories of survival.

INTRODUCTION

Valerie Sinason and Amelia van der Merwe

> And shall not pass them by
> Nor throw them crumbs
> > (From *A Soldier in Italy* by Corporal S. S. Segal, 1943)

> A new motto: "What have they done to you, poor child?"
> > (Freud, in Masson, 1985)

There is internationally the deep power of music, dance, and art with all the meta-understandings and meaning that come from them. However, our species depends on speech, on a voice to communicate. If a baby's cry did not resonate at a profound level, the baby would die, incapable of attending to her needs. We are constructed in a relational way, primed to hear and be heard. All around the world we are still dealing with the generational pain that was transmitted when a culture developed in which "children should be seen and not heard", where the unmet need of wounded adults meant there was no space for the actual child. And all around the world we are witnessing groups who cannot bear to hear the pain of others. Subjects are turned into objects by silencing them, not allowing them a voice. Sometimes "the other" is a child; sometimes the other is defined by gender, race, religion, sexuality, class, or politics.

Disability painfully enters here too as the child with a hearing impairment needs to be "heard" and the child with a visual impairment needs to be "seen" through other means. Our very language, even when trying to cover all, excludes and fragments.

The "other" who is the subject of this book is the child or adult with dissociative identity disorder (DID) and the adult or adults who professionally work with them. All experience society's fearful responses and discrediting processes that come uniquely with this subject. The fearful discrediting responses increase in relation both to the existence of DID itself, and to the nature of the abuse described as being part of the condition's aetiology together with the attachment pattern associated with it.

Van der Hart, Nijenhuis, and Steele (2006) brilliantly elucidated the nature of structural dissociation in which the ANP, the apparently normal part of the personality, in the dissociative system functions because the EP, emotional part of the personality, carries the pain and memory of the trauma, usually a child. In the DID field, itself an EP against the ANP of general trauma work, the situation changes yet again and ritual abuse (and mind control) become the EP. By the psychological processes of splitting and reversal, the emotional part of the personality then becomes experienced as the persecutory messenger, the perpetrator, the Voldemort (in Harry Potter language) who cannot be named.

Anna had presented us with a powerful memoir of ritual abuse. Ritual abuse exists around the world and yet evokes powerful negative responses. It was the ritual abuse she experienced which had led to her DID and both were equally denied. Even in professional circles that are concerned with DID there can be a wish to deny ritual abuse as part of its aetiology. Anna made us consider anew the social and clinical question—what does it mean if the abuse you experienced as a child or adult is not allowed to have a name and the condition it causes is equally denied? We are indeed seeing the power of our culture's difficulty in dealing with these subjects. However hard it is for the clinician or researcher, this pales into insignificance when compared to what it is like for the survivor.

Of course, the fact that ritual abuse exists does not mean that each narrative of such abuse is accurate, as Anna has been the first to agree. Similarly, the fact that DID exists does not preclude the possibility of confabulation, fictitious disorders, absorption, and so on. The same applies to narratives of mind control and specific groups (Illuminati/satanists, Celts, pagans, MK Ultra, Paperclip, Artichoke, etc.), and indeed any human enterprise. It must also be remembered that extreme trauma, particularly at an early age, can distort memory, and can be confused, merging with fantasy and magical thinking, which of course does not negate the existence of trauma, it just changes how it presents. However, it must also be noted that it is remarkable how little attention is paid, for example, to congressional records from the US, where, hiding in plain sight, the statements showing the ideology behind mind control experimentation can be found. Jose Delgado, professor of physiology at Yale University, was happy to publicly say (Congressional record No 262E, Volume 1178, 1974) that the liberal orientation concerning personal independence needed changing, as "Man does not have the right to develop his own mind. We must electrically control the brain." (Sinason, 2008).

Despite clinicians and researchers evaluating different kinds of abuse and their impact, and the neurological and psychological changes caused by DID, there are, as Van der Hart, Nijenhuis, & Steele (2006) point out, *ad hominem* attacks of a particularly vicious nature which false memory groups engage in, while Amelia Van der Merwe examines the nature of FMS responses. Our societal incapacity to deal with extreme trauma continues to haunt victims and survivors. Eli Somer, in writing about cross-cultural perspectives from Israel, underlines the importance of not being silenced and shamed and provides key international examples. Phil Mollon from the UK focuses on the impact of shame on victim and clinician alike. Vedat Şar provides a concerning and rigorous discussion of psychiatric comorbidities, and Kluft points out that "no single model has proven adequate" in treating DID. Hartcollis, in looking at culture and memory, shows how clinicians are turned from being co-authors of a narrative to sleuths in the face of social responses.

As a way of reflecting on voices that are compromised, we include fragments, poems, thoughts, and comments by a small range of survivors. Many different choices are made around levels of disclosure, of having a private or public voice, and there is no intrinsic right or wrong. Each human has to think of her own safety. We have tried to be representative in including an example of different choices made: anonymity, using a pseudonym, or using a real name. There are those who feel safest in their own silence, and who may never tell another and never go to a therapist. We hope they are represented as readers, although they are not authors in this book. Some feel safest in the full glare of public light, giving a full and graphic story complete with the exact names of abusers and details of abuse. The range of views printed here form a bridge between those two points in the hope of allowing survivors to consider their own options.

This first reconceptualised part of the book is now dedicated to all those whose voices, like Anna's, have been silenced. It contains contributions from adults with DID who tell us of the decisions they have made in order to have a voice. Some use their real name, and some a pseudonym. All give their own authentic reason for the choices they have made. All vary on what they tell of actual abuse and privilege us with their thinking. As their audience, we ask you to read their stories with open hearts and minds, and with respect for their bravery in sharing their stories. Many readers may recoil from some of the experiences they read, and disbelieve many of the—on the surface—unbelievable details, but we leave you with this thought: perhaps we react this way because of an intrinsic wish to continue believing in an essentially benevolent and predictable world, in a world many of us are familiar with and a world we know, which has none of the peculiar phenomena and evil surprises that Wendy Hoffman and Alison Miller, in particular, speak of. No one wants this fantasy world to be shattered, and many will fight, even illogically, blindly, to maintain it.

Part II provides a more academic response with key writers and thinkers from South Africa, the US, the Netherlands, Turkey, Israel, and the UK. Anna is not forgotten. All our professional contributors, noted clinicians in this field whose work had provided solace and inspiration for Anna in Part II, have now been shown her silent testament. Together with the thinking of the courageous survivors who have engaged with the issue of safety and speaking out in Part I, these two strands weave a banner of support.

A banner of support is needed for this subject. Our leading clinicians—Kluft, Van der Hart, Mollon, and Somer—who write in Part II have emphasised the powerful social fears surrounding these subjects and the discrediting process that clinicians face, both historically and geographically.

Our understanding of the psychological pain of others is not independent of the culture we live in. We take pride in our independent vision. Every day we fail people through the limits of our understanding.

Thus, we bring you this book to help expand our audiences' understanding. In 1966, while teaching infants, one of us (Sinason) commented on a "sexualised" drawing by a child, which was concerning and not fully understood for another twenty years. In the 1980s one of us (Sinason) published a paper about a child who spoke in different voices, not understanding she had DID until twenty years later. This brings about an internal shame quite separate from the shame experienced from outside attacks (the external response). In most subjects you can feel pride when you improve and learn more. In the therapy field, learning more means being aware that you failed previous patients. Mollon usefully emphasises the centrality of shame in this work, to the client, the therapist, and society. Let us try to unpack that a little more.

An adult patient comes to therapy with great shame and embarrassment. With great difficulty the patient manages to disclose that following the trauma of childhood abuse there has been nightly bedwetting, which has made the thought of any adult sexual relationship impossible. The therapist comments on how hard it was for this to be voiced and what a step forward to voice it. The therapist could have come from a range of different theoretical, cultural, and clinical backgrounds but the response is standard. Hopefully the painful sense of shame will have been momentarily relieved and a sense of non-judgemental positive regard will slowly be internalised. The concept of analytic neutrality was never intended to mean robotic or unfeeling. The point was that the therapist should not become the archaic persecutory figure in the patient's mind.

What would the impact have been on the patient if the therapist had replied, "It seems you have the perception you have been wetting the bed"? What would the impact on the patient be if a GP letter had also said, "Please see this adult who alleges nightly bedwetting"? What about an adult with a psychiatric diagnosis of PTSD being told by a senior police officer that they had "alleged" post-traumatic stress disorder and "alleged" flashbacks as the trauma had not been proven by law yet?

Let us take it to the ordinary human interpersonal sphere. A woman has just heard her mother died in a car crash. She rushes in to a friend's house, weeping with her news. The friend says, "I see. This woman who you say is your mother, you say has just died. Do you have the birth certificate to prove your parentage? Do you have your alleged mother's death certificate yet?"

We can see immediately that such a stance would mean the end of any friendship, unless the bereaved person sought out sadistic relationships. However, within the therapeutic sphere such a stance would also be profoundly anti-therapeutic. Yet when the presenting problem moves to the field of sexual abuse, all common sense disappears. Instead of accepting the patient's narrative, with internal understanding that any discourse is subject to error and distortion, some therapists feel compelled to sound like poorly trained lawyers or police officers.

Bedwetting, even if it is a psychological consequence of a crime, is not a crime. However, the lay therapist, faced with an increasingly litigious environment, can lose the relational link with the patient the moment a crime is mentioned. It is as if an adversarial non-psychological courtroom has entered the privileged space of the therapeutic relationship. Human relating is not the province of the courtroom, which has a different social task and function.

Of particular historical and legal note in the reduction of adequate therapeutic support and treatment in the field of trauma and abuse has been the impact of relatively small numbers of family members becoming spokespersons and prime movers for false memory societies (as Hartcollis, Van der Hart, Mollon, and Van der Merwe have written). Regardless of whether they are innocent or not, it is clear that their main attachment pattern is one of control as they seek to dominate the social discourse concerning the freedom of their adult children, largely daughters, to have a private reflective space. If they are not controlling the words and thoughts of these children they assume the therapist or other professionals are. The identikit of projection and reversal they conjure up—someone who ignores the sovereignty of the adult's mind, contaminates it with their own poisonous agenda, causes estrangement from the rest of society, and seeks to manipulate—is indeed that of a criminal abuser who recognises no generational boundaries.

This identikit is an accurate representation of the adult who continues an incestuous relationship right into adult life and, of course, there are a small percentage of therapists and other mental health professionals who fit this pattern and have committed a crime. However, it is of interest that false memory researchers rarely mention criminal therapists who sexually and financially exploit their patients or clients. Their focus is on those who, they consider, "believe" a narrative they, rightly or wrongly, do not accept.

In a context where, for example, in the UK eleven million citizens are considered by government to have had an abusive experience in their lifetime, and in South Africa 22,781 children reported sexual offences in one year (South African Police Services, 2013–2014), and 84% of those who were raped were raped by someone they knew (Vetten et al., 2008), the small number of allegedly innocent families in false memory groups have had to agree that abuse is more prolific than they originally considered. However, they can gain some validation by attacking the reality of more extreme kinds of abuse such as ritual abuse. Against a context in which the small number of allegedly innocent families appears to have a disproportionate impact as opposed to the eleven million citizens just in the UK who government consider could have an abusive experience within a lifetime, and the 22,781 South African children who report sexual offences, where does extreme abuse fit in?

In the UK the country was shocked by the multiple abusive acts of Jimmy Savile, a previously loved entertainer. Slowly it was accepted that he had abused physically and intellectually disabled children and adults while they were in hospital, he had abused emotionally disturbed teenagers, he'd had a key to wards in Broadmoor Hospital, and he engaged in necrophilia. But to abuse children and adults whilst wearing a cloak? No. That was not bearable.

For each step forward the public takes in recognising the extent and nature of paedophilia, there is one frontier that is too far to cross. Despite the amassed knowledge of ritual killings, especially of babies, across the ancient world, and the use of rituals or ritualistic behaviour in many kinds of abuse (Kahr, 1994), it would seem that the one way a paedophile can successfully commit a crime now is to wear a cloak and chant in Latin. Denial has to find a staging post, a place to state, "I can believe my country betrays its children so far, but surely not this far". The semi-secular society might find it more frightening to consider abuse within a framework of apparent belief. Even with mainstream religions, there has been enormous public fear at considering priests, vicars, mullahs, and rabbis could be guilty of abuse and using religious objects and words for that purpose. It is even harder to face the context of abuse in minority groups that are considered "way out".

Whether certain paedophiles are using aspects of religious ritual from a genuine belief system or to frighten their victims further is irrelevant. The fact is that it is successful. A terrified child internalises the threats of her abuser, especially when she is an attachment figure. As Childline pointed out in the UK in 1994, children do not ring a helpline saying they are being ritually abused, they talk about people frightening them who wear masks and cloaks.

Ironically, countries that are semi-secular or have a liberal existential sense of hell as an estrangement from God tend to react with more fear to the idea of ritual abuse within a belief system than countries that are Catholic or have malignant deities.

Perhaps it is the struggle between religious belief and disbelief, in a country which projects onto the reality of child abuse such a curious focus or fight. When we are asked, "Do you believe me?" by a traumatised child or adult, it is easy to answer, "Of course horrible things have happened to you. You would not be in this pain otherwise." There will be all kinds of distortions as memory cannot be total. However, to deny the existence of pain that caused a post-traumatic state is to take a very dissociative stance.

Anna has DID but she is not dissociative. Each part of her is alert and feels to the full. Slowly, in adult life, she has understood the tragic sequence of betrayal and pain that led to her condition. She is not a patient of ours. She is a person who privileged us with her presence. It feels obscene that her experiences are a subject of controversy, denial, discrediting, and shame. May this book allow others to voice their feelings or to feel that something in them has been acknowledged. Thanks, too, to the scientists and researchers who are finding other paths to social acceptance.

References

Kahr, B. (1994). The historical foundations of ritual abuse; an excavation of ancient infanticide. In: V. Sinason (Ed.), *Treating Survivors of Satanist Abuse* (pp. 45–57). London: Routledge.

Masson, J. (Ed.) (1985). *The Complete Letters of Sigmund Freud to Wilhelm Fliess 1887–1904*. Cambridge, MA: Belknap.

Segal, S. S. (1943). A Soldier in Italy. 8th army log.

Sinason, V. (2008). When murder moves inside. In: A. Sachs & G. Galton (Eds.), *Forensic Aspects of Dissociative Identity Disorder* (pp. 100–108). London: Karnac.

South African Police Services (2013/2014). *An Analysis of the National Crime Statistics: Addendum to the Annual Report 2013/2014*. http://www.saps. gov.za/about/stratframework/annual_report/2013_2014/crime_ statreport_2014_part1.pdf [last accessed 2 February 2016].

Van der Hart, O., Nijenhuis, E. R. S., & Steele, K. (2006). *The Haunted Self: Structural Dissociation and the Treatment of Chronic Traumatization.* New York: Norton.

Vetten, L., Jewkes, R., Fuller, R., Christofides, N., Loots, L., & Dunseith, O. (2008). *Tracking Justice: The Attrition of Rape Cases Through the Criminal Justice System in Gauteng.* Johannesburg: Tshwaranang Legal Advocacy Centre, South African Medical Research Council, and the Centre for the Study of Violence and Reconciliation.

PART I

VOICES

CHAPTER ONE

Remarks on the publication of detailed case studies

Richard P. Kluft

As originally conceptualised, the fulcrum and organisational focus of this book was to be a detailed case study. Stellenbosch University reviewed this proposal and declined to support it. This decision must have been difficult; both for the courageous woman who was prepared to share her personal experiences to facilitate the learning of others, and for Dr. Van der Merwe, who dedicated considerable time and effort to realising the book in that form.

Dr. Van der Merwe asked me to comment, knowing that my sympathies, however conflicted, concur with the university's decision. Granted, many have shared or permitted the use of their stories without apparent (or acknowledged) adverse effects. Their accounts have been invaluable in creating a more sympathetic environment for traumatised individuals and their treatment. It has been an honour to encounter many of these brave and generous individuals.

Sadly, I have met too many whose "going public" has had unwanted consequences, whose efforts to forge something constructive from the shambles of their tragic experiences became painful misadventures. In their zeal to tell their truths and achieve the praiseworthy goal of helping others, they often denied, underestimated, or misunderstood the risks associated with doing so.

The originally envisioned plan and format raise thought-provoking concerns which flow from extending "first, do no harm," the Hippocratic axiom, beyond the professional encounter between patient and healer to encompass a compassionate concern for the patient's overall future and quality of life. America's National Institute of Mental Health (NIMH) reviewed the problems associated with both giving and obtaining informed consent from a person suffering dissociative identity disorder (DID). The conclusion was reached that with regard to participation in a particular research project, if informed consent were given by any personality of a DID patient deemed competent by standard criteria for competence, that competent personality's informed consent would constitute sufficient legitmisation, across all personalities, for that DID patient's participation in that particular project (Putnam, 1984). That being said, I have profound concerns over the ecological validity of such consents for other matters and over time.

To explain further, the consent to participate in a research project rarely raises the risk of compromising confidentiality. Participation begins and ends within a discrete period of time. Usually, research results are expressed in pooled data. Individuals are described (if they are described at all) with no more than basic demographic data. In contrast, when one gives informed consent to expose a more detailed portrait of one's self to the professional and/or lay public, even skilfully disguised material may prove surprisingly revealing under certain circumstances. Further, once published or otherwise promulgated, it is public (or at risk for becoming public) forever. Many a DID patient looks back with severe regret and/or profound conflict upon a decision regarding personal privacy that seemed so straightforward and uncomplicated at the time it was made.

For example, a participant in a research project became worried that her taped interview would not be destroyed after scoring. Her tape was destroyed in front of her and her data expunged from the study. In contrast, a patient who had given informed consent for publication of some of her experiences as a victim of sexual trafficking in a professional publication told a trusted colleague that her treatment had been described in an article. Over time, that colleague and she had a parting of the ways. Litigation ensued. The colleague informed the colleague's lawyer, who claimed to have found her in the literature and attempted to intimidate her.

Hence, the ecological validity of the NIMH approach to informed consent when disseminated into clinical practice is questionable, and the capacity of DID patients to give informed consent in terms of understanding the possible future consequences of decisions to forfeit some or all of their personal privacy remains a matter of debate.

In the argument that follows, I am not terribly concerned about the possible conflicting opinions of various personalities. Conflict is a universal phenomenon. The clash of alters is only one manner in which conflict may be expressed.

Instead, my concerns encompass: 1) the cognitive distortions often concomitant with DID; 2) the transferential pressures toward compliance with the perceived demands inherent in the situation and toward enacting wishes to please particular individuals/types of individuals; 3) the difficulty many dissociative patients have in understanding the implications/passage of time; 4) the toxic impact of shame, often more devastating than the pain and hurt of a patient's actual traumatisation; 5) the fact that the patient who gives consent at one point in time may change significantly, and be very different from the more thoroughly treated patient who must live with the consequences of that consent; and 6) my distrust, based upon painful experience, of the judgement and discretion of third parties. My remarks here cannot do justice to the complexity and gravitas of these concerns.

Cognitive distortions and misunderstandings

A patient with dissociative identity disorder (DID) agreed to be interviewed by a prestigious television programme. Intoxicated by the prospects of appearing on national television, and grandiosely and/or altruistically and/or masochistically convinced that what she was doing would help others better understand DID, she dismissed her therapist's cautionary advice. She discussed her mistreatments in detail on camera and then informed her entire family, abusers included. Processes were set in motion that destroyed the social fabric of her life. She dwindled into a regressed and dysfunctional state, which has persisted for twenty-five years.

In comic counterpart to that tragedy, a DID patient of mine who was also a colleague gave me informed consent for the use of well-disguised verbatim notes on her sessions to teach a workshop at a conference she did not plan to attend. As I began my remarks, I saw her sitting in the front row of my audience. The trance logic inherent in her condition left her blind to the incompatibility of her firm statement across all alters that she would not attend with some alters' later decision to do so. I could not make my planned presentation. My desperate management of this dilemma is described elsewhere (Kluft, manuscript in preparation).

Another DID patient prepared an account of her experiences, including intrafamilial abuse and her sexual exploitation by a mental health professional, for publication. She understood herself to be an aggrieved victim entitled to tell her story. Her excellent manuscript was accepted for publication, but as her publisher's legal consultants researched the project, they learned that many easily identifiable others disputed her recollections. The mental health professional threatened legal action. Her book was never published. Feeling invalidated, she became flooded with guilt, shame, and uncertainty. She suffered years of profound turmoil.

Transferential contaminants to free will/informed consent

In conversations with several DID patients or patient/therapist dyads about going public, all too often it seemed that despite all other motivations and rationales, the patients were influenced by wishes or perceived needs to please their therapists (even if denied or unconscious). Once the endeavour gathered momentum, some patients, and even some therapists, feared rejection if they did not go forward. Sometimes both ultimately suffered serious consequences. Rarely the appearance of ostensibly successful therapies camouflaged boundary violations that would be omitted from the published accounts.

Difficulties understanding time (another cognitive distortion)

Traumatised individuals often have difficulty organising a meaningful understanding of their futures, a basic fact often overlooked by DID patients, therapists, and the media alike. Time itself is a difficult concept for the highly dissociative patient. Alters become inured to time loss, to being simultaneously in the past and the present, to making what is unpleasant go away and becoming amnestic for the missing time, and so on.

Dozens of my patients have uttered the same simple but profoundly important remark: "I don't do time." How can one give meaningful consent to the revelation of the intimate details of one's private life if one cannot anticipate the future as well as the current implications of such material's being in the public domain, however well disguised? One integrated DID patient's engagement was broken when her fiancé learned of the extent of her past sexual exploitations from an account she had written. The adolescent granddaughter of another came upon old tapes she had made and was devastated by what she learned. The children of another, to whom her abusive parents were adored and idealised grandparents, severed their relationship with their mother when she admitted that she was the patient described in a scientific article in which she had depicted her own parents as horrible people.

Consistent with their characteristic defences, DID patients often believe that their revelations belong to a moment in time that they can leave behind. But permanent records do not dissociate. Over time, some DID patients have recanted. Others have forgotten their revelations, redissociating both their experiences and the fact that they have revealed them. Unless a DID patient can think through the possible long-term consequences of the revelations that might be made in current moment, or grasp them with the help of an advisor, a powerful argument can be made that going public, anonymously or not, may be premature.

Shame

In addition to the pain and betrayal associated with traumatisation itself, the psychological sequelae, both immediate and delayed, must be considered. Not uncommonly, all the layers of pain and distress are not accessible at one time. Circumstances may require reprocessing and considerable time may elapse before the full force of the uncomfortable affects of shame, disgust, and dissmell (Kluft, 2007; Nathanson, 1992), almost invariably self-directed, make their way into awareness, either as they emerge from behind defences, expressed by a long-unavailable alter that has been containing or occasioning the affect in question, or they surface as patients' understanding of their experiences and their implications becomes more nuanced. When the patient who has gone public before these many layers have been addressed later experiences mortification and assumes that the world now knows how awful she actually is as a person (at least in the subjectivity of her own damaged self-esteem), the situation can become upsetting and fraught with peril.

Change

Simply put, the kaleidoscopic and complex mosaic that is DID must undergo profound transformations in order for those who suffer this condition to heal and enjoy an improved quality of life. Consent given when a traumatized and highly dissociated patient's demolished self-esteem does not allow that person to envision a productive future rarely can anticipate and take into account the consequences of that consent at a later date. One patient had made a phenomenal recovery. Years later, while running for public office, rumors vaguely related to published materials made withdrawal this person's most judicious choice.

The downside of trust

Ethical people often find it difficult to summon up and maintain sufficient suspicion to anticipate the nefarious efforts of those to whom ethical considerations are no obstacle to their pursuit of their objectives. DID patients often feel compulsive pressures to be "good". This may encompass the paradox of trying to think positively of others, notwithstanding their histories of traumatisation.

A patient allowed me to present her history and verbatim material to a scientific workshop. Both were distributed in a written form for study. Participants were advised both orally and in writing that this material had to be returned and destroyed at the end of the conference in order to protect the patient's confidentiality. Participants were also notified that for the same reasons, this conference would not be taped professionally, and could not be taped by individuals. Participants were also advised that there would be no discussion of the veracity of the patient's given history because the entire presentation would be made on the basis of incidents documented in legal and other official records—the only potential inaccuracies would be in items changed to further disguise the patient's identity.

A journalist attending the conference on a press pass surreptitiously taped the workshop. She did not return her printed materials. She included some of this material in a book purporting to be factual. She attacked me for not emphasising that the patient's memories probably were inaccurate and made myriad other inaccurate statements. I felt obliged to share with the patient what had occurred. When she read this person's remarks about her and the credibility of her documented accurate memories it destroyed our relationship, ended her treatment, and nearly occasioned her suicide. Confronted, this journalist became belligerent and threatened to make the confidential materials public.

While brief vignettes concerning patients offer valuable illustrations and often can advance the knowledge of the therapists who study them, my experience with more detailed and intimate accounts is that while they are far more instructive, they may have a problematic cost/benefit ratio for the patients. If an MPD patient wishes to write a first person account of her or his life, the act of authoring such a document may have profound healing power for the patient, and may facilitate treatment tremendously. But bringing that account into the public domain is a step fraught with peril, to be approached with great caution and with thoughtful consideration of possible worst-case scenarios. It may constitute a gesture of thanks to the therapist, better interpreted than enacted. Going public may constitute identification with a relatively benign aggressor, the therapist, and the effort to do something therapeutic for others. However, such identifications refer back to scenarios in which the aggressor does not have the patient's best interests at heart, so the patient's altruism in the moment may subsequently prove to be a sadomasochistic enactment.

My experience further suggests that if such a step is to be contemplated, it should be considered only when: 1) the treatment has accomplished its desired goals, and their stability is established; 2) the patient is strong, resilient, and well; 3) the patient has a stable life situation and a reliable support system; 4) if the patient's career goals necessitate graduate education, a terminal degree has been won, and prerequisite postgraduate experiences have been completed; 5) the patient's mind can engage in a diligent and searching exploration of the pluses and minuses of such a step; and 6) when private legal counsel has reviewed the situation in terms of possible negative consequences for the patient, both current and future. For example, the patient must knowingly forfeit "publication as payback", because undocumented accusations may prompt counterattacks and/or litigation. Detailed verisimilitude in the narrative may be associated with an unacceptable cost/benefit ratio in ways too numerous to count. It is of note that the DID author of a recent first person narrative, a prominent intellectual, went public to preempt his being "outed" in a hostile and destructive manner over which he would have no control.

Please note that I make no distinction between patients going public under their own identities or under disguised identities. Given the virtual lysis of privacy engendered by newer media, it is profoundly self-deceptive to proceed as if one's patients' identities can be concealed indefinitely, or with any degree of certainty. The names and identities of several famous patients, accounts of whose lives were disguised to protect their confidentiality, have made their way into the scholarly and lay media.

These are the times in which we live. For the sake of our patients, we must be mindful of their vulnerability and remember Hippocrates' sage advice.

References

Kluft, R. P. (2007). Applications of innate affect theory to the understanding and treatment of dissociative identity disorder. In: E. Vermetten, M. Dorahy, & D. Spiegel (Eds.), *Traumatic Dissociation: Neurobiology and Treatment* (pp. 301–316). Washington, DC: APA.

Nathanson, D. (1992). *Shame and Pride*. New York: Norton.

Putnam, F. W. (1984). The study of multiple personality disorder: general strategies and practical considerations. *Psychiatric Annals, 14*: 58–61.

CHAPTER TWO

Commentary on life writing from survivors

Annalise, Wendy Hoffman, Alison Miller, Mary Bach-Loreaux, Paula Bennett, Amelia van der Merwe, Kim Noble, and Joanna

Between the personal contributions that follow, we have inserted autobiographical excerpts from another survivor, Annalise, who has written many pieces on the subject. In these excerpts we include the hardest point of all. This is harder than the horror story of the B movie organised abuse can turn into. It is harder than any description of war torture. It is the L word—the twist at the start of everything: love and attachment.

Many themes so central to the suffering of those with DID are covered in the excerpts, like survivor guilt, body shame, rage, the reality of conflicting alters, memory, and the practical realities of living with DID. But the most recurring and penetrating theme is the deep and complex ambivalence towards the perpetrator. Mourning for the perpetrator is the core of everything—the heart of the bondage that holds so many survivors captive and unable to experience true compassion and love for themselves, which is the true beginning of healing.

The mirror

Annalise, writing under pseudonym

In the film, "The Neverending Story", the deadliest challenge the protagonist, Sebastian, must face is the mirror. Sebastian is as brave as brave can be. Many people run from this mirror before they can even see their silhouette, but I look into it every single day. Sometimes it feels as if the mirror is shattering, sometimes it feels like I am shattering, but I still go back and look because there is work to be done. So I approach the mirror, I glance at it, confront it, touch it tentatively, and eventually slip slide through the mirror, the looking glass, and glide into the deadliest of fractured memories.

Wendy Hoffman—survivor, and Alison Miller—witness

This section begins with the writing of Wendy Hoffman, ritual abuse and mind control survivor, and author of *The Enslaved Queen: A Memoir of Electricity and Mind Control* (2014), as well as *White Witch in a Black Robe: A True Story about Criminal Mind Control* (2016), and *Forceps: Poems about the Birth of the Self* (2016), who chose to write her story in her own name. The section ends with her therapist, Alison Miller's, narrative on how it felt to be named in *The Enslaved Queen*.

On writing a scary memoir and using my own name …

Wendy Hoffman

For almost seven decades, I had no idea that I had no clue about who I am and what my life contained. I thought I was simply a child of a middle-class golf-loving lawyer-father and a repressed, frustrated, creative housewife-mother. I went to college, and then married a thoughtless man (whom my controllers assigned to me), and who left me for one of his students after I had put him through graduate school. So many people have troubles like these in their lives. At least my husband didn't give me AIDS. Never did I suspect what emerged as I approached seventy years of numbed half-living.

I don't think I scratched for my hidden life or the secret memories I contained until I reached forty-three years old. At that moment, I had achieved a high point, not a low point, in my life. My father called me back from Chicago to New York City, supposedly because he had a heart attack and wanted me close, but I suspect he used that as a cover story. I had done the forbidden: I had formed a dance company and theatre. Mind control programmes in me kept breaking, and I had started to become who I am. The perpetrators who controlled me thought I needed to be re-sealed and watched more intensively.

During these years of my return to New York City, I began remembering the strangest things. I still did not know I had dissociative identity disorder, but I knew I had discovered a truth so severe that I vomited in an outdoor garbage pail on the corner of Columbus Avenue one morning. I had remembered black robes and body parts.

I ploughed through my life uncovering incest and sexual abuse by many people. I wondered why the pinky finger on my left hand looked deformed. And look at all those scars on my body! Nice Jewish girls from Queens don't have scars on their faces and thighs. Bold clues glared at me, but three more decades passed before I found out at last what they meant.

I felt ashamed (I still do) when I discovered that my family for generations back has been involved in ritual abuse and mind control. However, for me, and many others, I believe, knowing foul truths is better than icy ignorance. I would rather know. Never did I have an inkling of how horrendous the information would get. Conspiracy shows try to unravel some of these problems, but don't take in the extent of inconceivable evil. What adults in authority can do to children and the world would stagger anyone's mind.

I have been kept from knowledge of myself for my whole life. Every time the part of me assigned to live my ordinary here-and-now life peeked over barricades and sniffed something else within, every time I came close—they closed me down. My perpetrators sent me to specialists who sealed off my awareness of my true life.

In the early years of this kind of abuse being known, some people glided into positions of authority in the mental health field. They seemed to know a lot, and we victims felt desperate for any information. In retrospect, how did they know so much, before their survivor-patients and clients knew much consciously? The information was supposed to have come from the surviving victims. How did some of the pioneer experts get ahead of us? That kind of person—a plant, a double agent, a distorter—erased my mind again and again while on the surface pretending to help.

I wanted to share what I had discovered with society. I talked, exhibited art, lectured, presented multimedia performances, and started lawsuits against two of my perpetrators. But the professionals closed me down in a brutal fashion, in ways worse than what the United Nations protests against.

The human spirit can be like a branch cut off a flowering fruit tree. It lies on the ground and still sprouts buds. I lay on the ground, cut off from the trunk, but I still talked. Spring buds burst out of my dead selves, and some river in me still flowed with life. But I needed help. Had I not had copious, constant closedowns thwarting my path, I think I might have been able to unravel this mind control myself. But I didn't have that luxury. Thorns prevented every tentative, shocked step.

And then the sky opened. True, some force had kept me alive all these decades but I hadn't exactly had blessings. And then I did. My friend from decades ago, E. Sue Blume, author of *Secret Survivors: Uncovering Incest and Its Aftereffects in Women* (New York: John Wiley and Sons, 1990), persuaded Alison Miller, a psychologist experienced in treating mind control survivors, to talk with me on the phone. We talked late one night eastern time. If my destiny had many arrows, they would have all been pointing to this moment.

I was sixty-nine years old and talking for the first time to a specialist in this field who was not a double agent, who would not try to erase my mind and torture me. I had contact with a genuine human being. At least thousands of survivor victims need help and there are few genuine therapists. Here I was, an ordinary-front person knowing almost nothing, but straining to know the truth. At the same time, many insiders clamoured because the leaders wanted them dead: there is a mandate to murder me at the age of seventy-two. According to the beliefs of this anti-religion, their queens have to die at the international ritual called "Feast of the Beast" which occurs worldwide every twenty-seven years. I broke the rule and did not attend my death ceremony in 2009. That is when the leaders decided that I would be abducted and killed when I reached seventy-two years.

After asking me several questions, Alison informed me that my programmes were active, that my fully intact mind control needed treatment, and that she was starting to plan for her retirement. *All right,* my front person thought, *I'll work on my own.* But the insiders knew I faced danger and had to run for my life. Alison and I kept up an email conversation for about six months, and then the heavens opened again.

She changed her mind and said she would help me. I felt somewhat bad about interfering with her plans for retirement, but I had discovered my role as one of the designated queens of the Illuminati. The Illuminati is a secret society that attempts to direct the spiritual and psychic course of the universe. Its satanic kingdom divides the world into thirteen "counties", each having a designated king and queen. Prophecies and bloodlines determine who will hold these positions of royalty, often against the chosen victim's will. This person becomes a figurehead but, if he or she has psychic abilities, as most do, will also be a leader.

As a queen, I had been discarded long ago, but I retained a glimmer of wanting to help my "people". I wanted to be free so that I could help others. I didn't want children to suffer as I had. Maybe naive, but sincere. I wanted to turn hopelessness into hope. I knew no one else who could help me. Later, whenever Alison looked tired, I felt guilty. I used up a great deal of her time and energy.

With Alison's help and support, I discovered within myself sexual slaves, murderers, cult reporters, mules, terrorised children, Illuminati heads, resident queens, psychics, cult therapists, soldiers, porno actors, spies, thieves, memorisers, to name just some of those in tightly sealed communities and ghettoes that resided within my squeezed brain.

Some of that information came out as I had email correspondence with Alison and travelled from Baltimore to Victoria every several months for a week of intensive therapy. Even before I made the temporary move to Victoria BC, I journaled all my memories and sent them to her both for safe keeping and so that she could keep track of my progress and alert me to any implanted deceptions.

From the beginning, she encouraged me to write my story down, including the shame, fears, and humiliations. As long as I was writing it, I wanted my book to be published.

One of the big questions became whether to use my own name. This issue had come up before. I had done public work earlier and signed my work with my real name. I had never thought twice about it. I had appeared on stage during my travelling multimedia performances of INCEST: *remember & tell*; had often stood in the art galleries when I curated a group art exhibit, and later my own exhibit on satanic abuse; and had given lectures around New York City. It's easy to make a quick decision when you know little. I had also written a clinical book on ritual abuse and mind control, gleaned from my remembered experiences and those of my clients. The publisher had asked if I wanted to use my own name and I had said yes. With my permission, the publisher had even photographed me for its back cover. My perpetrators punished and tortured me for this bold move, but the parts of my brain that made the decision to be public didn't know of the torture sessions. I remained a blind robot at that time. This publisher withdrew the book before publication as the false-memory movement gained momentum.

When I first had contact with Alison, she was working on putting the finishing editorial touches to her clinical book for therapists, *Healing the Unimaginable: Treating Ritual Abuse and Mind Control* (Miller, 2012). I made a tiny contribution to that work and had to decide whether to use my own name then. Was this not my purpose in life—to expose this abuse, to make an effort to get it to stop, to devote my life for the sake of the future? Isn't this why I am alive? I asked whoever, if anyone, inside listened at that moment. I didn't know that I had just taken the first monumental step to break out of the mould of terrified slave and into the world of humanity.

The soldiers lunged forward and said, "Use my name, of course", but less militant others inside heard and said, "What are you doing?!" That disagreement alone began the panic. I could panic because I knew what my life contained and what the possible repercussions of speaking out would be. This time—because I had disappointed them, because they wrote me off and wanted me dead badly, because I passed my expiry date—this time, I knew I would provoke them to action. The internal pieces of me debated whether they could emerge from a thirteen-year closedown and try to belong to myself. Thirteen years earlier, my controllers had sent me to Maryland to a specialist in sealing off memories. She had kept me for seven years and had succeeded in making most of my life experiences inaccessible to me.

My insiders kept deliberating. Many sections of my atrophied brain protested. "Have we not been tortured enough?" "Do you want an agonising death?" "Do you want more electroshock—ice—head vices—drugs?" The children in me felt so terrorised, they couldn't speak. The vacillation began between wanting to be forthcoming and use my real name, and not wanting to be ostracised by my peers and society and maybe tortured and killed. My internal leaders did not want more torture, which unfortunately they got, but my purpose in life shone before me like a silver statue in rarefied air. In gasps, I communicated my fears to E. Sue, who communicated them to Alison and told her that she had better talk with me. Alison, whom I hardly knew then, told me to do whatever I wanted to do. She could use my information with or without a real name. Or I could withdraw my contribution.

A civil war waged within. For days, I rode on the crest of panic attacks. I felt dizzy from mental spinning inside me, coming from parts who had received training to spin my brain should I ever even contemplate freedom or telling. The angel who appears to lead me to suicide sprang up in my mind—another programme deliberately placed inside me as a failsafe measure. Both programmes blasted out because telling and trying to escape coated the air. During the day, I staggered to my job with difficulty.

Alison's publisher's deadline encroached. At the time, I did not realise what a life-changing decision I grappled with.

What is a life of slavery worth? That realisation represented a turning point for me.

"Use my real name," I said. Even after Alison's book was printed, anxiety continued. My inside parts worked through the programming without the "front" here-and-now sections of my brain even knowing I had been programmed not to reveal "on penalty of death" (that's how mind controllers talk). Eventually, the anxiety subsided and I became a chick breaking out of a shell. The shell represented tortuous mind-erasing-smashing-and-filling imposed on me for all of my unfortunate life. Those in me who took the cruel hits wanted no more. Those who discerned the future erupted. That the going-forwards won this battle had miraculous ramifications. I moved towards transforming into who I am today. With that urgent decision, I gave birth to myself. Months passed before I realised that I had made the right choice.

I have worked full time on recovery since my earth-shattering decision. At Alison's request, I wrote more for her second book, *Becoming Yourself: Overcoming Mind Control and Ritual Abuse* (Miller, 2014), which is for survivors rather than therapists. For *Becoming Yourself*, I never considered not using my real name. The decision flowed as easily as the first one stuttered out with difficulty. Some writers have excellent reasons to prefer a pseudonym. They may have small children they want to protect from reality or retribution, a career, or other good reasons. They may simply want to avoid what they consider public knowledge or disgrace.

On track to knowing what lurked inside, without conflict, I let pieces of me write their stories. I wrote about half of it before the move across the country. I sent an early bulky chapter to a New York City agent to whom one of my writing teachers, Kim Dana Kupperman, referred me. He appreciated the writing, even quoted some of it back to me, but he could not think of a single publisher who might touch the material. I scratched off New York. I sent it to Alison's publisher, Karnac Books in England, whose editors have the social consciousness to publish books on mind control and ritual abuse. The publisher agreed to take *The Enslaved Queen: A Memoir about Electricity and Mind Control* (2014). My jaw dropped open. I could not believe it. I wrote a thick book and was asked to cut it in half. I cut it in half, reluctantly eliminating many episodes and thoughts I wanted to include.

The question emerged again: What name do I use? Earlier I had ploughed forward not knowing what I dealt with. But now I had real knowledge and saw Goliath clearly. Three considerations sprung to mind: safety, possible lawsuits, and integrity. All that took deep thought. I also had to think through the issue of whether to name the perpetrators. And should I name the helpers, Alison and E. Sue?

In terms of safety, I was grateful to E. Sue for helping me at the crucial moment when she introduced me by telephone to Alison and advocated for me. I didn't want to dishonour her by not stating her name. I didn't have to worry about E. Sue's safety. I thought that the fact that Alison became my therapist would not put her at as much risk as her publishing her own two books and her many presentations at conferences on mind control. Alison said they don't usually take the chance of harming outsiders and exposing themselves to public scrutiny. What they want is secrecy. I asked them both if I could use their names and both said yes. I wanted to honour Alison without whom I do not believe that I would be free now. Why hide who she is? If either had felt their privacy would be invaded, I would have made up names for them, something like Eugenia Stein and Mary Turner. Making up names can also be a way of joking and having fun.

If I had used a pseudonym for myself, I might have been safer. But I didn't want the kind of safety that comes from hiding. I had done that for six decades. I thought, *Who are they to take away the rights to my name also? Who are they to make me cower?* And so I called to myself. I took my hand. I led my being, my soul, out of slavery. I shed the devastating lack of self-esteem they, my controllers, prison guards, and relatives, forced on me. I straightened my spine. I took steps in freedom. Light shone on me, covered my shoulders. My mouth opened. I told my story. I protected my telling by cementing my mind into one piece.

I am not who they made me into. I am not artificial. I am real. I needed my real name.

To some degree, whether to use a pseudonym is a moot issue for me. Even if I had used a false name, my perpetrators would have recognised my story. My sibling would have recognised my written voice. So the enemies who could endanger me would have spotted my identity anyway.

Also I hoped to name some names. If I wanted to use some of the real names of some of the perpetrators, shouldn't I then use my own real name?

Lawsuits would involve not only myself but also my publisher. I would have preferred to name everyone. Perhaps not the victims because they have to decide for themselves whether they want to be known in life. I don't think that perpetrators who severely damage others' lives and minds have that right. However, they can sue. And when they sue, they often sue the publisher. So the publisher has the last word. My editor thought naming perpetrators would only distract from the bigger issues, and no one can disagree with that reasoning. Moreover, there are larger issues than any one individual's identity. But if Alison Miller or I die in any way that could possibly be construed as suspicious, then a list of people's true identities will be released. Twelve individuals who live around the world are in possession of this list and will make it public.

I listed my deceased grandfather and father's first name, Max. He lived as an infamous mastermind controller who destroyed many young minds. He travelled around the world torturing children. I feel uneasy about having to change perpetrators' names. Here I am revealing the truth but having to disguise (and therefore protect) the bad guys. Most of the perpetrators would not have been criminal without extensive torture and mind control. Some took to it readily. Others hated it but could not conceive of a way out. Many people die trapped in these prisons. They die ashamed of the lives they lived and the legacies they've left though they may not even consciously know what their lives were like, what they were forced to endure and do.

A pseudonym can be more truthful than a real name. You can highlight a trait of a person and play on that trait. For example, if a character is full of herself, you can think of a name which suggests that. In *The Enslaved Queen*, I called a character who is self-absorbed and selfish "Marlene". I renamed some government buildings "palaces", the site of a military post used for closedowns, "Purple Fields". I had difficulty finding a substitute title that had not been used already for a Christian counselling centre that functioned as a front for a training ground for torturers. The evangelical church, which underneath is a satanic assembly, was changed to "Acres of Grapevine Church". Still, I would prefer to name accurately.

In terms of integrity, people don't want to hurt those they love, especially not their children. Out of the eight children I gave birth to, to my knowledge only one survived. I don't know the fates of five of my children. They were stolen from me as infants. The one I am sure of has a different family name from mine. He kept his father's. I didn't when I divorced. So people will not know he is my child. Therefore I don't have to worry that using my real name will hurt him, for he won't be linked to me. If we used the same family name, I would probably have deliberated more. The truth, however, is the only thing that can bring people back to their senses. I would have liked to name my son's father, my ex-husband, who is deceased and well known in the sports world. Alison points out that if I did, my son might have sued me. *How much should I care about that?* I wonder.

He and I haven't been in touch since I had to disappear and go into hiding. I am in hiding not because of the memoir that I wrote or my writing that appeared in Alison's books. It is because of the mandate on me, which I hope to prevent from happening. They would try to make my possible death look like a suicide. I am not suicidal and am in good mental and physical health. Or they might stage an accident.

I grew up under the command not to tell about my mind-control-created thousands of false selves with names and combinations of names and numbers added to crazy names. My goal is to find my real self, the one they extinguished and buried and tried so hard to burn out. Using my real name, even though my parents gave it to me, is symbolic of my transforming and belonging to myself, not to my controllers and abusers.

I could have written a novel about my life. People find fictionalised violence more palatable than real-life violence, but I am at long last exposing the truth, not continuing the make-believe. My many interior personalities chiselled from sections of my brain artificially chopped up have artificial names. My brain is no longer butchered like a dead cow's meat, and I have only one name.

I have endured the gruelling, albeit exhilarating, work of discovering my internal world, mostly to help others. I cannot leave this world without doing all I can for the people born into the web of evil and who suffered what I suffered. A prophecy, decades before my birth, named me as one of the queens of the worldwide Illuminati. Perhaps I still feel some of the responsibility of that role in life. My role now is to help people get out.

I am a salmon swimming upstream. I am compelled to lay this egg. I am old anyway. Even if I were young, I would do the same thing. Death will follow at some point no matter what.

Because of my past and who I am and what they put in my brain, I have had the impression that I don't fit into the world. Having written a book that some people read gives me more of a connection to life than I would have had otherwise. My life could have so easily been wasted. I could have been controlled, tortured, and killed with no record. Having some of the events of my life on paper documents that I lived, endured, and survived, and gives the message to others that they too can pursue freedom.

In *The Enslaved Queen*, I wrote about infant parts of me registering their experiences and holding on to the information, and then when my mind aged and developed, other pieces of my brain putting the infants' encapsulated memories (sights, sounds, sensory impressions, and emotions) into language.

Some readers of *The Enslaved Queen* have difficulty with the idea that anyone can remember what happened when they were so young. According to Allan Schore (1994), the only memories of the first year and a half of life that are available to us as adults, are "somatoform" memories (i.e., crude memories of bodily sensations or feelings). Because the part of the brain (the left hemisphere) that controls verbal memory and logic does not develop until eighteen months, "explicit memory" (also known as autobiographical memory) is not yet possible. Research to date shows that there is no autobiographical memory earlier than eighteen months. As Daniel Siegel (2001) notes, "the maturation of the hippocampus in the medial temporal lobe does not occur until after the first birthday, and is thought to be essential for explicit encoding" (p. 74).

Early memory may be different for the traumatised and non-traumatised mind. Here is how I learned to hold on to information until it became ready for words.

I was between infancy and two when my mother smeared faeces over me and placed me in a bassinet. My father/grandfather Max strangled me. He told me that he wanted me to remember everything he said. I registered the feeling that came out of him. My infant selves saw his face and his fingers, and heard his tone and his voice.

"Cynthia, write this down. I want her to memorise everything I say." My mother wrote down everything he said.

To me, he said, "I want you to memorise everything I say."

He put a screw in my scalp and said, "I want you to memorise everything I tell you." My scalp bled a little as he combined physical torture with verbal commands. He twisted my left leg from the hip. "I want you to remember everything I say." My mother continued writing on a pad of paper.

Mrs Twartski, my first handler-programmer, sat behind me by the windows and wrote in what I would learn later was my black book, the official record of my mind control.

Floater parts of me who had attached themselves to the baby-me and grew up with my body gave this information about the training to memorise. They must have matched the feelings to the sound and then the meaning of the words later. The perpetrators embedded the command to be a memoriser in my very young emotional state that I identified later as hopelessness. I knew what Max wanted, somehow, even though I didn't know what "memorise" meant.

My bassinet faced the wall but it was on wheels. Max said this to me every day in different locations within the apartment. He squeezed my neck. I floated away. The floaters watched him and me very closely. They decided to stay with this baby. They felt very bad for the baby, and decided to take it on. This cluster of floaters overhead resembled the dog in the nursery, guarding the baby. As they grew up, they did a lot of matching words and facial expressions and assigning them meaning. Most of me was in the body being the baby. The memorised words had a sound and a meaning and a little spit. Children like myself grow up very fast. There is much in my memoir that goes against what is publicly known.

Memories come out in scattered pieces. Writing a memoir helps put the many parts in order. I journaled my memories longhand, and then typed them into the computer. Still I could not hold it all in my head. Writing them as a piece of narrative helped me to understand, organise, and contain. I wrote in moderate detail because my memories came forth in a detailed way and because a real healing requires the whole story, no matter how excruciating.

It may benefit most survivors of abuses of this nature to write down their stories, to observe the reality of their lives on paper, and to tell someone, even if not many, who they are. Grasping reality can be like standing barefoot on burning barbed wire but it can also be liberating and fill people with joy.

When I finished this memoir, I thought I would take a nice rest, maybe spend time at the beach, but more memories and information kept pouring out of me. Just because I now knew a lot about my interior world didn't mean my insiders had finished telling. I recently—it is 2015 now—found children in my brain who were so terrified that they could not speak or move. They communicated with me in emotions and visual images. They must have been at least part of my panic attacks with agoraphobia (fear of leaving the house). They were too paralysed to join in the large wave of my integration process, which occurred in 2014 after almost a year of intensive therapy in Victoria. They had to be carried out and suctioned into the mass.

I never thought I would feel joy. Alison said her other, mostly integrated clients, feel it and I will too. I look in the mirror. My face sags and I look weary. But since the giant wave of integration, I have felt among many other emotions, a happiness, solidity, and expansion. In other words, it pays to go through the gruelling process of full healing.

I have told a good part of my story in writing, not so that people will know the bad things that happened to me, but so that the distortions of society will be known. These malpractices go up to the highest level of government, organised religion, in every field. I wrote *The Enslaved Queen* to encourage victims to come forward, not to be too ashamed to speak, not to blame themselves, not to think something is inherently wrong with them. We are the way we are because of what was done to us, and at an extremely young age. I also wrote to encourage society at least to take a peek at what really is sapping the environment, children, and citizens of strength and beauty.

Entangled attachments

Annalise, writing under pseudonym

The last enduring theme associated with my main perpetrator, aside from his role in my torture and ritual abuse, was his need for emotional enmeshment, to compensate for his profound abandonment terror, which resulted in my highly disorganised attachment patterns that have persisted into adulthood. That is, for example, what made him

very nearly kill me, when I showed signs of independence as an adolescent. My main perpetrator could not tolerate being alone. He needed
me to be fused with him, to complete him (because he felt hollow and
empty), to need him, and to "fix" him. It was an impossible task.

My main perpetrator alternated between profound closeness which
manifested as intrusions such as, for example, sexual abuse, which
was concealed as a means of "protecting" or "preparing" me for the
dangers of adulthood, and allowing absolutely no privacy (in the bath
or shower, in the toilet, on the phone, etc.) to the ice-cold dismissal and
disregard of me; complete disinterest and fearful, paranoid distrust of
me. This can evoke an urgent need for love and acceptance, which may
lead to trusting others indiscriminately and becoming very compliant
with others in an attempt to prevent abandonment from them. This of
course increases the chance that chronically traumatised people like me
will be emotionally or physically or sexually abused by others again.

The function of this extreme dysregulation in intimacy for me, aside
from giving me a please-love-me and extra compliant nature, was hyper-
vigilance. I had to be able to predict my main perpetrator's next move
at any given moment, so that I could protect myself. Was he comfortable
with me, trusting me; or was he starting to get angry-paranoid, slip-
sliding far away from me, usually into never-never land where he is so
deeply psychotic I cannot retrieve him? This alternation or dysregulation
has implications for my livelihood. Whether he will start on his tirades,
day and night long tirades; whether I will not sleep for days and nights;
whether I will go to school; how often or how severely he will drug me;
whether I will eat. So I became extremely intuitive. If I knew what I
was dealing with, I could protect myself better. I can smell a mood long
before it has landed. A hint of madness, and it sticks to me like Velcro.
I have been trained to track a change in the psychic air, to detect a switch
or a slippage, grab it by the neck, and stare it squarely in the eye.

Reflections on having my name used

Alison Miller

I first met Wendy Hoffman in 2011 by telephone and then email, as
she lived on the other side of the continent from me. My online colleague, E. Sue Blume, had known Wendy in the 1980s, when E. Sue
published one of the groundbreaking books on incest, *Secret Survivors*

(Blume, 1998). Wendy was then trying to write a book on ritual abuse, and touring with a multimedia performance piece on incest. After that Wendy had become more or less invisible for many years, working quietly as a therapist, and her first book was never published. As she recounts in her memoir, *The Enslaved Queen: a Memoir about Electricity and Mind Control* (Hoffman, 2014), she renewed contact with E. Sue in 2011 when questions about her own past began to resurface. At that time E. Sue was helping to edit my book for therapists on ritual abuse, *Healing the Unimaginable* (Miller, 2012), and her admiration for Wendy's early attempts to reveal this most hidden abuse led her to recommend me and make the introduction. Approaching my seventieth birthday, I was trying to wind down my practice. I was no longer taking new clients with dissociative disorders or histories of organised child abuse, because the extent of their trauma means the therapy process takes several years, and also, to be honest, because twenty years of hearing about unspeakable evil was wearing me out.

But E. Sue is something of a bulldog, and she wouldn't give up. She said that Wendy had been her teacher back in the 80s, and she owed her this. I could at least talk with Wendy, couldn't I? Smart woman, E. Sue; she knew that it's much harder to decline to help a person once you've actually started getting to know them. I remember my first conversation with Wendy, who is just two years younger than me. Between her years of active advocacy and her years of quiet therapy practice, Wendy had spent seven years and about $100,000 engaging in therapy with an alleged expert on ritual abuse. She asked me whether I thought all her "programming" was now inactive. Programming is one of the words that organised abusers use to refer to their splitting a child's mind and training different parts to perform various tasks they assign them, tasks that would be abhorrent to their conscious mind. I asked Wendy, by telephone, a number of questions. And then I told her, apparently emphatically (as she remembers it), that there was no evidence that any of her programming had been disabled; I believed it all to be active. Whatever her "expert" therapist had done, it hadn't in any way destroyed the mind control. Apparently this statement of mine gave hope to her hidden internal leaders.

We corresponded by email and the occasional telephone call. Eventually Wendy arranged to come here for an "intensive" week of therapy, and when she did we quickly discovered that her previous therapist had been working for the abuser groups who believed Wendy to be their property. Wendy described the way the therapist dismissed "demons" and "human spirits" by waving her hands a certain way, and I asked her to show me these movements. I suspected these were cult-created hand signals. I asked what had happened to the internal beings who were supposedly being dismissed as alien to Wendy, and discovered that these signals had locked them away in imaginary internal prisons, installed in her mind by her abusers in childhood. I asked to meet one of these parts, and discovered the internal gatekeeper, whom the other therapist had labeled a "human spirit" because it was named after an early abuser. Wendy remembers me saying, "Now we're getting somewhere." This insider (that's what I prefer to call the hidden internal personalities rather than "alters"), along with other internal leaders, has set the pace and agenda for Wendy's healing. I later discovered that the "Christian therapy" of this supposed therapist was supplemented by torture sessions to make sure Wendy's memories were completely closed down, so that they would never be accessible to her in everyday life.

I was amazed by Wendy's determination to recover, to tell the world about the abuse, and to help the next generation of survivors. And of course, I was hooked. How could I not agree to help someone with this degree of dedication to healing? I had no idea when we started that Wendy's story would take us into the higher-up circles of the secretive Illuminati, and to abuse by well-known public and political figures.

As I completed writing my book for therapists and embarked on a second book, *Becoming Yourself* (Miller, 2014), this one for survivors of mind control and ritual abuse, Wendy began her memoir. I was still refusing to take her as an ongoing client, but after she flew here for two more "intensives", we both realised that she could do her work best if she lived here. In the autumn of 2012, she left both her jobs, sold her house, and moved here, to live in hiding while working on her recovery and her memoir. Between our thrice-weekly therapy sessions, I read her journal and memoir entries to help me understand what she had gone through and was still dealing with.

Wendy and I spent many hours together through an intense and grueling course of therapy over a relatively short time period. At the age of seventy, she could not afford to take her time once she had found a therapist who was not involved with the abuser group. All she did, for a year, was work through her memories and write her memoir. These two things were the purpose of her life.

As Wendy's therapist, I listened to her decision-making process regarding whether to name names in her memoir, which describes unimaginable abuses she endured throughout her life. Quite honestly, I shuddered as I heard some of the names she mentioned to me, because they were public figures, and some of them are admired. The point of her memoir was not to blame individuals or to create a sensation, but to expose the rot underlying some of society's institutions, the evil that continues to be perpetrated on small children, and to show how it works through her own case. As I understood her reasoning process, Wendy wanted readers to know she was telling the true story of her life experiences rather than making things up, but at the same time she didn't want to endanger anyone, and she did not want to risk a lawsuit or any other form of retribution from anyone who abused her or whom she witnessed abusing others. Her final decision was to name only a few people, including me. She asked me whether it would be acceptable to me for her to use my real name.

Having spent many hours watching Wendy agonise through the re-experiencing of seventy years of traumatic memories, I did not want readers to think she could possibly be coming up with these events through simply a "vivid imagination". I had watched her begin each new piece of memory work with the bodily sensations of the particular form of torture she was beginning to remember, these sensations coming up days before our therapy session. She would also go into an emotional state congruent with the devastating experience. Finally, in the therapy session, she would access the "story line", the visual and auditory experiences, and the words that were said to her by her family members and/or handlers. Each bodily or emotional memory would culminate in a narrative of what happened on a particular occasion, or set of related events. The way the process unfolded simply did not allow for her to have made up these stories, something that would take planning in an organised state of mind. In any case, no one could think up such things; they are indeed stranger than fiction, and the Machiavellian planning that her abusers engaged in would be impossible for this vulnerable woman to invent while on my couch. Although Wendy's writing is clear and well organised, her vulnerability as she accessed each memory was very apparent to me, sitting across from her and recording whatever she said. Wendy's process was actually atypical compared to other such clients

I have treated, but it was very effective for her, as we did not have to struggle to reintegrate all the emotions and body sensations after knowing the content of a memory. She was going through all this in order to expose the abuser groups, who had believed they owned her for her entire life, and to give vital information and hope to other survivors.

I felt that Wendy needed my support not only in accessing her memories but in her important life goal of making them public—support which could be best expressed by allowing my name to be revealed as the name of the therapist who had witnessed and assisted in her recovery process. Since my name is now known in the field, it may lend credibility to Wendy's account, for those open-minded readers who do not come to her memoir with the agenda of disparaging whatever she says because it is about ritual abuse. At the very least, it means she did not invent the therapist who helped in the recovery process she describes in the memoir. On the other hand, the inclusion of my name may give those readers who disparage accounts of organised abuse more ammunition with which to discount what she or I have to say on the subject. People often come to this subject with fixed agendas rather than open minds. I imagine them saying, "Oh, Miller, you can't trust anything she writes, she was the therapist for the woman who wrote that unbelievable memoir", or conversely, "The events described in Wendy Hoffman's memoir aren't likely to be real, because her therapist was Alison Miller, who is obviously biased, and must have suggested such things to her". Let me state clearly that I never suggested Wendy's memories to her. If I'd known that she was at such a high level in an international abuser group which involved government and elected officials, I would have had to think even longer and harder about whether or not to take her on. But the journey of memory exploration has no route map available at the start, only a method of travel.

My two books on mind control and ritual abuse are practical guides for therapists and survivors. My own work as a therapist therefore needs to stand up to the scrutiny of readers of my client's memoir. Having shared in this unique experience with Wendy, I owe it to her to allow my name to stand as the witness to her process of memory recovery. Her memoir demonstrates her determination, courage, and sheer brilliance in the face of overwhelming odds, and her story needs to be known, as it elucidates so much of the history of organised ritual abuse. She is leading the way, as a true liberated queen would do, to recovery for other survivors.

After I wrote the words above, I encountered some evidence (through telephone calls made to me and to another therapist, which appeared to be from some kind of bounty hunter) that Wendy's abuser group was attempting to hunt her down. I began to wonder about whether I had made the wrong decision in allowing Wendy to tell the world that I was her therapist, especially since the abuser group has decided her "expiry date" and probably has a price on her head. My location is known. I mentioned my doubts to Wendy, and she responded, "I don't want them to control me like that. I would rather take my chances than be silenced just because they are tracking me." Although this worries me, ultimately Wendy's decision about her safety has to be in her own hands. She is no longer a mind-controlled slave. She is free, and she wants the world to know that freedom is possible and is worth the risk.

Precious

Annalise, writing under pseudonym

My first alter, in age, Precious, sheds a great deal of light on my under-standing of my complex, confusing main perpetrator. I will never get back what Precious had: pure, linear, coherent, three-dimensional, colourful, and lively memory. So re-experiencing my past through Precious is terrifying because there is no dissociative glass pane. No filter; no pathological fracturing. As my first alter, Precious had not been abused before, so her abuse was experienced as much, much more grave, shocking, and incomprehensible. She was softer, more sensitive, and more vulnerable, and less able to defend herself than the other, later, alters. She was all delicate and new. She had not learnt to dissociate yet, so when I have flashbacks, I actually feel her physical pain. She did drift in and out of consciousness, although I think this drifting was because she was dying, which is the physical equivalent of dissociation. Since I developed DID, and more alters emerged, most of my memories have had a surreal quality. I remember when I first saw The Persistence of Memory by Salvador Dali during adolescence; I slept with the art book that depicted it, because to me it was exactly how I saw the world. I think Surrealism is the artistic articulation of dissociation. So that's how my memories have been. Like reliving things with a warped goldfish bowl over my head. Some of the time, I don't remember day-to-day memories like that anymore, but most of the time I still do. The world can seem random and disconnected, flat and colourless, warbled and warped. Or when I have flashbacks, it can come screaming at me in screeching colours and textures that leave me exhausted. DID causes the landscape of life to change frequently. Every day a different landscape greets me. I have learnt that what comes comes, and to dedicate my life to the dissolution of the glass pane of dissociation that has protected me so well so far, so that I may experience this changing landscape, dissolve into it, and live.

Mary Bach-Loreaux, American poet, artist, and survivor,
writing in her own name

I don't ever publicly name my tormentors, and yet I experience vandalism, phone harassment, accessing, and intentional and unintentional retraumatisation. All of this makes me want to go and hide and never create again. I know that revisionist tactics still thrive in publishing and other media and I have been called evil in the art world for art that suggests that the effects of sexual abuse can affect the victim for life. No matter how good the therapy and the personal support received. No matter how sophisticated we are and insightful into our own backgrounds.

In internet and other instantaneous communication, information about me goes out a piece here and a piece there. It can be combined with information slips and cult knowledge, electronic surveillance or hacking. I have had them all, or so I believe. And I have written a fair amount of anonymous material ... And even put subtle clues into poetry in my own name, hiding it in plain sight, although my poetry isn't all biographical. But what happens with all this leakage is that it gets harder with each passing day to protect myself, my reputation, and my personal knowledge and wisdom. I have no retirement safety. Little chance of having it, so I am writing in my own name to have a legacy in the world. My intellectual property and the tears of my heart. I want to have a name, even in a world where I know that even some survivor vigilantes try to silence the rest of us.

My methods, psychological and spiritual beliefs, and healing style all differ from those of the majority of survivors who are using simple PTSD methods or cognitive behavioural therapy alone and where there is no depth psychology to aid in self-building. I am far more concerned with understanding myself as a foreign creature in a world that offered me no incubator or Petri dish or greenhouse to grow in. It is fine with me for integration to mean a certain ability to hold an awful truth in however many semi-permeable containers. I don't care how many I am when I die. How many we are. If I can understand the sequelae of trauma of any sort in another person, then surely God can and will know what to do. I am so thankful to have learned to weep, which I believe God does. Wouldn't I rather have been happy and clueless to evil? I don't know. That isn't an option for people born into holocausts, as children are throughout the ages. But when evil is made secret and denied, there is nothing for the children to become.

> the artists and poets in me are dying
> because my friend has demanded that i make her smile
> with every contact. shall i grab the corners of her mouth
> and pull them into position?

> shall i hold the hand of the child being
> stabbed in a piece of cultic theatre and pull
> it from the hands of the murderer and nail
> it to the other wall. what will it do
> to the soul of my friend when her pulled
> back mouth seems to be a grin at the
> spread and pierced child before her.

> i can't be a grandmother.

> suppose grandma moses had a mentor
> who helped her become an insider artist
> with grants and forms? suppose her dress had been pulled off
> and she had been dressed in the singer tissue paper
> dressmaker's pattern. showing that her skin
> was creped and she had been stood in front of
> the coliseum of critics and teachers
> and made to be rembrandt, both old
> and traditional. where would be the breath and the light?

> oh, god, thank you for not letting me meet van gogh.
> what would it have done to his soul
> when i told him what i always say ... "van gogh
> is said
> to be

an
ac
a
de
mic
ar
tist,
but have you noticed his bed doesn't sit on the floor?"

i know i would have helped him. maybe another ear
fallen to the floor
or bullet in the grass
years earlier.
But
what if i had paid him
for one of his paintings. yes,
poor of course. i am poor,
but suppose
just suppose that theo
had paid for the canvas and paint
and vincent had labored in love
and then i had paid him something
for his labour, for his intellect,
for a bit of his tortured soul.

and suppose he had taken my pittance
and bought some soup to wet his mouth
and bread to refresh him.

still no meat for his muscles
to keep
his heart beating.

his heart was a muscle, and
he was filling museums while hungry
and discouraged and with
his
narcissistic
wound.

What
if i had given vincent van gogh

twenty-five dollars for his thirty hours
of work, i'd have been laughed out of arles
for feeding a beggar whose brother
had paid for the materials.

art is a hobby. painting is being a dilettante.

in 2014 printers
are paid well enough
for copying fine art to hang
on the walls of the middle class
who feel no guilt at paying
for that but wouldn't
have paid the wild man
of arles or grandma moses
dressed in a paper pattern
with cutting and pinning marks
as her only covering.

i have creped skin
and holes in my jeans
and because
of the critics
unpaid dilettante
critics, busying their bodies
with unwitting heart stabs

because i can't
do anything with my poetry
and eschewing my low
self-esteem and failure
to make a grandmother smile,

i have to learn
about creativity from my
life mentor, the gifted poet
who dares not say when she likes
something i write because i will think
she doesn't love me if i can't write well
the next time. and so i can't let her
heal my wound
because i'm too old

and didn't buy my own supplies or
remember to eat and sleep.
instead i must hide from her
in the back row of her arts talk
in a shining city
as it chokes and sputters for bandwidth
and there i am allowed to learn from her
without having to fear i
will
cut
off
my
ear.
and the
reproduction companies
are respected.

with my paper pattern dress ripped
and my fear xeroxed and tattooed
on my broken skin
i am bringing me to my poet healer
and she will hold me with her voice
and believe i will become free
i will let her see
that my naked half-hid skin
was tattooed in layers for years
and i will read her books and wait
because she mustn't give me cheap praise
but her heart is moved and her words
and voice and lent out walls
will contain and heal me.

and she and i will encircle the dying
poets and picture makers with our dreams
and our anger and respect
and we will with that hard hard work
heal me. prevented from throwing
the slash of demand, with smiles,
into the fire, we won't erase the spread,
pierced child dying. we will remember her

and mend her, stitching her along dotted lines
and wailing at the walls—in freedom
we will grieve for her and god will smile,
thankful to hold her to his breast.

Glass prison

Annalise, writing under pseudonym

At the end of *Life of Pi* (Martell, 2002), the interviewer asks the narrator which version of his story is "true", and the protaganist answers: "Which story do you prefer?" I will fight the "truth" I do not prefer, which still prevails; my first alter's simple "story" that I loved my main perpetrator, that he loved me, and that he and others hurt me because I was and am bad, and that I have to be punished for the rest of my life. I prefer an alternative "story" where I complexly and paradoxically love my main perpetrator; that I long-yearn-ache for him, but he cannot love me. He hurts me because he is unconsciously playing out his own hurt, and that I don't have to suffer because of it anymore. I no longer have to be punished. For this to happen, I have to get angry. Reject the "story" I do not prefer, the one where I have my identity cracked-splintered-fractured and moulded forcefully to the point that I sometimes sit night after night with murderous feelings towards my constructed, but authentic, shamed self, daring myself to die.

Irrespective of which "story" I choose, the fact is I have lost my main perpetrator, who played such an important role in my life. The words still taste strange in my mouth. It is a statement so deep and profound it leaves me achingly, suffocatingly speechless. This longing, this loss of my many-faced perpetrator, the life-long grief process I have only just begun to glance at, leads me to night after night of dissociative fugue states. They begin with me, switched to a little girl(s) of about four or five, talking in my sleep at night, sometimes all night, to my stony-faced perpetrator. I am trying to get him to listen to me.

Wake up!! I speak to him quietly at first, but as the night progresses and I get no response from him but a glassy-eyed stare, I begin to get panicky and I talk more urgently. I talk all night. I keep my husband awake. I begin to sleepwalk, and I have absolutely no idea whose house I am in. I am looking for my main perpetrator. I realise, gradually, that what I am trying to do is undo the past, prevent it from happening by waking my perpetrator up and warning him, and ensuring that he at best, prevents any further torture from happening, and at least, that he provides me with his protection. I am hammering at the glass pane between me and him to tell my perpetrator what is going to happen if he doesn't wake up from his trance, which he would remain in for the duration of my torture. I am desperate terror-stricken driven half mad scratching biting like a lunatic in my sleep pulling bits of my hair out to make what is to come STOP. I stop speaking. I start screaming please listen please please. I start to beg plead choke in my sleep and my body goes stiff, arms thrown backwards, back arched from the stress of my failed attempts to reach him. I wrestle struggle fight with a "claustro-phobic terror of (his) muteness" (Frank, 1995, p. 109).

I decide to tell my psychiatrist, who puts me on a sleeping pill that makes me sleep so deeply that I cannot engage in my dissociative dialogue with my imaginary perpetrator. But one night I take it too early, and at four in the morning, it all starts, but with a difference: I am there, the Annalise part of me. It is a simple dream-hallucination. "I" am two of my young alters, Ruby and Lilly. They have endured unspeakable things. They are around four or five. In the dream-hallu-cination they have melted into one, and they are pushing an old-fash-ioned pram up and down, up and down. Inside lies a baby, who is half me, half my sister. It is my task to protect the baby. I remember every detail of the pram. It is navy blue, its hood is up, and it has a water-proof mattress with bunnies and balloons on it. Behind it stands my main perpetrator, frozen, his facial muscles slackened as they do when he dissociates. Ruby and Lilly are at first talking and then screaming garbled terror, and then giving up, defeated. They decide that maybe they could reach him if they talk about less threatening things. So they start telling him about their day, and about what they observe around them. But tears are streaming down their face, because my perpetra-tor's paralysed face does not move. At this point, out of these two little parts, grows Kali, who is my last alter, the part of me with the heart of a fighter. She tries with violence to reach my perpetrator. Screams, threats, terrorisations, intimidations. But my perpetrator remains deaf, blind, fish-bowl eyes. It is only then that the adult me, Annalise, walks up behind all three of these parts of me, with the tears pouring down their face and strokes their faces, closes their eyes, dries their tears, and tells them to "shh, shh, he is never going to hear". I could not undo what was to happen. It will always turn out to be the heartbreaking catastrophes they were, but for me only. It was the catastrophes he did not see, hear, or consciously experience in his silent, slackened, dead-paralysed glass prison.

Paula Bennett, UK writer and survivor,
writing under pseudonymn

I believe that it is important to write about our trauma and experiences so that other people out in the world do not feel they are going through these things alone. The most important thing is that we always use a pseudonym and do not use any name that can be recognised by those who may read a book, paper, or chapter. It is particularly important not to name places where you were abused and say where you are writing from at the time. There is always an element of fear when exposing our past, especially within cult families who programmed such fears in us from childhood and made threats concerning people who we love and care for also being in danger. This increases the anxiety of telling and not being believed, and like this survivor—Anna—being forced to keep quiet because she will be in further danger and possibly be sued.

The danger and trauma we experienced through our abusers within our cult families, either through satanic ritual abuse or ritual satanic abuse and mind control was so traumatic for the survivors that being forced to stay silent becomes a way of life. There needs to come a time when those who have been through their journey long enough realise that most of the threats spoken were not carried out after all, and were basically scaremongering and a way of keeping those who are speaking out under a continuous wave of deep-rooted fear.

Yes, many of us may still have our cult family members, or people who are linked to our past, alive and well around us, and some of the people still going back under duress do need to be careful and possibly wait until they are stronger mentally and emotionally, and are physically distanced from their abusers before taking such a huge step in speaking out. I believe that there has to come a time for some of us to have our voices heard and unleash the hold that has kept us under all our lives. This has to be an individual's choice and most importantly, the person or persons must have had, or must still be getting, the support needed to face this milestone event because, although one wants to be brave and speak out, underneath there is always going to be some anxiety and pressure from within and even more pressure, perhaps, without.

In the last few years I made the decision to speak out against my abusers in professional groups concerned about ritual abuse. I felt that it was time for me to go against what I was always taught, which was to keep silent because no one would believe me, or they would think I was mad. I had written a few papers on my personal experiences by this time, but I came to a place where that was not enough anymore. I came to believe it was time to stand with others with dissociative identity disorder and tell my story, hoping it would help others like myself. It was an extremely big thing to do and I was very fearful and anxious, as I had never talked publicly before about the horrific abuse I was made to suffer. It was daunting but I was helped by my therapists at the time and got massive support. I managed to speak and keep eye contact, which was rather a big issue for me personally. This was due to thinking I would not be believed, or would be punished for breaking the long silence that was ground into me from very early childhood. I received a very good response after I spoke where colleagues came up to me and said that they either cried or something in them was stirred deeply. I found myself thinking with shock that this really happened to me and wondering how I survived.

After the seminar I was asked if I would write a chapter on my experiences of satanic ritual abuse and I found myself saying I would. As I started to write my chapter I realised I was doing it in a very detached way so that I could actually do the piece of writing asked of me. The writing of the chapter seemed to just flow easily and after a good friend helped me with the grammar and sentence structuring and proofreading it was finished. That was when I had a complete reality check; this was my life written in black and white for many to read. I only hoped that others who had also gone through what I did could find their voices and be brave enough to seek the help they might badly need, like I did.

Recently when a news-breaking story came out exposing the late Jimmy Savile for many offences of sexual abuse and more against young girls all over the country, I knew it was time to talk to the papers. I had been abused by him in a satanic ritual abuse ceremony and knew there was more to him than the papers were saying. I felt it was extremely important to support those who had been brave enough to speak of the atrocities he caused to hundreds of young girls and to speak up alongside these brave women who had taken years to expose him. I was fortunate to be able to speak to a journalist with the *Sunday Express* and give my account of the trauma and abuse he had put me through, as I knew I would not be the only one to suffer this sort of sick abuse. For me it was not about selling my story but about giving as accurate an account as possible to show other people what the man had been capable of over the decades. This was a very significant time for me; I had just terminated with my therapist of nearly nine years and had taken on a new therapist, and I realised it was through them that I now had the courage to speak out against my abusers. I no longer wanted to keep quiet and live under secrets forced on me from childhood. This decision took a great deal of courage and I couldn't quite believe I had done this after so many years of keeping quiet. I felt there is a time when you are ready to speak out and this was an important step for myself and the other victims of Jimmy Savile.

After this milestone I decided that I had to go to the police who were investigating Jimmy Savile under operation Yewtree, so I went with two people for support on the day of the interview to give a detailed account to the people who were running the investigation. This was not easy by any means and I knew this was a risky thing to do, but knowing what I did, I could no longer keep quiet. I had been to the police before in my local area and wider afield and received good support that has kept me safe and alive for over a decade now. I know I would not have been able to take such courageous steps as I have done over the last few years if I did not have the support I do, so this has made it easier to speak out. I am very aware that not all survivors can take such steps, so if I can then I will do so for those who cannot for whatever reason. This does not mean others who don't speak out are weak, instead they are being wise and mostly keeping themselves and their families safe, and this is okay too. It has taken me many years of hard work in therapy to get to this place and even now at times I still get nervous over the fact that I have spoken out so boldly, but in myself I knew that for me this was the right time.

For myself, I have come to a place where those who were my abusers have done all the damage to my life that they can do, and nothing they try to come up with now to make me think I am missing out on anything surprises or shocks me. Yes, I confess there is a large element of pain I still experience but I now tell myself that I am bigger than them, that it is sad if that is all they have to get my attention. They must live a very boring and empty life if all they do is continue to try to get me back to the cult, when they know nothing they have threatened me with so far has enticed me or sent me back to their evil sick lives. Sadly and tragically many people are given a false sense of hope, such as, if you come back you will be able to see your child or something very precious to you. Basically it is a very bitter pill because no such offer is real—just another chance to cause further atrocities to you personally, and so many times we are so desperate to see a loved one we sadly get pulled in to that trap.

Among the many good bits of advice I was given through my time in therapy was to make yourself known, get out there and let people recognise you, put yourself in places that are safe and you will see, people often do not forget a face. This I found a very important thing to take on board eventually, and now I am out of therapy and moving on I am making sure, first, that I am safe, that I find good people around me and very importantly, letting those who care for me know where I am going and with whom. I am standing firm in my life choices and wanting to get out into the world, and hopefully be a pioneer for those who are still fighting to stay away from their abusers and for those who never got the chance. I will take every opportunity I can to speak up and against those who damaged my life and to be a voice to those still struggling to stay away. This is no easy feat because to do this one sometimes has to let go of those we love, which we all need and are entitled to. Walking away can leave you feeling desolate, isolated, and extremely lost and orphaned, but the most important thing I have learnt over the years is that it is safe to make my own friends and good support networks which I know I can go back to if I have any concerns, anxiety or fear. You sadly cannot change your past as it has already happened but one does have the chance to change the present and future; it does not have to remain the same. It is very important not to put yourself in high-risk situations and to make sure you are alert at all times, especially around bad dates or personal dates that trigger you personally, but don't let these times govern your life. You are not a survivor for nothing. Always remember that, make your own precious memories, ones that will give you a smile or a laugh.

Please, fellow survivors do not give up writing, speaking, and telling your stories: this is so important. There will always be people out in the world, who don't want to believe, but there are many who are suffering such abuse even in today's world, and sadly this is happening more and more. Those who work with satanic and ritual abuse and mind control, need us, the ones who lived it and are still doing so, to stand together and stop this happening to further generations of our families and loved ones. We, the survivors, need to stand and say, "Enough is enough." This has to end here, this is my goal—that others do not suffer like I did for so many years, taking a long and traumatic journey to healing so that I can live the next phase of my life the way I choose to. It is not always easy and I still panic at times, but I know now I can live through it and get out the other side because I know where I have come from and where I now wish to go.

A pane of glass

Annalise, writing under pseudonym

There is a staggeringly beautiful quote by the author Martha Beck (2005b), who in her recent autobiography refers to her identification with Virginia Woolf, who was never able to free herself from the bondage, the paralysis, the numbness of dissociation. Beck says:

> I am endlessly grateful for the fact that I was lucky enough to learn something Virginia Woolf never realized: glass can melt. It melted for me when I began allowing myself to know what I already knew, to feel consciously the pain I'd been ignoring almost all my life … Call it awakening, call it being born again, call it whatever you like; but the sensation of my disowned self moving back into my body was so strange and delicious that it occupied much of my attention for many months. In the words of another female writer, Emily Dickinson, "to live is so startling it leaves little time for anything else". (Beck, 2005, p. 220)

I don't want to take away from the beauty of this quote, but I think it is dangerous for some, perhaps not for others, this notion of psychic glass melting. I don't want my glass to melt. I do not want to "integrate", become one person, although I have great respect for those who do aspire to this goal. Dissociation has saved my life, and continues to do so. I have been through too much trauma for one person to contain or to bear. I am aiming for co-consciousness—where all the alters know about each other, I am able to hold them in consciousness, and live alongside their memories to the best of my ability, hopefully most of the time, without being catapulted into hell.

Imagine not having those dissociative barriers. I would never emerge from an eternal descent into a hellish madness. As it is, I have a significant disability, and I am extremely privileged in terms of psychiatric, psychological, and social support. I've learnt to live with it. So do those around you, if they love you enough. I have to fight every day to live with my shame, my survivor guilt—a hopelessly inadequate term. I have to fight every day to believe I have the right to live. I have to fight the instinct not to give in to that seductive perpetrator-defined identified identity; the internalised voice that whispers to me, *punish yourself punish yourself you know you do not deserve to live.* Every day. I struggle deeply and pervasively with owning the beautiful house I live in, my education, my ability to eat and buy clothes whenever I want. I still sometimes have to hold onto my plate of food, thinking it is going to disappear. And I always, always, buy too much food during our weekly grocery shopping, so much so that my fridge is always bursting. And sometimes I still have to binge shop because I am scared the money will suddenly run out and I will be left with nothing.

At the time that I was processing memories, DID affected my daily life, and those around me, in profound ways. When things were hard I didn't drive because sometimes I switched and the little parts didn't know how to drive and this led to very dangerous situations. I was in daily psychiatric or psychological treatment during which, at times, we processed memories that caused such immense emotional upheaval that I had to be sedated afterwards. That meant that I had to sleep on those days and struggled to stay up after eight o'clock at night. It was very difficult to explain to people to whom I was not necessarily emotionally close enough to want to share my diagnosis, particularly colleagues. I had to come up with countless lies why I couldn't attend meetings, or other collegial get-togethers. Luckily I work extremely fast, and I was highly productive in the moments I snatched when I was awake. Things changed though, and I have to work through memories less and less, and I have to be sedated to the extent that I have been in the past, just in order for me to live, far less frequently. I will not be defined by my past. I have, despite considerable distress, completed my studies. I have managed to keep a job throughout my journey through the past, and I have excelled. I have married a wonderful man, and I am blessed with an exceptional family. I am not "just" a survivor. I have many other identities in which I am invested. And my next identity to embark on is my identity as a mother. I have always known, that by some means, I will make it possible to have a child of my own. When I think about this miraculous possibility, my heart tears with joy. Producing life, which thrusts me forward into the future, is one way in which I can compensate for the death I see when I habitually look over my shoulder, into my past. For the first time in at least four generations of abuse, I will hurtle-dance-leap into the future with my still-ghost of a child, bright white, unblemished by the hell on the other side of the looking glass.

The case of Martha Beck's Leaving the Saints: How I Lost the Mormons and Found My Faith, writing in her own name

Interpreted by Amelia van der Merwe

Martha Beck's memoir, *Leaving the Saints: How I Lost the Mormons and Found My Faith*, is an excellent example of the risks of life-writing. In her book, Dr. Beck accuses one of Mormonism's most prominent religious scholars, her father, Hugh Nibley, of sexually abusing her. She also critically and satirically scrutinises the protectively private Mormon religious community. The memoir details how the author, a sociologist and therapist, recovered memories in 1990 of her ritual sexual abuse more than twenty years earlier, by her father. He was professor emeritus of ancient scripture at Brigham Young University and considered the leading living authority on Mormon teaching. Dr. Nibley denied all allegations, and Dr. Beck's seven siblings have condemned her assertions and hired a psychologist and lawyer specialising in lawsuits against therapists practising recovered-memory therapy once the book was published (Wyatt, 2005).

The memoir was not well received among the Mormon community in particular, although dissent was widespread and defensive responses were abundant. Dr. Beck was accused of factual distortions, hyperbole, distortion, unsubstantiated allegations, inconsistencies, and outright lies. Signature Books' marketing director, Tom Kimball, called the book "problematic" and "most likely heavily laced with fiction" (Wyatt, 2005). Sunstone's reviewer, Tania Lyon, came to the conclusion that "Martha's case against Mormonism is ... exaggerated and shallow, the accuracy of her narrative style ... suspect, and her use of hyperbole in such a devastating accusation ... misplaced" (Petersen, 2015). Affirmation, the gay Mormon Alliance, declared that "Martha Beck's credibility as an author is now in question" as *Leaving the Saints* "is being criticized for its alleged inaccuracies" (ibid.). The Mormon Church issued a statement condemning the book, calling it "seriously flawed in the way it depicts the church, its members and teachings". Hugh Nibley's main supporter said that Dr. Beck had no evidence that her allegations were true and therefore nothing could be proven (ibid.).

I cannot comment on the truth of these claims, but of course the real issue here is that the naysayers do not want the memoir to be true, and that is the real reason for these criticisms. Interestingly, for those who say that Dr. Beck has no evidence that her story is true, Dr. Beck's childhood was characterised by unexplained depression, anorexia, and despair, which sometimes left her suicidal. Long before she retrieved the memories of sexual abuse, she suffered unexplained pain and bleeding between her thighs at the age of five. In her teenage years and in her twenties, several doctors commented on unusual scar tissue in her vaginal area, which she cites as physical evidence of abuse; the vaginal scarring was not the result of childbirth. This certainly points to the truth of her story (Wyatt, 2005).

A central debate in the backlash against Dr. Beck is how she retrieved her memories. Many have argued that induced memories are fictions created by hypnosis. Dr. Beck did use self-hypnosis, which can result in the creation of false memories, but that was after having recovered her memories. It is important to note that most leaders in the field of memory agree that memories of early childhood abuse that have been forgotten can be retrieved and remembered later (Wyatt, 2005).

It is interesting to note the tone of the criticisms of Dr. Beck's work. Critics are clearly outraged. Criticisms of her memoir are peppered with emotional name-calling and insults such as "treacherous daughter", "shoddy memoir". The personal nature of the attack on Dr. Beck is evidenced in the following: Dr. Beck has received death threats, and Mormons around the country have participated in an email campaign against the book, sending more than 3,500 messages to Oprah Winfrey, who featured the memoir on her internet site and in an issue of her magazine, *O* (Wyatt, 2005).

However, one brave family member of Dr. Beck, who has only agreed to speak anonymously after threats of violence against her, has said: I believed Martha from the beginning because the memories she had of elements of the abuse—memories that never went away and were always part of her history—also fit with the outward signs of the abuse I saw in her growing up." Speaking to Dr. Beck's parents about it since, she said, "has only served to strengthen my belief in the veracity of her reporting of her experience" (Wyatt, 2005).

But sentiments like these are few and far between. It is clear what dangers are inherent in life writing, especially when tackling controversial subject matter. However, despite this ordeal, Dr. Beck has gone on to be highly successful, and is now a public figure doing writing and therapeutic work.

Chasing peace

Annalise, writing under pseudonym

In a dream, I sit on a Daliesque concrete slab floating above an exquisite turquoise pool. As an outgrowth of me, I have a continually mutating and revolving set of perpetrators, whispering horrors about me into my ear. When I look behind me I realise the slab has connected to a labyrinthine set of party venues, but sadistic, or sado-masochistic ones; ones which reflect the emotional climate of my torture venues. There is a blank in the dream, and then suddenly, to my utter joy, I look down and notice I am heavily pregnant, and despite the messages of my morphing perpetrators, I decide to show everyone I can find how proud I am of being pregnant. Even if it means I have to enter the labyrinth, black and filthy. In such a place, no one cares, no one sees. And my excitement and pride and joy slowly diminish, and I am defeated—I am so easily defeated—until I get to a crackhouse bathroom and start smoking crystal meth, watching my stomach deflate, my body wracked with grief. I stumble into the next room and see a woman who is part me part a friend from school mainlining heroin. She is unconscious, face down on the bed, hair spread over her vomit-soaked face. This image of self-destruction wakes Anna up and I shake her, roll her over—"why do you keep doing this to yourself?? WHY DO YOU KEEP DESTROYING YOURSELF?? LIVE!!! LIVE!!!" To her vacuous face and to the revolving, mutating perpetrators who are now sitting out on the slab, I say, "I have a big waterproof backpack. There is space for all the little alters, and there is space for my unborn child. There is food and water. I can look after you. We won't drown if we jump into the water. We must just believe we deserve to survive." An eternity passes as I contemplate whether I can really do this. Whether I deserve such an encounter with beauty, and ultimate survival. And then I jump with my enormous backpack. I hear my perpetrators hissing, "You have the children who died during your torture on your shoulders" over and over and over and over and I sink and I think I am going to drown and I sink and I think I am going to drown but I hold onto that backpack like a tigress and we get to shore.

And now, I would like to hand back these children, with love, love, love, to my perpetrators. I will always remember and cherish you, but your deaths rest on the shoulders of others. I remember you, even though your faces disappear in a fog, and your time will come. And then I will publicly name you. I say with too little conviction that it is on many of your shoulders, that all these deaths rest.

And for that reason, in my imagination, I line you up against a wall. I make you strip. I make you stand in the hot sun for days without water. Gun to your heads. And then, just when you are about to slip into unconsciousness, I shoot and I shoot and I shoot and shoot, and God forgive me, I will rejoice.

Kim Noble, writing in her own name

It would have been a lot easier for me had I used a pseudonym, and I could have said more had it not been my real name. So I do understand people wanting to go anonymous, as there is a safety issue. But, as a reader, I personally do not know if it is true when the real name is not given. So when I read a biography I personally prefer one with the real name, or I worry the person is not ready or someone could have made it up. If the publisher or editor vouches for the truth of the account, that helps, but it is still not the same.

Safety does have to be taken seriously. The author of *Today I am Alice* used a pseudonym and could not be on television so people could not see her face, but then she was on the radio and I worried if her voice had been altered to protect her.

When it is a novel—that is completely different obviously—anything can be said, but with a factual book I have problems. Because when I read something under a pseudonym I am aware that anything can be made up—abuse, domestic violence, anything with a stigma. I could go under a different name and make everything up. On the one hand you want people without a voice to be heard, but if it is under another name you could be reinforcing the fact that it is shameful to speak out.

That does not mean you have freedom when you use your real name. In my case, in the UK it was down to the book publisher and its legal team as to what could be said. That team said anyone who could be identified had to be removed even though I had gone public with my name and not used a pseudonym.

If you not only have to change their name, but places where it happened, and so on, and there is too much you have to change, it gets a bit ridiculous. When I read parts of my book I began to think, "Who is that person?" and then I remembered who the real person was. It did not have meaning to me when I read it and I was not happy with it. If you change names and "they" reckon they did not do it they would not see it as relating to them. Only if they knew it was them could they make a legal case. If I said Bob Smith came to my house and attacked me and it was Fred Brown and not Bob Smith, then why would Fred Brown want to take action? So I can understand just changing the abuser's name but nothing else.

Initially when I went public it was about trying to promote my artwork so I could not hide. But I have not felt frightened. I am more upset about how the legal department changed things so what I wanted to say was hidden. For example, there are cases in the headlines now that linked to me, and people do not know because that was hidden. It was all in the press when it was just me as a witness and not believed, and twenty years later it is in the press and I am nowhere to be seen. Looking back now with all that has been exposed about Jimmy Savile and people like that, it was all taken out.

Nobody would know from the book where it happened or who did it, so legally I am covered. But if it got to court in the future and someone said it was different in the book, I don't know if that legal care could act against me. So someone could accuse me of lying in my biography through not being clear enough about the truth. And legal aid would probably not pay for me. Looking back again, would it have been safer under a pseudonym? Then if it went to court and there was a case against my abusers no one could say I had said anything different in my book. But that is looking years on.

So there is a problem with legal issues. Realistically, if anyone tried to sue me they would have to prove I was lying and they can't because I am telling the truth. But I don't think it is so much the issue today that people sue. I think it is more a matter of human rights that you have privacy. Any real person you name has a right to their privacy. At the end of the day it is human rights. People have a right to privacy. For example, I could not put in the book that my dad had cancer. It was a fact. How could he sue if it was the truth? But he can because he has a right to privacy. So with human rights it is harder and harder to write a book.

I don't like watching myself on TV or hearing my voice on TV or radio but I have not been fearful. Once it is out there it is out there, and because of the changes in society that does make you safer.

With regard to abuse details—I don't think it is necessary personally to include all the details. It is the other things like being programmed or DID which people don't know about. Your feelings and thoughts and how it left you feeling is what I could do, but not the details. The book, for me, was about the experiences of DID and how I was treated in institutions. We were severely abused, but why should anyone know the details? There are lots of books on that, but not on the DID aspects of it.

For the paintings it was better to use my real name and to try to take away the stigma by speaking out, which I think is the main thing. Shame is such a thing from abuse but when you write under a pseudonym, for me the shame will still be there.

I am pleased to say I am not ashamed I have a mental health issue and that I have been abused. I still don't understand Anna's situation properly. I think her team have over-reacted. But we haven't got a crystal ball and every survivor has got to do what they think is best for them.

Note: Kim Noble, the artist, has published a book, *All of Me*, in her real name, and her art is in her name and the names of the personalities who are artists. As she shares in the Foreword to Alison Miller's new book on mind control for survivors, this meant she had to face the shock of mind control sites analysing her work all over the web, sometimes correctly, sometimes not, and sometimes where she, as a main personality, cannot be sure.

Kali

Annalise, writing under pseudonym

Kali, my final alter, is named after the Hindu goddess of destruction. She is my defender. If I look closely, I see that Kali destroys the bad much more often than she destroys the good. She is what has turned me into the Bobo doll. The one who nurses the broken, flattened me until I can stand, bounce up again, teeth bared, hissing at the perpetrators, when I have been desperately hurt. And I always stand up again, with Kali holding my hand. She is the part of me who is responsible for the best decisions I have made, for my physical and psychological survival. While I carry the weight of my own torture and the burden of the dead, I have also accumulated wealth in every possible way. My life is rich-drenched in love.

The African culture is rooted in oral tradition. One of those traditions is the praise song, which is typically in the form of a spoken poem about a person. Each line in the poem gives one "praise name". A praise name is a vivid description of distinctive features of the person. The praise song could be chanted to a drumbeat or performed as a song. I thought this kind of poem would be appropriate for describing Kali in this chapter dedicated to her, because it is she who kept me alive and allowed me to reach adulthood.

My name is Kali.
I have the heart of a warrior.
My function is to defend, crush break kill destroy anyone who
threatens me or those I love.
I am viciously protective of those I love.
I am resilient.
I am strong.
I am brave.
I am fearless.
I am sometimes, mostly, capable of hating the perpetrators
instead of myself, which allows me to stand up and walk again,
each time I am knocked down.
I love the other child parts as best I can, and look after them
and want what is best for them.
I am able of making decisions based on self-love.
I know that I deserve good things despite what I saw and par-
ticipated in.

I have learnt to instil fear in those who threatened me and
those I love.

I have sometimes fought hard and dirty but I believe I did not
lose my moral compass; I did these things for the right reasons, or
more often, because I had no choice or alternative.

I am just, and integrous.

I am able to endure and persist until I have achieved my goal.

I adapt myself according to the requirements of the situation no
matter how dangerous it is.

I am capable of understanding and accepting profound darkness, in others and myself.

I am able to see humour in that profound darkness.

I am able to accept love from others because I understand I am
not all bad.

I am beginning to understand that I can rely on a life that is still
sometimes, often, painful, but also good.

I don't have to fight alone anymore. I don't have to be my own,
my child parts' army.

But I am still Kali.

Crush kill destroy.

Inherently, essentially, I remain a fighter.

Deadly.

Watch your back.

A British survivor, Joanna, writing under pseudonymn

Writing anonymously for me doesn't mean I write un-named. I know the
name. I have chosen it, I can identify with it. So I am not sure if by writing anonymously my writing loses integrity. Is my writing less valid? Or
does using my real name make it more true to those who read it?

So why don't I choose to write openly, freely using my own name?
Maybe, just maybe, one day I will, if ever my place in the world is less
fragile. If ever the world within my mind is less fragile. You see, my
fight for survival as a survivor is tough enough …

Writing using my own name would in many ways be like stepping
out into the "light" and would be like putting a final stamp on the
dreadful truth of the first twenty-one years of my life; now that takes
inner courage on a huge level. Writing in my own name would have to

be survived, yet again a gamble with my mind and my life. It would also mean a real *in your face* look in the mirror … could I withstand the pain even then? I would like to think I could, if I can get that far, I could withstand anything.

But you know, that is the tip of a dangerous iceberg in writing in my own name. It would be like creating a minor earthquake amongst those around me, not only those I care about deeply, but also those who would still seek to harm me and punish me for speaking out. They watch my silence. You see, she tried it once … punishment, a beating and burning … tried it again five years later … punishment, a beating and death threats. Hiddenness, that is their agenda, at all costs. So speaking out breaks the rules. The rules must not be broken. Fear is the key, and it runs deep like a blueprint, a programme from birth. But by writing this I am breaking rules, I am moving forward in recognition and becoming a real person, and that is good.

Writing anonymously is a paradox … I want to be free. Would writing under my own name give me that freedom and the healing I crave? Would it help me find a place to fit in? You may think so.

The sting in the tail is that exposure in a world that would much rather deny the atrocities of ritualised abuse could cause a retreat into the hiddenness; now that would be pain. It may be an end and not a beginning. What a risk to take. How would the damage to those I have tried to protect all my life be dealt with? Would they survive? I fear not. I know not.

Writing anonymously still allows me to strike back. I would like to believe one day I will speak out in my own identity, but it would mean being strong enough to trust that a world which did not protect me once would now be able to.

Triumph

Annalise, writing under pseudonym

Invictus

Out of the night that covers me,
Black as the pit from pole to pole,
I thank whatever gods may be
For my unconquerable soul.

In the fell clutch of circumstance
I have not winced nor cried aloud.
Under the bludgeonings of chance
My head is bloody, but unbowed.

Beyond this place of wrath and tears
Looms but the Horror of the shade,
And yet the menace of the years
Finds and shall find me unafraid.

It matters not how strait the gate,
How charged with punishments the scroll.
I am the master of my fate:
I am the captain of my soul.
(William Ernest Henley, 1888)

There is a team of medical and therapeutic professionals who have begun to undo what others in their professions have done to me. They are, first and foremost, my current psychotherapist, Karen, and my psychiatrist, Noa. They are drops of golden light, but I reserve a special place for them, because their role in my life is different from those of friends and family. They form the basis of my therapeutic and medical army. They take me, each day, staring down the rabbit hole, beyond the looking glass, with an openness to accept whatever unspeakable horror might emerge, with emotional generosity, dedication, kindness, gentleness, consistency, and they hold my hand as I repeatedly visit this place of wrath and tears. They do not shrivel-crumble or judge-defend at the horror of the shade, they stand bravely, occasionally falter with me, but unflinchingly remain.

They have not run from DID, denied its existence, because to believe breaks down the foundation of a common but false belief that the world cannot be filled with the depth of such atrocity. That it is essentially a good, safe, and benevolent place. It means suspending this fictional, defensive reality, and they have, for me. We constantly negotiate boundaries, we struggle with my abandonment terror without compromising their integrity or breaking the hearts of the little alters irreparably. This takes immense commitment and conviction in their ability to care for me in a way I have never been cared for, without pathological enmeshment, without co-dependence. Sometimes it is so new it hurts me like the severing of my heart from my main perpetrator, but I guess that is the point. They are teaching me to love in a new way, me kicking and screaming all the way. I abhor anything new, I yearn for the familiar and predictable so I cannot be hurt again; better the devil you know. But it is worth noting that I too am not running; running from what is new—my terrifyingly, sparklingly beautiful, different future. I have formed attachments to these women. Anxious attachments, but attachments nonetheless, which means I am investing in the changes that are necessary to catapult me forward. It is because of Karen and Noa that my head is bloody, but unbowed.

One other member of my astonishing medical team is my gynae. When I first saw her two years ago, she had received three referral letters about me and my condition and said as a result she found me a rather intimidating patient. But I intuitively liked her because she was sensitive and treated me with respect. I went back two days ago. I told her I needed a cervical smear. Cervical smears evoke Evelyn, one of my alters, because of her abuse; the process is so similar although the intentions are so different. I am in the same physical position and there are instruments inside me. So I switch and my instinct as Evelyn is to kick. This makes me a very attractive gynaecological patient. But I try to soothe Evelyn before, and I have my dad in the waiting room, and my friend Gemma is on her way. Then the most unexpected thing happens. Carren's manner with me/Evelyn is so calm, so confident, yet sympathetic and sensitive, so soft-efficient, yet respectful, that I relax and I don't switch. I lie on the hot pad on the bed after I have taken my clothes off and wait, a peculiar kind of dissociative calm flooding over me. Carren came back into the room and showed me the instruments she was going to use. She put it up inside me and then she did something extraordinary. She said, "Push me out". She said she wasn't going anywhere until I used my pelvic muscles to push her out. And I push and as I push I visualise my perpetrators and I grit my teeth and in my head I am screaming to them, shaking my head hysterically, no no NO NO NO. She does the same with the internal examination. She said she is not taking her hand out until I push it out. I am exhausted from the previous triumph, but I try and try again. And I do it. And she says to me, "You see, you aren't help-less anymore, you are in control." Each time I tell this story the tears roll down my cheeks. I pushed every perpetrator out of me. I am the master of my fate: I am the captain of my soul. I am victorious. I am huge. I said NO.

References

Beck, M. (2005). *Leaving the Saints: How I Lost the Mormons and Found my Faith*. New York: Three Rivers.

Blume, E. S. (1990). *Secret Survivors: Uncovering Incest and Its Aftereffects in Women*. New York: Wiley.

Frank, A. (1995). *The Wounded Storyteller: Body, Illness and Ethics*. Chicago, IL: University of Chicago.

Henley, E. H. (1888). Invictus. In: *A Book of Verses* (pp. 56–57). London: D. Nutt.

Hoffman, W. (2014). *The Enslaved Queen: a Memoir about Electricity and Mind Control*. London: Karnac.

Martell, Y. (2002). *Life of Pi*. Edinburgh: Canongate.

Miller, A. (2012). *Healing the Unimaginable: Treating Ritual Abuse and Mind Control*. London: Karnac.

Miller, A. (2014). *Becoming Yourself: Overcoming Mind Control and Ritual Abuse*. London: Karnac.

Petersen, B. (2015). *As Things Stand at the Moment: Responding to Martha Beck's Leaving the Saints*. www.fairmormon.org/perspectives/publications/as-things-stand-at-the-moment-responding-to-martha-becks-leaving-the-saints [last accessed 11 March 2015].

Schore, A. N. (1994). *Affect Regulation and the Origin of the Self: The Neurobiology of Emotional Development*. Hillsdale, NJ: Erlbaum.

Siegel, D. J. (2001). Toward an interpersonal neurobiology of the developing mind: attachment relationships, "mindsight", and neural integration. *Infant Mental Health Journal, 22*(1–2): 67–94.

Wyatt (2005). *A Mormon Daughter's Book Stirs a Storm*. www.nytimes.com/2005/02/24/books/a-mormon-daughters-book-stirs-a-storm.html [last accessed 2 February 2016].

PART II

TESTIMONIES

INTRODUCTION TO PART II

Valerie Sinason

Anna has read the second part of this book. As an intelligent woman pursuing a university path, she is bilingual. She can read and write with the raw feelings of a sentient being whose freedom was bruised, whose right to nurture was cruelly withheld. However, she can also read, write, research, and welcome the language of professionals, the concepts of diagnosis, treatment, outcome, co-morbidities, and brain scans. Anna is therefore a survivor and a professional. Many professionals are also secret survivors, and then there are those who publicly call themselves survivor-professionals. Similarly, the non-survivor professional also speaks different languages when presenting court reports as opposed to advocating for a patient's rights. Multiple states and languages are demanded of all of us.

Amelia and I thought long and hard about the impact Part II of this book would have. Was it even ethically right to split the book into two? How would a survivor feel at reading of their experiences translated into formal terms? Was this our own dissociative process—to use formal language to prevent us from feeling survivors' pain? Were we colluding with the academic demands of a dissociative formal prose style in including learned formal contributions at all? Was that a separate book? On the other hand, how would professionals feel at having their careful evidenced statements held in a book that contains first person accounts? Would they even be willing?

However, truth is more complex. Some survivors can write of their experiences in a way that contains the unbearable, whilst some professionals, saturated with toxic secondary traumatisation, cannot. There are also different kinds of formal writing from professionals. Alison Miller's workbooks for survivors of mind control are deliberately written in straightforward language with all the reading and research implicit in them, just like her chapter here. Others provide a myriad of explicit references to enable survivors and professionals to utilise academic research in a different way.

Just as there is no one way for survivors (who may or may not be professionals) to write, anonymously, under pseudonym or using their real name, there is also no one way for professionals (who may or may not be survivors) to write.

In the interests of true rich multiplicity of opinion we decided to hold within the covers of this book the different emotional experience of the languages of communication. To our delight, all were keen on such collaboration. All were concerned for the plight of Anna.

May all survivors reading Part II (whether professionals or not) take on board our deep intention for voices to be heard, for toxic silences to end, and may all professionals (whether survivors or not) appreciate the genuine moral commitment that underlies the academic and research contributions. Such collaboration, we felt, with Anna's agreement, provided common sense, and common sense, as the psychoanalyst Bion always said, is not common.

So let us bring together a range of voices to aid all in this field who are facing threats and pressures for silence, whether from the powerful voice of perpetration hidden in professional scepticism, the unscientific proponents of false memory, or even, more heartbreakingly, in victims who have not yet been safe enough to leave their identification with abusers.

The voices of this book are international. Cruelty to children is international, but then, so is courage.

and when we speak we are afraid
our words will not be heard
nor welcomed
but when we are silent
we are still afraid
So it is better to speak
remembering
we were never meant to survive

(Audre Lorde, *The Black Unicorn: Poems*, 1995)

CHAPTER THREE

History of trauma-related dissociation, with a focus on dissociative identity disorder

Onno van der Hart

Jeanne Fery was a twenty-five-year-old Dominican nun believed to be possessed by devils and demons. Her exorcists produced a detailed account of the manifestations of this "possession", mentioning a history of childhood trauma, and described her treatment through exorcism that took place in Mons, France, in 1584 and 1585. Jeanne Fery wrote her own account of her affliction and treatment. Originally published in 1586, the French description of her treatment course was republished in the late nineteenth century by Désiré-Magloire Bourneville (1886), a doctor at the Pitié-Salpêtrière hospital in Paris, who diagnosed Jeanne's disorder not as a case of possession but as the most severe form of hysteria. Her hysteria was characterised by a "doubling of the personality [dédoublement de la personnalité] ... in its most perfect type" (ibid., p. iii). Among her symptoms described in the original text, Bourneville mentioned, among other things, convulsive attacks (pseudo-epileptic seizures), visual, auditory and olfactory hallucinations, mutism, dissociative blindness, refusal to eat, anesthesia, longlasting extases, physical pains, and visceral sensations which she believed were caused by a snake having entered her body.

What was, in Bourneville's time, the "most perfect type" of doubling, or dissociation of the personality, that is, the dissociative disorder

61

most clearly manifesting its symptoms? Described at the time by different names, it was multiple personality disorder (MPD); Bourneville was able to notice the similarities of Jeanne Fery's disorder with the then famous cases of MPD, such as Félida X (Azam, 1876) and Louis Vivet (e.g., Bourru & Burot, 1885; cf., Faure, Kersten, Koopman, & Van der Hart, 1997). Central to Bourneville's diagnosis of MPD was Jeanne Fery's switches to what we would now call a child alter or child part, while her experiences of the devils and demons, who could also speak through her throat and mouth, were subsumed under the label of hysterical psychosis, now known as dissociative psychosis. Nowadays we would also regard these as dissociative experiences of persecutory alters or perpetrator-imitating parts, and her hallucinations of Mary Magdalene as an "inner self-helper" part. Jeanne Fery indicated that some of these dissociative parts inhabited and disturbed particular body parts, such as her blasphemous tongue, her blind eye, and her painful throat. While acknowledging the true nature of Jeanne Fery's MPD, Bourneville noticed that various experiences in her dissociative psychosis were influenced by sociocultural factors, such as those of the Catholic church, including the mass and its commandments, and sacred hierarchy. While not highlighted by Bourneville, Jeanne Fery's case presents indications of early physical abuse and, possibly, sexual abuse (Van der Hart, Lierens, & Goodwin, 1996).

In a sense, Bourneville's late nineteenth century view on Jeanne Fery's MPD, now known as dissociative identity disorder (DID) (APA, 1994, 2013), was a precursor of the DSM-5's main diagnostic criterium. Uniting dissociative and possession phenomena, it states:

> Disruption of identity characterized by two or more personality states, which may be described in some cultures as an experience of possession. The disruption in identity involves marked discontinuity in sense of self and sense of agency, accompanied by related alterations in affect, behavior, consciousness, memory, perception, cognition, and/or sensory-motor functioning. (2013, p. 292)

In this chapter, a brief, selective history is presented of dissociation as manifested in various dissociative disorders, in particular MPD/DID. Relevant developments in Europe, especially in France, and subsequently in North America, will be emphasised. For more extensive historical discourses, the reader is referred to Dorahy and Van der Hart

(2007) and Van der Hart and Dorahy (2009). Both works distinguish two conceptual approaches to dissociation: so-called narrow and broad conceptualisations. As highlighted in the understanding of DID, the narrow conceptualisation refers to a trauma-induced division of the personality into dissociative parts (known also by many other terms) which manifest in a range of dissociative symptoms. As early as the nineteenth century, these symptoms had been distinguished into bodily and mental manifestions, currently described as somatoform dissociative symptoms (e.g., anesthesia, tics) and psychoform dissociative symptoms (e.g., amnesia, hearing voices). These are further divided into positive (intrusions) and negative (functional losses) symptoms (cf., Janet, 1889, 1907, 1977; Nijenhuis, 2004, 2015; Van der Hart, Nijenhuis, & Steele, 2006). Bourneville (1886) described many such symptoms in Jeanne Fery. In principle, a hypnotically induced division of the personality can also be distinguished, and the question is how or whether this temporary division relates to trauma-related dissociation of the personality.

The broad conceptualisation, in contrast, focuses on a wide variety of phenomena thought to be more or less dissociative, regardless of whether or not these phenomena stem from a dissociation of the personality. Examples not directly related to such an underlying division include absorption and related alterations of consciousness. However, in line with nineteenth-century understanding, this chapter adheres to the narrow conceptualisation which involves a dissociation of the personality.

The nineteenth century

During much of the nineteenth century, it was not the existence of multiple personality that was highlighted, but rather double personality, also known as double conscience (double consciousness). Although the first reports of double personality in Germany and the United States were published at the end of the eighteenth century, the main thrust in the development of the study of dissociation, double personality and DID took place in nineteenth century France. Perhaps the Marquis de Puységur's discovery, in 1784, of the existence of a lucid state or artificial somnambulism in one of his patients, involving a dissociation or division of consciousness, was the first. He observed that an individual able to enter a somnambulistic state displayed two separate streams of thought and memory, in which one stream operated outside conscious awareness. Although opinions differed, most students of this artificial somnambulism regarded it as an abnormal, morbid state, clearly related to hysteria. However, whether or not this abnormal state developed from traumatic experiences was usually not explored.

Most of the dissociative cases were presented in the framework of the double personality. Even when patients presented signs of the existence of more than two dissociative parts, the dissociation of the personality was formulated in terms of this Procrustean bed. This was the case, for instance, with the well-known North American case of Mary Reynolds, who was described as having double consciousness (Mitchell, 1816). In France, Azam's famous case Félida X was a prime example (Azam, 1876; cf., Carlson, 1986), while Breuer and Freud (1893) invariably adhered to the concept of double conscience.

However, sometimes the manifestations of different dissociative parts unavoidably required the diagnosis of MPD/DID. This was the case with Jeanne Fery, mentioned before, as understood by Bourneville in 1886. The most famous case of a DID patient during the first half of the nineteenth century was Antoine Despine's young patient Estelle, who manifested many dissociative parts and a whole range of somatoform and psychoform dissociative symptoms. She had experienced some traumatising events during childhood, which Despine did not regard as etiological factors. Nevertheless, he was able to cure her, as the book he wrote about her testifies (Despine, 1840; see also Ellenberger, 1970; Janet, 1889; Kluft, 1984; McKeown & Fine, 2008).

During the second half of the nineteenth century the French DID case of Louis Vivet received, nationally and internationally, much attention. Known for his fugue states, among other psychoform and somatoform dissociative symptoms, he often disappeared from the psychiatric institutions he was admitted to, only to emerge in some other part of the country, and thus he was treated by a number of different clinicians. Camuset, his first psychiatrist, diagnosed him as having a double personality (Camuset, 1882), while subsequent clinicians found manifestations of multiplicity (e.g., Bourru & Burot, 1885). They eventually distinguished ten dissociative parts in the patient. Given the fact that a lot of experimental studies have been carried out with him, it has been suggested that Louis Vivet was a case of iatrogenically induced DID (Merskey, 1992). However, a careful study of the original medical files and original publications clearly contradicts this interpretation (Faure, Kersten, Koopman, & Van der Hart, 1997). Many original reports on

Louis Vivet indicated that he suffered from extended childhood traumatisation, including physical abuse, severe neglect, and, from age seven on, abandonment and wandering, with the need to steal food, subsequent arrest, and imprisonment.

At the end of the nineteenth century, Alfred Binet (1896) summarised the situation with regard to double and multiple personality as follows:

> In general observers have only noted two different conditions of existence in their subjects; but this number two is neither fixed nor prophetic. It is not perhaps, even unusual, as is believed; on looking closely we find three personalities in the case of Félida, and still a greater number in that of Louis V—that is sufficient to make the expression "double personality" inexact as applied to these phenomena. There may be duplication, as there may be division in three, four, etc., personalities. (ibid., p. 38)

Pierre Janet

Pierre Janet (1859–1947) was unquestionably the greatest student of dissociation in patients suffering from hysteria, that is a broad range of mental disorders characterised by a more (as in MPD/DID) or less complex division of the personality. In his early clinical work and experimental research, with his famous doctoral thesis *L'Automatisme Psychologique: Essai de Psychologie Expérimentale sur les Formes Inférieures de l'Activité Humaine (Psychological Automatism: Experimental-psychological essay on the inferior forms of human activity)* (Janet, 1889) as a landmark, he systematically explored the fundamental characteristics of hysteria. Besides the dissociation of the personality and related negative dissociative symptoms (mental stigmata) and positive dissociative symptoms (mental accidents), these include a retraction of the field of personal consciousness, that is, a reduction of the number of psychological phenomena that the individual can simultaneously perceive (Janet, 1907, 1977).

Janet regarded both the dissociation of the personality and the retraction of the field of consciousness as the results of integrative failure. Hysteria, therefore, was as an "illness of personal synthesis" (Janet, 1907, p. 332). Constitutional vulnerability could play a role, as could physical illness and exhaustion. However, he regarded the vehement emotions inherent in traumatic experiences as the primary cause of this integrative failure. And the more intense these emotions are, the longer they last, and the more they are repeated, the stronger their disintegrative effects (Janet, 1909). This entails an ever more complex dissociation of the personality, that is, an increasing number of dissociative parts—with DID as the most complex form of dissociation. Janet found that so-called hysterical attacks constituted the re-activation of some of these dissociative parts—he spoke of "systems of ideas and functions" or "existences"—and the traumatic memories they contain. In these re-enactments, patients, or rather specific dissociative parts, are "continuing the action, or rather the attempt at action, which began when the [trauma] happened; and they exhaust themselves in these everlasting recommencements" (Janet, 1919, p. 663).

Janet developed a phase-oriented approach and created a wide variety of techniques for the treatment of these patients (cf., Van der Hart, Brown, & Van der Kolk, 1989), which are reflected to this day in the current standard of care (e.g., Brown, Scheflin, & Hammond, 1998; ISSTD, 2011). At the base of the increasing recognition of Janet's views on trauma and dissociation lies the publication of Henri Ellenberger's masterpiece, *The Discovery of the Unconscious*, in 1970, which includes a most impressive chapter on Janet's personality and work.

Sigmund Freud and Joseph Breuer

Freud and Breuer originally followed Janet and other French contemporaries in understanding hysteria in terms of dissociation, which they referred to as a splitting of consciousness. In their joint work, *On the Psychical Mechanism of Hysterical Phenomena: Preliminary Communication*, they stated:

> We have become convinced that *the splitting of consciousness which is so striking in the well known classical cases under the form of* "double conscience" *is present to a rudimentary degree in every hysteria, and with it the emergence of abnormal states of consciousness … is the basic phenomenon of this neurosis*. (Freud & Breuer, 1893a, p. 12; italics in orginal)

This illustrates that Breuer and Freud were still trying to fit all dissociative cases in the Procrustean bed of double consciousness or personality. Even though they assumed that all cases of hysteria, and thus of dissociation of the personality, are rooted in early trauma, Freud downplayed Janet's understanding of integrative failure as the root of trauma-induced dissociation. Rather, he emphasised its role as a defence mechanism. However, Freud soon abandoned the view that hysteria was rooted in trauma as well as the accompanying dissociation theory. Thus, on the rare occasion that he mentioned double consciousness, he treated it "like a hot potato, anxious to get rid of it and forget all about it as quickly as possible" (Zemach, 1986, p. 132):

> Depersonalization leads us to the extraordinary condition of double conscience, which is more correctly described as split personality. But all of this is so obscure and has been so little mastered scientifically that I must refrain from talking about it anymore. (Freud, 1936a, p. 245)

For a long time, psychoanalysis bore the stamp of this unfortunate and puzzling switch in perspective. For instance, the psychoanalytically informed English physician William Rivers (1864–1922), who was highly experienced in the treatment of military men traumatised during the Great War, stated about hysteria: "In the absence of any evidence of alternate consciousness, it is doubtful whether anything is gained by bringing hysteria within the category of dissociation" (Rivers, 1920, p. 134). But a most shocking example of the intentional silencing—clinically, politically, and personally—of a testimony of dissociation and its traumatic antecedents took place a decade later, with Sándor Ferenczi (1873–1933). Orginally one of Freud's favourite students and one who treated survivors of childhood traumatisation, he returned to a dissociation perspective on childhood traumatisation (Ferenczi, 1949). During his address to the Twelfth International Psychoanalytic Association Congress in September 1932 in Wiesbaden, he stated: "If the shocks increase in number during the development of the child, the number and the various kinds of splits in the personality increase too" (Ferenczi, 1949, p. 229), thus referring to the relationship between complex childhood trauma and dissociative disorders, including DID. Subsequently he was ostracised from the psychoanalytic movement because of his return to the original concept and emphasis on the pathogenic influences of child abuse. Fortunately, a revival of interest in his work is currently taking place (e.g., Howell & Itzkowitz, 2016).

William James

In the United States, the philosopher and psychologist William James (1842–1910), professor at Harvard University, closely followed the European, in particular the French, studies in hysteria and dissociation. His acute understanding of dissociation is exemplified in his magnum opus *Principles of Psychology* (James, 1890) and in his clinical lectures on exceptional mental states, presented in 1898 (Taylor, 1984). His view on dissociation is perhaps best summarised in the following statement:

> It must be admitted ... *that in certain persons*, at least, the total pos-sible consciousness may be split into parts which coexist but mutu-ally ignore each other, and share the objects of knowledge between them. More remarkable still, they are *complementary*. (James, 1890, p. 206; italics in the original)

James admired Janet's pioneering work, and in his own work he high-lighted several of Janet's case studies (cf., James, 1890; Taylor, 1984). He regarded Breuer and Freud's *Preliminary Communication*, mentioned above, "as an independent corroboration of Janet's views" (James, 1894, p. 199). In short, together with his own studies of hypnosis, automatic writing, and double personality—for instance, the famous case of Ansel Bourne—James was a great synthesiser of what was thus far known on dissociation.

The twentieth century

Around the turn of the century a number of well-known authors pub-lished important studies on dissociation. The Englishman Frederic Myers (1843–1901) was a psychical researcher and one of the founding members of the Society for Psychical Research. He held the view that the ordinary waking or supraliminal self is only a small segment of the subconscious or subliminal self; that is, the source of all our capacities could be disintegrated into secondary personalities. His posthumously published *Human Personality and its Survival of Bodily Death* (F. Myers, 1903) is the great synthesis of his studies. It is a treasure house of all that was known so far about dissociative phenomena. Boris Sidis (1867–1923) and Morton Prince (1854–1929), both based in the United States, were among the most important early twentieth century students of DID. Sidis was originally focused on studying hypnosis and hypnoidal states and concluded that in every person there coexists two streams of consciousness, involving two selves: the waking self and the subwaking self (Crabtree, 1986; Sidis, 1902; Sidis & Goodhart, 1905). He observed how in certain individuals this dissociation, within the realm of subconscious selves, becomes more severe and complex. Among the factors involved, traumatic experiences played a major role. These experiences could take place at a subconscious level or in the waking state. Thus, Sidis (1902) stated that when the latter occurs:

> [T]he dissociated system sinks into the obscure, dreamy, subwaking region of the subconscious, and from thence causes psychomotor disturbances in the normal waking state. (ibid., p. 273)

Such "dissociated" or subconscious selves may develop more self-awareness and become self-conscious personalities (Crabtree, 1986). Multiple personality was his prime example, but he interpreted "functional psychosis" in the same way. Unlike his French colleagues, Prince did not solely regard dissociation as a pathological phenomenon (e.g., Prince, 1906). He substituted the concept of coconscious for Janet's concept of subconsciousness, which he found confusing, as he did even more Freud's use of the unconscious. For Prince, the simultaneous and conscious activity of two or more systems of consciousness in one individual is the key element in dissociation (Crabtree, 1986).

In Switzerland, an influential development, with far-reaching implications for mental health, took place during the beginning of the twentieth century, when Bleuler (1911) used the constructs of splitting (*Spaltung*) and dissociation to describe the essence of the mental disorder which he called schizophrenia: a diagnostic category which seemed to comprise both the older diagnostic category of dementia praecox and hysteria. As Bleuler stated: "The splitting is the fundamental prerequisite condition of most of the complicated phenomena of the disease" (ibid., p. 362). He regarded splitting and dissociation as denoting more or less the same phenomena (cf., Moskowitz, 2008; Ross, 2004), albeit attributing an extra meaning to the latter concept, that is, a constriction of consciousness: an extension with which Janet (1927) subsequently disagreed. Jung, who was influenced by Janet, also compared these two concepts (cited by Moskowitz, 2008, p. 40):

> We have taken over from French psychology a similar concept which initially was true for hysteria—namely, "dissociation". Today, the name means a "splitting" of the self ... Hysteria is primarily characterized by dissociation and because dementia praecox also shows splitting ("Spaltung"), the concept of dissociation seems to "run into" the concept of schizophrenia. (Jung, 1908, p. 335)

An unfortunate result of this position was, and still is, that many patients with dissociative identity disorder have been wrongly diagnosed as suffering from schizophrenia and thus have received ill-judged treatment (cf., Ross, 2004). Meanwhile, the concept of dissociation has been formally disassociated from schizophrenia, which is no longer regarded as a dissociative disorder.

Although, at the beginning of the twentieth century, a few more cases of double personality and DID were reported internationally, it was World War I that intensely stimulated the study and treatment of trauma-induced dissociation, for obvious reasons. (It should be remembered that Ferenczi had functioned as a military psychiatrist during this war, and had described a number of dissociative cases.) Among those with the most influence during and after World War I were Charles Myers (1873–1946) and William McDougall (1871–1938). Myers, who introduced the diagnostic category of shell-shock and soon regretted it, clearly described trauma-induced disorders—such as those later conceptualised as acute stress disorder and post-traumatic stress disorder—as being dissociative in nature (C. S. Myers, 1940). He observed in acutely traumatised service men the alternation between a so-called emotional part of the personality (EP—engaged in the re-experience or re-enactment of the war trauma) and a so-called apparently normal part of the personality (ANP—more or less functioning in daily life). Myers recommended a treatment that, essentially, consisted of reintegrating these two parts of the personality, including the original traumatic memories of the EP.

While Myers was focusing on cases of "double personality", McDougall covered the whole range of dissociative complexity, including DID. In his *Outline of Psychopathology* (McDougall, 1926), he stated that DID ("the major cases") lends itself better to investigation than do the "minor cases" (such as simple dissociative disorders of movement and sensation), with all of them having a dissociation of the personality:

> In all ... major cases, we find the dissociated activity to be ... the self-conscious purposive thinking of a personality; and, when we study the minor cases in the light of the major cases, we see that the same is true of them. (ibid., pp. 543–544)

Unlike the attention that trauma-induced dissociation received during World War I and its aftermath, during the 1930s, and subsequently during World War II and its aftermath, it had become a much-neglected subject.

The high level of interest in dissociation of the early 1900s died down for a number of reasons (Hilgard, 1977), a major one being the dominance of psychoanalytic theory and practice. The 1950s saw publications about the famous DID case of "Eve" (e.g., Thigpen & Cleckley, 1957). It was only near the end of the 1960s that a rise in academic, nonclinical interest in dissociation (or, at least, dissociation-like experiences) took place (Van der Hart & Dorahy, 2009).

As mentioned before, the publication in 1970 of Ellenberger's monumental work may have stimulated academic (e.g., Hilgard, 1977) and clinical interest in dissociation and DID, while the appearance of *Sybil* (Schreiber, 1974) drew enormous attention from the general public and clinicians alike. This famous DID case, incidently, has been subject to severe criticism (e.g., Rieber, 1999) and has been used by some to question the validity of the diagnostic category of DID (e.g., Hacking, 1995). Bowers et al. (1971) published a remarkable but unfortunately rarely cited article on the treatment of multiple personality. Greaves (1993) commented that this article outlines a canon of rules for such treatment, "most of which almost every expert in the field follows scrupulously to this day" (ibid., p. 363).

The 1980s

Clinical studies of DID, then MPD, and related disorders during the 1970s, culminated in the inclusion of a group of dissociative disorders in the DSM-III (APA, 1980), with DID as the most complex one. Curiously, the somatoform manifestations of dissociation were not recognised as such and were subsumed under a group of somatoform disorders. Following the appearance of the DSM-III, a veritable tide in clinical and research interest took place, particularly in DID. A series of books, written by the pioneers of that time, appeared on the diagnosis and treatment of DID (e.g., Bliss, 1986; Braun, 1986; Kluft, 1985; Putnam, 1989a; Ross, 1989). Ross (1989) also included a diagnostic instrument for the DSM dissociative disorders, that is, the Dissociative Disorders Interview Schedule (DDIS). In 1988 Richard Kluft, as editor-in-chief, started the journal *Dissociation: Progress in the Dissociative Disorders*, that is, the official journal (until 1997) of the International Society for the Study of Multiple Personality and Dissociation (ISSMP&D), which was founded in 1984. This journal emphasised the study of DID. With his background in hypnosis, psychoanalysis, and a host of other treatment modalities, Kluft has become one of the great masters in the diagnosis and treatment of traumatised and dissociative patients.

While the focus on DID could still be seen as belonging to the narrow conceptualisation of dissociation, further research at the time followed a broad conceptualisation. The most important example is the development of the Dissociative Experiences Scale (DES) (Bernstein & Putnam, 1986; Carlson & Putnam, 1993), still the most often used instrument in the field. One of the original authors, Eve Bernstein Carlson, subsequently testified to this broad conceptualisation, which includes phenomena that do, and some that do not, stem from a dissociation of the personality (Carlson, 1994):

> The definition of dissociation incorporated into the DES was intentionally broad .... There are items inquiring about amnestic experiences, gaps in awareness, depersonalization, derealization, absorption, and imaginative involvement. (ibid., p. 42)

Apart from the rather exclusive focus during the 1980s on DID, the value of Janet's original dissociation theory for understanding and treating traumatised individuals was more widely recognised. This manifested in a number of publications celebrating the centennial of his thesis, *L'automatisme Psychologique* (e.g., Nemiah, 1989; Putnam, 1989b; Van der Hart & Friedman, 1989; Van der Kolk & Van der Hart, 1989).

The 1990s

In this decade further progress was made in the diagnosis of DSM-IV dissociative disorders. Marlene Steinberg developed the Structured Clinical Interview for DSM-IV Dissociative Disorders (SCID-D)

(Steinberg, 1994), which is widely used internationally. Loewenstein (1991) published an excellent article on a modified version of the Mental Status Examination for complex dissociative symptoms and MPD, which is a must for clinicians. Spiegel and Cardeña (1991) published a most influential article on dissociation and dissociative disorders. Although not much noticed in North America, the publication of the *ICD-10 Classification of Mental and Behavioural Disorders* (WHO, 1992) was a milestone with regard to the classification of dissociative disorders. While its formulation of DID was weak, its advantage over the DSM-III-R, which had appeared in the meantime, was the recognition of the dissociative nature of "conversion disorder". Conversion disorders were not considered dissociative in the DSM-III-R and subsequent DSM-IV, and were thus included under somatoform disorders. Neither did Spiegel and Cardeña (1991) pay attention to their dissociative nature. However, in the ICD-10 they were re-named as "dissociative disorders of movement and sensation". Further research into somatoform dissociative phenomena, conducted by Nijenhuis and colleagues (Nijenhuis, 2004), including the development of a Somatoform Dissociation Questionnaire, brought this dissociative dimension further home. Eventually, the DSM-5 (APA, 2013) did include alterations in sensory-motor functioning among the diagnostic criteria of DID: a step forward, but still insufficient.

In the first half of the 1990s a so-called memory war began. Partially spurred by court cases in which some parents were accused of abuse, certain cohorts of these parents along with some academicians developed strategies to challenge the validity of delayed memory recall of childhood sexual abuse, in particular those reported by patients with DID (see Brown, Scheflin, & Hammond, 1998, for an overview). During this time attempts were made to discredit the validity of the DID diagnostc category. Accused parents and their sympathisers made vicious legal and *ad hominem* attacks against prominent American clinicians involved in the treatment of DID patients, and the dissociation field suffered tremendously. A reasoned discourse on the subject eventually prevailed in the scientific community for the most part, but not before much damage to reputations and to the field. Richard Kluft wrote in 1996:

> [T]he fact that one aspect of the traumatic memories of a patient with dissociative identity disorder may be disproven does not allow one to draw the conclusion that the rest of the reported memories

are erroneous; similarly, the fact that part of the recollection of a patient with dissociative identity disorder may be documented does not allow one to be certain that the rest of what has been said is accurate. (Kluft, 1996, p. 105)

A sitting duck in attempts to discredit DID patients and their therapists were patients' reports of satanic ritual abuse (SRA) and mind control. Sceptics believed that these reports were manifestations of mass hysteria and iatrogenic suggestibility, and some stories may well have been. However, clinicians working worldwide with patients with DID who had never heard these stories, continued to stumble upon patients who made the report. Clearly, these could not be considered a case of mass hysteria or of iatrogenic suggestion (cf., Fraser, 1997; Sinason, 1994). There may be many meanings to these reports, but that is no reason to discredit the field for working with patients who make the reports.

During the 1990s, a number of major books appeared in the field. Among them, *Clinical Perspectives on Multiple Personality Disorder* (Kluft & Fine, 1993), and the *Handbook of Dissociation* (Michelson & Ray, 1996). The Michelson and Ray handbook covers most dimensions, except dissociation in children. However, this was remedied in the following year by the publication of *Dissociation in Children and Adolescents* (Putnam, 1997). Ross published a new edition of his earlier book on MPD, now under its new name, *Dissociative Identity Disorder* (Ross, 1997).

In the 1990s, within the psychoanalytic movement, some awareness of the importance of trauma-generated dissociation started to grow. This re-awakening was rooted in the recognition that returning Vietnam veterans had been highly traumatised and were often dissociative, having "hysterical" problems. Furthermore, in the wake of the Women's Movement, it was noticed that many children and women had been traumatised by child sexual abuse and spousal abuse. Inspired by the pioneers on dissociation and MPD/DID, such as Richard Kluft and David Spiegel, some psychoanalytic authors became aware that many of these trauma survivors were dissociative as well (e.g., Davies & Frawley, 1994). Psychoanalytic reformulations also included the insights of Breuer and Freud's original understanding of trauma and dissociation of the personality, as well as those of Janet, in particular, and other French contemporaries. More recent examples are the publications of Bromberg (1998, 2006, 2011), Chefetz (2000, 2015), and Howell (2005, 2011), and a forthcoming reader on psychoanalysis and dissociation edited by Howell and Itzkowitz (2016).

One aspect of the meeting of psychoanalysis and the field of dissociation was a discussion of the similarities and differences between the psychoanalytic concept of repression and the construct of dissociation (e.g., Singer, 1990). One corollary was the development of the tendency to speak more often of dissociation, where before "repression" was used, in particular with regard to (traumatic) memories for which the individual has amnesia.

In 1991 Peter Barach published a groundbreaking article in which he described MPD/DID as an attachment disorder (Barach, 1991). This was followed by a series of clinical and research papers, which continued to be published in the twenty-first century, on the relationship between so-called disorganised attachment (D-attachment) and dissociation. Giovanni Liotti argued that D-attachment patterns in infants might lead to the development of dissociation later in life. He noted the parallel between such patterns and dissociation, and eventually regarded D-attachment in itself as dissociative in nature (e.g., Liotti, 1992, 1999, 2009). In longitudinal studies, D-attachment in the infant was indeed found to be a precursor of dissociative symptoms in late adolescence (Lyons-Ruth, Dutra, Schuder, & Bianchi, 2006; Ogawa, Sroufe, Weinfeld, Carlson, & Egeland, 1997).

The twenty-first century

The year 2000 saw the start of the *Journal of Trauma & Dissociation*, that is, the successor to *Dissociation* and the official journal of the International Society for the Study of Trauma and Dissociation. DID remains an important subject in this journal, but in contrast with its predecessor, *Dissociation*, many more articles represent the wider field of trauma and dissociation, including peritraumatic dissociation, psychosis, and military trauma. Spiegel (2005) edited a book that discussed the various fields in which dissociation has become a key concept. Ogden, Minton, and Pain (2006) published a groundbreaking book presenting, among other things, an extraordinary integration of Janet's and the authors' understanding of trauma and dissociation and its application in Sensorimotor Psychotherapy. An important follow-up was published in 2015 (Ogden & Fisher, 2015).

In the twenty-first century a number of other important clinical and research developments took place in the dissociation field; a field which may have continued to be hampered by a confusion of tongues, regarding the definition of dissociation and thus the scope of its manifestations.

There appear to be two major types of conceptualisation. The first one, in line with the original nineteenth-century views, is the so-called narrow conceptualisation of trauma-related dissociation as a post-traumatic division of the personality (Van der Hart & Dorahy, 2009). Perhaps McDougall's (1926) statement, cited above, was the most important summary of this view. A more recent book, *The Haunted Self: Structural Dissociation and the Treatment of Chronic Traumatization Dissociation* (Van der Hart, Nijenhuis, & Steele, 2006), represents this conceptualisation and emphasises the existence of dissociative parts that are either trauma-avoident or trauma-fixated: a view probably more accepted outside than within North America. This book constitutes an attempt to integrate Pierre Janet's dissociation theory and psychology of action with modern developments in the trauma and dissociation field. A major line of research based on the narrow conceptualisation was initiated by Ellert Nijenhuis. With the first study published by Reinders et al. (2003) and more recent ones by Schlumpf et al. (2013, 2014), this neuroimaging research with DID patients investigated and found different responses of dissociative parts functioning in daily life (ANP's "apparently normal parts of the personality") and parts stuck in trauma (EP's "emotional parts of the personality") to neutral and trauma-related memories, and to neutral and threat-related cues; findings that could not be simulated by other subjects who were not dissociative.

The other perspective is the so-called broad conceptualisation of dissociation (Van der Hart & Dorahy, 2009). In this view, emerging already in the 1980s—for instance in the construction of the DES—a wide range of phenomena, whether based on a divided personality structure or not, are subsumed under the label dissociation. Thus, it includes alterations in consciousness, including absorption and imaginative involvement, which are not *per se* related to structural dissociation of the personality. *Traumatic Dissociation: Neurobiology and Treatment*, edited by Vermetten, Dorahy, and Spiegel (2007), and the most impressive reader, *Dissociation and the Dissociative Disorders*, edited by Dell and O'Neil (2009), represent both conceptualisations and show that North American researchers and clinicians, in particular, adhere to a broad conceptualisation.

Within the domain of the broad conceptualisation, two developments are especially notable. The first pertains to the study of so-called peritraumatic dissociation as a predictor of PTSD, beginning in 1994 (Marmar et al., 1994). A significant relationship has indeed been found in many (but not all) studies (cf., Lensvelt-Mulders et al., 2008), but the conceptual base of the peritraumatic dissociation construct remains unclear.

The second development involves a line of research in which a so-called dissociative subtype of PTSD is distinguished. This subtype was eventually included in the DSM-5 as "PTSD with dissociative symptoms" (APA, 2013, p. 272). As a number of research studies have shown (e.g., Lanius et al., 2010), this "dissociative subtype" is characterised by elevated levels of depersonalisation, derealisation, and hypo-arousal. These symptoms are exclusively regarded as dissociative symptoms, whether or not they stem from an underlying dissociation of the personality. However, the so-called nondissociative subtype of PTSD is also characterised by (positive) dissociative symptoms, such as dissociative flashbacks "in which the individual feels or acts as if the traumatic event(s) were recurring" (APA, 2013, p. 271), which are clearly stemming from a dissociation of the personality. Thus, distinguishing a dissociative subtype of PTSD appears to constitute an anomaly in the understanding of PTSD's dissociative nature, in general (Nijenhuis, 2014).

With regard to diagnostic procedures and treatment, Dell's Multidimensional Inventory of Dissociation (MID) (Dell, 2006) became a welcome addition to the field. A milestone was the publication of the third revision of ISSTD's official guidelines for the treatment of DID (ISSTD, 2011) in the *Journal of Trauma and Dissociation*. Furthermore, a large, long-term naturalistic study of treatment of DID patients was initiated, resulting in a number of important publications (e.g., Brand et al., 2013; cf. Brand, Loewenstein, & Spiegel, 2014). A second generation of this study is now in progress. Kluft published a monograph on the treatment of traumatic memories in patients with complex dissociative disorders (Kluft, 2013). Meanwhile, the eye movement desensitisation reprocessing (EMDR) world was becoming more and more oriented to adaptations in the treatment of such patients (e.g., Fine & Berkowitz, 2001; Gonzalez & Mosquera, 2012; Twombly, 2000). More attention was paid to diagnosis and treatment of dissociative disorders in children and adolescents (e.g., Silberg, 2013; Wieland, 2011). As highlighted in the DSM-5 (APA, 2013), cultural aspects of the dissociative disorders also received more attention (e.g., Van Duijl, Nijenhuis, Komproe, Gernaat, & De Jong, 2010). Finally, the role of trauma and dissociation in psychosis was highlighted with the publication of *Psychosis, Trauma and Dissociation: Emerging Perspectives on Severe Psychopathology* (Moskowitz, Schäfer, & Dorahy, 2008). Special mention should be made of the many epidemiological and related studies that emerged from Turkey (e.g., Şar, 2011; Şar, Gamze, & Doğan, 2007; Şar, Koyuncu, & Öztürk, 2007).

As for international organisational developments, in Europe, ISSTD's sister organisation, the European Society for Trauma and Dissociation, was formed in 2006 and instituted bi-annual meetings. In Germany a separate German-language dissociation organisation had previously existed for a much longer period. This society is chaired by Michaela Huber, the leading clinician, instructor, and author in German-speaking countries (e.g., Huber, 2010). While not all international developments manifest in the establishment of professional societies, still much is going on in clinical and research activities in various parts of the world. An important international development, started by Peter Barach in 1997 and since 2003 moderated by Richard Chefetz, is the ever-growing online Dissociation Disorders Discussion Forum for professionals (www.dissoc.icors.org). On this invaluable electronic mailing list, which is not affiliated with any organisation, all topics related to the practice of psychotherapy as it concerns trauma and or dissociation are discussed, including anonymous case vignettes, typically representing situations of impasse or confusion. At the end of August 2014, the Forum had 1,180 members.

Dissociative identity disorder and sociocultural influences

A thorn in the side of the dissociative disorders field has consisted of curious attempts to discredit the validity of the DID diagnosis. Although some psychiatrists (e.g., Merskey, 1992) and adherents of a so-called sociocognitive model of DID (e.g., Lilienfeld et al., 1999) engaged in these attempts have been highly vocal, their view that DID is not a true mental disorder but rather is a social construction caused by therapist cueing, media influences, and broader sociocultural expectations, has been refuted by a number of empirical studies (cf., Dalenberg et al., 2012, 2014; Brand, Loewenstein, & Spiegel, 2014; Dorahy et al., 2014; Reinders et al., 2003; Schlumpf et al., 2013, 2014). Of course, there are sociocultural influences in the manifestation of this disorder, as in any mental disorder, as the sixteenth-century case of Jeanne Fery, presented at the beginning of this chapter, and the DSM-5 diagnostic criteria of DID testify. However, they do not explain the underlying, trauma-related dissociation of the personality. While those who express the belief that DID does not exist have done harm to the proper diagnosis and treatment of patients with complex dissociative disorders, the positive effects of their fixed ideas include the challenge and stimulation of ever more sophisticated research in the field.

Conclusions

This chapter on the history of dissociation, with an emphasis on DID, is inevitably a highly selective one. Nevertheless, it shows that complex dissociative disorders have been observed across history and cultures, regardless of the understanding of their etiology and the various names they received. It also demonstrates that international attention to dissociation and the dissociative disorders has grown rapidly during the last three decades. The phenomenological and neurobiological characteristics are much better understood, as well as the relationship between trauma and dissociation. Diagnostic and treatment procedures are improved, with outcome studies regarding phase-oriented treatment emerging. However, much work still needs to be done. A further worldwide dissemination of all that has been learned is strongly needed, as childhood maltreatment and thus trauma-induced dissociation are endemic across societies, nations, and cultures. Research, such as prevalence studies, should be conducted in many more countries around the world. With regard to the definition of dissociation, conceptual house cleaning remains an urgent challenge. However, this task might not be realised soon, if at all, as many researchers remain strongly attached to their own particular views, which may or may not be related to the original understanding of dissociation as a division of the personality. Perhaps a better knowledge of the history of the concept might facilitate the acceptance of a common conceptual denominator.

References

American Psychiatric Association. (1980). *DSM-III*. Washington, DC: APA.
American Psychiatric Association. (1994). *DSM-IV*. Washington, DC: APA.

American Psychiatric Association. (2013). *DSM-5*. Washington, DC: APA.

Azam, E. (1876). Le dédoublement de la personnalité, suite de l'histoire de Félida X. *Revue Scientifique, 18*: 265–269.

Barach, P. (1991). Multiple personality disorder as an attachment disorder. *Dissociation, 4*: 117–123.

Bernstein, E. M., & Putnam, F. W. (1986). Development, reliability, and validity of a dissociation scale. *Journal of Nervous and Mental Disease, 174*: 727–735.

Binet, A. (1896). *Alterations of Personality*. New York: Appleton.

Bleuler, E. (1911). *Dementia Praecox or the Group of Schizophrenias*. J. Zinkin (Trans.). New York: International Universities Press, 1950.

Bliss, E. L. (1986). *Multiple Personality, Allied Disorders, and Hypnosis*. New York: Oxford University.

Bourneville, D. (Ed.) (1886). *La possession de Jeanne Fery (1584)*. Paris: Progrès Médical/A. Delahaye et Lecrosnier.

Bourru, H., & Burot, P. (1885). Un cas de la multiplicité des états de conscience chez un hystéro-épileptique. *Revue Philosophique, 20*: 411–416.

Bowers, M., Brecher-Marer, S., Newton, B. W., Piotrowski, Z., Taylor, W., & Watkins, J. (1971). Therapy of multiple personality. *International Journal of Clinical & Experimental Hypnosis, 22*: 216–233.

Brand, B. L., Loewenstein, R. J., & Spiegel, D. (2014). Dispelling myths about dissociative identity disorder treatment: an empirically based approach. *Psychiatry, 77*: 169–189.

Brand, B., McNary, S., Myrick, A., Classen, C., Lanius, R., Loewenstein, R., Pain, C., & Putnam, F. (2013). A longitudinal naturalistic study of patients with dissociative disorders treated by community clinicians. *Psychological Trauma: Theory, Research, Practice, 5*: 301–308.

Braun, B. G. (Ed.) (1986). *Treatment of Multiple Personality Disorder*. Washington, DC: APA.

Bromberg, P. M. (1998). *Standing in the Spaces: Essays on Clinical Process, Trauma, and Dissociation*. Hillsdale, NJ: Analytic.

Bromberg, P. (2006). *Awakening the Dreamer: Clinical Journeys*. Mahwah, NJ: Analytic.

Bromberg, P. (2011). *In the Shadow of the Tsunami*. New York: Routledge.

Brown, D., Scheflin, A. W., & Hammond, D. C. (1998). *Memory, Trauma Treatment, and the Law*. New York: Norton.

Camuset, L. (1882). Un cas de dédoublement de la personnalité: Période amnésique d'une année chez un jeune homme. *Annales Medico-Psychologiques, 40*: 75–86.

Carlson, E. B. (1994). Studying the interaction between physical and psychological states with the Dissociative Experiences Scale. In: D. Spiegel (Ed.), *Dissociation: Culture, Mind, and Body* (pp. 41–58). Washington, DC: APA.

Carlson, E. B., & Putnam, F. W. (1993). An update on the Dissociative Experiences Scale. *Dissociation, 6*: 16–27.

Carlson, E. T. (1986). The history of dissociation until 1880. In: J. Q. Quen (Ed.), *Split Minds, Split Brains: Historical and Current Perspectives* (pp. 7–30). New York: New York University.

Chefetz, R. A. (2000). Disorders in the therapist's view of the self: working with the person with dissociative identity disorder. *Psychoanalytic Inquiry, 20*: 305–329.

Chefetz, R. A. (2015). *Intensive Psychotherapy for Persistent Dissociative States: The Fear of Feeling Real*. New York: W. W. Norton & Co.

Crabtree, A. (1986). Explanations of dissociation in the first half of the twentieth century. In: J. M. Quen (Ed.), *Split Minds, Split Brains: Historical and Current Perspectives* (pp. 85–107). New York: New York University.

Dalenberg, C. J., Brand, B. L., Loewenstein, R. J., Gleaves, D. H., Dorahy, M. J., Cardeña, E., Frewen, P. A., Carlson, E. B., & Spiegel, D. (2014). Reality versus fantasy: reply to Lynn et al. (2014). *Psychological Bulletin, 140*: 911–920.

Dalenberg, C. J., Brand, B. L., Gleaves, D. H., Dorahy, M. J., Loewenstein, R. J., Cardeña, E., Frewen, P. A., Carlson, E. B., & Spiegel, D. (2012). Evaluation of the evidence for the trauma and fantasy models of dissociation. *Psychological Bulletin, 138*: 550–588.

Davies, J. M., & Frawley, M. G. (1994). *Treating the Adult Survivor of Childhood Sexual Abuse*. New York: Basic.

Dell, P. F. (2006). The multidimensional inventory of dissociation (MID): a comprehensive measure of pathological dissociation. *Journal of Trauma and Dissociation, 7*(2): 77–106.

Dell, P. F., & O'Neil, J. A. (Eds.) (2009). *Dissociation and the Dissociative Disorders: DSM-V and Beyond*. New York: Routledge.

Despine, A. (1840). *De l'emploi du magnétisme animal et des eaux minérals dans le traitement des maladies nerveuses, suivi d'une observation très curieuse de guérison de névropathie*. Paris: Germer Ballière.

Dorahy, M. J., Brand, B. L., Şar, V., Krüger, C., Stavropoulos, P., Martínez-Taboas, A., Lewis-Fernández, R., & Middleton, W. (2014). Dissociative identity disorder: an empirical overview. *Australian & New Zealand Journal of Psychiatry, 48*: 402–417.

Dorahy, M., & Van der Hart, O. (2007). Relationship between trauma and dissociation. In: E. Vermetten, M. J. Dorahy, & D. Spiegel (Eds.), *Traumatic Dissociation: Neurobiology and Treatment* (pp. 3–30). Arlington, VA: APA.

Ellenberger, H. F. (1970). *The Discovery of the Unconscious*. New York: Basic.

Faure, H., Kersten, J., Koopman, D., & Van der Hart, O. (1997). The 19th century case of Louis Vivet: New findings and re-evaluation. *Dissociation, 10*: 104–113.

Ferenczi, S. (1949). Confusion of tongues between the adult and the child. *International Journal of Psycho-Analysis, 30*: 225–230.

Fine, C. G., & Berkowitz, A. S. (2001). The wreathing protocol: the imbrication of hypnosis and EMDR in the treatment of dissociative identity disorder and other dissociative responses. *American Journal of Clinical Hypnosis, 43*: 275–290.

Fraser, G. A. (Ed.) (1997). *The Dilemma of Ritual Abuse: Cautions and Guides for Therapists*. Washington, DC: APA.

Freud, S. (1936a). A Disturbance of Memory on the Acropolis. *S. E., 22*: 239. London: Hogarth.

Freud, S., & Breuer, J. (1893a). *On the Psychical Mechanism of Hysterical Phenomena: Preliminary Communication. S. E., 2*: 3. London: Hogarth.

Gonzalez, A., & Mosquera, D. (2012). *EMDR and Dissociation: The Progressive Approach*. Charleston, SC: Amazon.

Greaves, G. B. (1993). A history of multiple personality disorder. In: R. P. Kluft & C. G. Fine (Eds.), *Clinical Perspectives on Multiple Personality Disorder* (pp. 355–380). Washington, DC: APA.

Hacking, I. (1995). *Rewriting the Soul: Multiple Personality and the Sciences of Memory*. Princeton: Princeton University.

Hilgard, E. R. (1977). *Divided Consciousness: Multiple Controls in Human Thought and Action*. New York: Wiley.

Howell, E. F. (2005). *The Dissociative Mind*. Hillsdale, NJ: Analytic.

Howell, E. F. (2011). *Understanding and Treating Dissociative Identity Disorder: A Relational Approach*. New York: Routledge.

Howell, E. F., & Itzkowitz, S. (Eds.) (2016). *The Dissociative Mind in Psychoanalysis*. New York: Taylor & Francis.

Huber, M. (2010). *Multiple Persönlichkeiten: Seelische Zersplitterung nach Gewalt*. Paderborn: Junfermann.

International Society for the Study of Trauma and Dissociation (ISSTD) (2011). Guidelines for treating dissociative identity disorder in adults, third revision. *Journal of Trauma & Dissociation, 12*: 115–187.

James, W. (1890). *Principles of Psychology (Volumes 1 & 2)*. New York: Dover, 1950.

James, W. (1894). Review of Breuer and Freud, "Ueber den psychischen Mechanismus hysterischer Phänomene". *Psychological Review, 1*: 199.

Janet, P. (1889). *L'Automatisme Psychologique: Essai de Psychologie Expérimentale sur les Formes Inférieures de L'activité Humaine*. Paris: Alcan.

Janet, P. (1907). *The Major Symptoms of Hysteria*. London: Macmillan.

Janet, P. (1909). Problèmes psychologiques de l'émotion. *Revue Neurologique, 17*: 1551–1687.

Janet, P. (1919). *Psychological Healing*. New York: Macmillan, 1925. (Original French publication in 1919.)

Janet, P. (1927). *La Pensée Intérieure et Ses Troubles*. Paris: L'Harmattan, 2007.

Janet, P. (1977). *The Mental State of Hystericals: A Study of Mental Stigmata and Mental Accidents*. Washington, DC: University Publications of America. (Original publication in 1901.)

Jung, C. G. (1908). On dementia praecox. In: *The Symbolic Life: Miscellaneous*. London: Routledge & Kegan Paul, 1977.

Kluft, R. P. (1984). Multiple personality in childhood. *Psychiatric Clinics of North America, 7*: 121–134.

Kluft, R. P. (Ed.) (1985). *Childhood Antecedents of Multiple Personality*. Washington, DC: APA.

Kluft, R. P. (1996). Treating the traumatic memories of patients with dissociative identity disorder. *American Journal of Psychiatry, 153* (Festschrift Supplement): 103–110.

Kluft, R. P. (2013). *Shelter from the Storm: Processing the Traumatic Memories of DID/DDNOS Patients with the Fractionated Abreaction Technique*. North Charleston, NC: CreateSpace.

Kluft, R. P., & Fine, C. G. (Eds.) (1993). *Clinical Perspectives on Multiple Personality Disorder*. Washington, DC: APA.

Lanius, R. A., Vermetten, E., Loewenstein, R. J., Brand, B., Schmahl, C., Bremner, J. D., & Spiegel, D. (2010). Emotion modulation in PTSD: clinical and neurobiological evidence of a dissociative subtype. *American Journal of Psychiatry, 167*: 640–647.

Lensvelt-Mulders, G., Van der Hart, O., Van Ochten, J. M., Van Son, M. J. M., Steele, K., & Breeman, L. (2008). Relations among peritraumatic dissociation and posttraumatic stress: a meta-analysis. *Clinical Psychology Review, 28*: 1138–1151.

Lilienfeld, S. O., Lynn, S. J., Kirsch, I., Chaves, J. F., Sarbin, T. R., & Ganaway, G. K. (1999). Dissociative identity disorder and the sociocognitive model: recalling the lessons of the past. *Psychological Bulletin, 125*: 507–523.

Liotti, G. (1992). Disorganized/disoriented attachment in the etiology of the dissociative disorders. *Dissociation, 5*: 196–204.

Liotti, G. (1999). Disorganized attachment as a model for the understanding of dissociative psychopathology. In: J. Solomon & C. George (Eds.), *Attachment Disorganization* (pp. 232–256). Hove: Psychology.

Liotti, G. (2009). Attachment and dissociation. In: P. F. Dell & J. A. O'Neil (Eds.), *Dissociation and the Dissociative Disorders: DSM-V and Beyond* (pp. 53–65). New York: Routledge.

Loewenstein, R. J. (1991). An office mental status examination for complex chronic dissociative symptoms and multiple personality disorder. *Psychiatric Clinics of North America, 14*: 567–604.

Lyons-Ruth, K., Dutra, L., Schuder, M. R., & Bianchi, I. (2006). From infant attachment disorganization to adult dissociation: Relational adaptations or traumatic experiences? *Psychiatric Clinics of North America, 29*: 63–86.

Marmar, C. R., Weiss, D. S., Schlenger, W. E., Fairbank, J. A., Jordan, K., Kulka, R. A., & Hough, R. L. (1994). Peritraumatic dissociation and post-traumatic stress in male Vietnam theatre veterans. *American Journal of Psychiatry, 154*: 173–177.

McDougall, W. (1926). *An Outline of Abnormal Psychology*. London: Methuen & Co.

McKeown, J. M., & Fine, C. G. (Eds. & Trans.) (2008). *Despine and the Evolution of Psychology: Historical and Medical Perspectives on Dissociative Disorders*. New York: Palgrave Macmillan.

Merskey, H. (1992). The manufacture of personalities: the production of multiple personality disorder. *British Journal of Psychiatry, 160*: 327–340.

Michelson, L. K., & Ray, W. J. (Eds.) (1996). *Handbook of Dissociation*. New York: Plenum.

Mitchell, S. L. (1816). A double case of double consciousness, or a duality of persons in the same individual. *Medical Repository, 3*: 185–186.

Moskowitz, A. (2008). Association and dissociation in the historical concept of schizophrenia. In: A. Moskowitz, I. Schäfer, & M. Dorahy (Eds.), *Psychosis, Trauma and Dissociation: Emerging Perspectives on Severe Psychopathology* (pp. 35–49). London: Wiley-Blackwell.

Moskowitz, A., Schäfer, I., & Dorahy, M. (Eds.) (2008). *Psychosis, Trauma and Dissociation: Emerging Perspectives on Severe Psychopathology*. London: Wiley-Blackwell.

Myers, C. S. (1940). *Shell Shock in France 1914–1918*. Cambridge: Cambridge University.

Myers, F. (1903). *Human Personality and its Survival of Bodily Death (Volumes 1 & 2)*. London: Longmans, Green.

Nemiah, J. C. (1989). Janet redivivus: the centenary of *L'automatisme psychologique*. *American Journal of Psychiatry, 146*: 1527–1529.

Nijenhuis, E. R. S. (2004). *Somatoform Dissociation: Phenomena, Measurement, and Theoretical Issues*. New York: Norton.

Nijenhuis, E. R. S. (2014). Ten reasons for conceiving and classifying posttraumatic stress disorder as a dissociative disorder. *Psichiatria e Psicoterapia, 1*: 74–106.

Nijenhuis, E. R. S. (2015). *The Trinity of Trauma: Ignorance, Fragility, and Control*. Göttingen, Germany/Bristol, CT: Vandenhoeck & Ruprecht.

Ogawa, J. R., Sroufe, L. A., Weinfeld, N. S., Carlson, E. A., & Egeland, B. (1997). Development and the fragmented self: longitudinal study of dissociative symptomatology in a nonclinical sample. *Development and Psychopathology, 9*: 855–879.

Ogden, P., & Fisher, J. (2015). *Sensorimotor Psychotherapy: Interventions for Trauma and Attachment*. New York: W. W. Norton & Co.

Ogden, P., Minton, K., & Pain, C. (2006). *Trauma and the Body: A Sensorimotor Approach to Psychotherapy*. New York: Norton.

Prince, M. (1906). *The Dissociation of a Personality*. New York: Longmans, Green.

Putnam, F. W. (1989a). *Diagnosis and Treatment of Multiple Personality Disorder*. New York: Guilford.

Putnam, F. W. (1989b). Pierre Janet and Modern Views of Dissociation. *Journal of Traumatic Stress, 2*: 413–429.

Putnam, F. W. (1997). *Dissociation in Children and Adolescents: A Developmental Perspective*. New York: Guilford.

Reinders, A. A. T. S., Nijenhuis, E. R. S., Paans, A. M., Korf, J., Willemsen, A. T., & Den Boer, J. A. (2003). One brain, two selves. *Neuroimage, 20*: 2119–2125.

Rieber, R. (1999). Hypnosis, false memory and multiple personality: a trinity of affinity. *History of Psychiatry, 10*: 3–11.

Rivers, W. H. R. (1920). *Instinct and the Unconscious: A Contribution to a Biological Theory of the Psycho-neuroses*. Cambridge: Cambridge University.

Ross, C. A. (1989). *Multiple Personality Disorder: Diagnosis, Clinical Features, and Treatment*. Toronto: Wiley.

Ross, C. A. (1997). *Dissociative Identity Disorder: Diagnosis, Clinical Features, and Treatment of Multiple Personality*. New York: Wiley.

Ross, C. A. (2004). *Schizophrenia: Innovations in Diagnosis and Treatment*. New York: Haworth.

Şar, V. (2011). Epidemiology of dissociative disorders: an overview. *Epidemiology Research International* (article ID 404538). Available at: http://dx.doi.org/10.1155/2011/404538 [last accessed 12 November 2015].

Şar, V., Gamze, A., & Doğan, O. (2007). Prevalence of dissociative disorders among women in the general population. *Psychiatric Research, 149*: 169–176.

Şar, V., Koyuncu, A., & Öztürk, E. (2007). Dissociative disorders in the emergency psychiatric ward. *General Hospital Psychiatry, 29*: 45–50.

Schlumpf, Y. R., Nijenhuis, E., Chalavi, S., Weder, E. V., Zimmermann, E., Luechinger, L., la Marca, R., Reinders, A. A., & Jäncke, L. (2013). Dissociative part-dependent biopsychosocial reactions to backward masked angry and neutral faces: an fMRI study of dissociative identity disorder. *NeuroImage: Clinical, 3*: 54–64.

Schlumpf, Y. R., Reinders, A. A. T. S., Nijenhuis, E. R. S., Luechinger, R., Van Osch, M. J. P., & Jäncke, L. (2014). Dissociative part-dependent resting-state activity in dissociative identity disorder: A controlled fMRI perfusion study. *PLos ONE, 9*(6): e98795.

Schreiber, F. R. (1974). *Sybil*. New York: Warner.

Sidis, B. (1902). *Psychopathological Researches: Studies in Mental Dissociation.* New York: Strachert.

Sidis, B., & Goodhart, S. P. (1905). *Multiple Personality: An Experimental Investigation into the Nature of Human Individuality.* New York: Appleton.

Silberg, J. (2013). *The Child Survivor: Healing Developmental Trauma and Dissociation.* New York: Routledge.

Sinason, V. (Ed.) (1994). *Treating Survivors of Satanist Abuse.* London: Routledge.

Singer, J. (Ed.) (1990). *Repression and Dissociation: Implications for Personality Theory, Psychopathology, and Health.* Chicago: University of Chicago.

Spiegel, D. (Ed.) (2005). *Dissociation: Culture, Mind, and Body.* Washington, DC: APA.

Spiegel, D., & Cardeña, E. (1991). Disintegrated experience: the dissociative disorders revisited. *Journal of Abnormal Psychology, 100*: 366–378.

Steinberg, M. (1994). *Structured Clinical Interview for DSM-IV Dissociative Disorders (revised).* Washington, DC: APA.

Taylor, E. (1984). *William James on Exceptional Mental States: The 1896 Lowell Lectures.* Amherst, MA: University of Massachusetts.

Thigpen, C. H., & Cleckley, H. (1957). *The Three Faces of Eve.* New York: McGraw-Hill.

Twombly, J. H. (2000). Incorporating EMDR and EMDR adaptations into the treatment of clients with dissociative identity disorder. *Journal of Trauma & Dissociation, 1*(2): 61–80.

Van der Hart, O., Brown, P., & Van der Kolk, B. A. (1989). Pierre Janet's treatment of posttraumatic stress. *Journal of Traumatic Stress, 2*: 379–396.

Van der Hart, O., & Dorahy, M. (2009). Dissociation: history of a concept. In: P. F. Dell & J. A. O'Neil (Eds.), *Dissociation and the Dissociative Disorders: DSM-V and Beyond* (pp. 2–26). New York: Routledge.

Van der Hart, O., & Friedman, B. (1989). A reader's guide to Pierre Janet on dissociation: a neglected intellectual heritage. *Dissociation, 2*(1): 3–16.

Van der Hart, O., Lierens, R., & Goodwin, J. (1996). Jeanne Fery: a sixteenth-century case of dissociative identity disorder. *Journal of Psychohistory, 24*(1): 18–35.

Van der Hart, O., Nijenhuis, E. R. S., & Steele, K. (2006). *The Haunted Self: Structural Dissociation and the Treatment of Chronic Traumatization.* New York: Norton.

Van der Kolk, B. A., & Van der Hart, O. (1989). Pierre Janet and the breakdown of adaptation in psychological trauma. *American Journal of Psychiatry, 146*: 1530–1540.

Van Duijl, M., Nijenhuis, E., Komproe, I. H., Gernaat, H. B. P. E., & De Jong, J. T. (2010). Dissociative symptoms and reported trauma among patients with spirit possession and matched healthy controls. *Culture, Medicine & Psychiatry, 34*: 380–400.

Vermetten, E., Dorahy, M., & Spiegel, D. (Eds.) (2007). *Traumatic Dissociation: Neurobiology and Treatment.* Arlington, VA: APA.

Wieland, S. (Ed.) (2011). *Dissociation in Children and Adolescents: Clinical Case Studies.* New York: Routledge.

World Health Organization (1992). *ICD-10.* Geneva: WHO.

Zemach, E. (1986). Unconscious mind or conscious minds? *Midwest Studies in Philosophy, 10*: 121–149.

CHAPTER FOUR

Cross-temporal and cross-cultural perspectives on dissociative disorders of identity

Eli Somer

> I swore never to be silent whenever and wherever human beings endure suffering and humiliation. We must always take sides. Neutrality helps the oppressor, never the victim. Silence encourages the tormentor, never the tormented. (Ellie Wiesel: Nobel acceptance speech, 10 December, 1986)

I first planned to write this chapter as a purely academic project aimed at reviewing culturally divergent manifestations of altered states of consciousness and identity that I saw as pertinent to dissociative identity disorder (DID). I knew, then, that the book was planned to include a first-person account of DID and that my chapter would be part of its scientific backdrop. However, when I read the memoir I realised not only the courage of the writer but also the atmosphere of secrecy, silencing, and scepticism that surround the experiences of victims of child abuse in general and ritual abuse in particular.

For a long time, an atmosphere of doubt and delegitimisation has haunted survivors, their therapists, and scholars of dissociation. Memories of childhood abuse, rooted in serious crimes, have been labeled false by the accused families, therapists have been charged with implanting false memories, and scholars have been attacked for propagating scientifically unfounded concepts, false diagnoses, and harmful therapies.

In the prologue to her memoir the anonymous author wrote: "The continued belief in false memories leads to shame-based self-esteems and limits opportunities for the mistaken belief that the self is bad, deserving and responsible for the abuse, to be challenged." After reading these words I decided that this chapter would be written as a response to the stigmatisation of severe dissociative psychopathology (and those who suffer from it) as iatrogenic, extremely rare, or even feigned. My commitment to this project doubled when I realised that the story of the memoir's author will not be included in this book because of fears of retribution from the perpetrators. Although the safety of the survivor-author was given priority here, the dissemination of knowledge on the reality of severe child abuse and its outcome cannot be silenced. This chapter is dedicated to the author of the unpublished memoir and to the countless victims of childhood abuse in Africa and around the globe.

DID has been reliably diagnosed in a variety of mental health settings in countries across the globe (Martínez-Taboas, Dorahy, Şar, Middelton, & Kruger, 2013). Epidemiological data show that up to 1.5% of the general population meet diagnostic criteria for DID (Şar, Akyüz, & Doğan, 2007). Despite the evidence showing that the disorder is neither rare nor limited to particular societies, arguments are still raised that because DID is "an absurd fad", it is ignored by most psychiatrists (Paris, 2013, p. 357). The socio-cognitive model of DID understands the disorder as a series of role enactments which are directed towards achieving social reinforcements by therapists who create and maintain these maladaptive behaviours (Lilienfeld & Lynn, 2003; Spanos, 1996) in susceptible individuals who are fantasy prone (Lynn, Rhue, & Green, 1988). The alternative post-traumatic model of DID maintains that the disorder is an outcome of childhood neglect and abuse and that traumatised children compartmentalise their intolerable and inescapable experiences into alternate personality states (Putnam, 1997; Ross, 1989). Proponents of the post-traumatic model of DID have tended to reject the socio-cognitive model and to ignore the various historical and cultural expressions of disorders of identity (e.g., Dell, 2006; Gleaves, 1996). I agree with Lilienfeld et al. (1999) that the existence of social, cross-cultural, and historical influences on the manifestations of identity alterations may represent an area of common ground between the socio-cognitive and the trauma models (ibid., p. 520). I also maintain that this sort of influence cannot be unique to DID and that similar influences are probably exerted on other forms of psychopathology. Culture-bound disorders of identity probably reflect not only societal oppression and the personal trauma of the ailing individual but also those idioms of distress that are sanctioned in that particular culture (Somer, 2006).

In this chapter, dissociative disorders of identity are explored mostly from an etic perspective. Behaviours or beliefs will be presented not only from a socio-cognitive viewpoint, which regards the investigated psychological phenomena as products of the norms and expectations of the cultural milieu in which they occur, but also from a trauma and dissociation stance which will be more culturally neutral. Evidence to be presented in this chapter about the existence of dissociative disorders of identity in various cultures, some of which may have never been exposed to any systematic dissemination of knowledge regarding dissociative disorders, could suggest an independence of these syndromes from popular or specific professional Western influence. Evidence showing that disorders of the sense of agency and identity among oppressed segments in traditional patriarchal cultures could imply that these phenomena are less related to short-lived Western fashions but perhaps reflect attempts to cope with societal or personal oppression.

Cross-temporal perspectives on dissociative disorders of identity

Cultures do not only vary across geographical and ethnic boundaries. A regional culture and its conceptual frames of reference typically evolve along the axis of time. In this section I review generational trends in the understanding of disowned psychological experiences. The oldest records of "alter" control of a human being by spirits that cause mental disturbances are probably those mentioned in the Old Testament. These spirits were understood to be sent by God to torment people. For example: "behold, the Lord hath put a lying spirit in the mouth of all these thy prophets" (1 Kings 22:23), or "But the Spirit of the Lord departed from Saul, and an evil spirit from the Lord troubled him" (1 Samuel 16:14). The belief in Satan and his army of demons first appears in Jewish writings after 300 BCE. At the time of the first century CE, it is a well-developed concept in the Land of Israel. There are literally dozens of passages referring to demon possession causing mental and physical illnesses in the New Testament. A major feature of Jesus' ministry is portrayed as curing people of demonic possession through exorcism. For example:

> Jesus rebuked the foul spirit saying unto him, "Thou dumb and deaf spirit, I charge thee, come out of him, and enter him no more." And the spirit did come out after shrieking aloud and convulsing violently. (St Mark 9, 25–27, cited in Moffatt, 2013)

A more detailed discussion of possession trance will follow.

Accounts of dissociative identity changes have been published in eras that preceded any knowledge about dissociative disorders. For example, the successful exorcism in 1586 of Jeanne Fery, a nun who was possessed not only by harmful "devils", but by benign devils who protected her in childhood when being beaten, and also by a cooperative personality alter named Mary Magdalene (Van der Hart, Lierens, & Goodwin, 1996). Another example is the tale of Italian nun Benedetta Carlini, who was possessed by three angelic boys who took over her body, spoke different dialects, produced specific facial expressions, and caused her chronic pain. Benedetta had amnesia not only for these appearances but also for her sexual relationship with Sister Bartolemea, who was assigned to her cell for protection (Brown, 1986). Sixteenth-century eyewitness accounts of dissociative identity alterations associated with dybbuk possession described women from Safed, Israel who were possessed by male spirits whose chosen loci of the entrance and exit were highly suggestive of sexual intercourse (Somer, 2004). Descriptions of identity alterations that were not presented as possession cases first emerged in the late eighteenth and the beginning of the nineteenth centuries.

Following are illustrative descriptions of dissociative disorders of identity from the last 200 years, all from an era preceding current popular or academic knowledge about dissociative disorders.

- In 1791 Eberhardt Gmelin published a case he named *umgetauschte Persönlichkeit* (exchanged personality) in which he describes the reaction of a young German woman from Stuttgart to her encounter with aristocratic refugees from the French Revolution (Gmelin, 1791). The woman suddenly exhibited a personality who spoke perfect French and otherwise behaved in the manner of a Frenchwoman of the time. She would periodically enter these states and then return to her normal German state. Her new alter personality spoke in elegant, idiomatic French and struggled when she attempted to speak German. The two states had no direct knowledge of each other.

- A description of identity alterations during a brutal murder of a stranger followed by amnesia was provided by Anselm Feuerbach. In 1828 Sörgel, an epileptic young German shepherd, killed, butchered, and cannibalised a man he met in the forest while collecting wood. "He then returned to the village, quietly related what he had done, and returned a while later to his normal state of consciousness in which he seemed to recall nothing at all" (Ellenberger, 1970, p. 124). Similar cases were much discussed during the nineteenth century and were sometimes interpreted as instances of transient multiple personality.

- Despine, a general practitioner, described the successful treatment case of Estelle, an eleven-year-old Swiss girl, who demonstrated a dual personality (Despine, 1840). In one she was paralysed, suffering from intense pain, low appetite and showed respect to Despine, and in the other she was able to walk, run and play, and eat abundantly, and was disrespectful to both Despine and her mother.

- Another case was described in Kerner's notable description of the girl from Orlach (1834). Here is an excerpt of Kerner's description:

> The girl loses consciousness, her "Self" disappears or rather leaves in order to make place for another "Self". Another spirit now takes possession of this organism, of its sense organs, of its nerves and muscles, speaks with this throat, thinks with these brain nerves … It is just as if a stronger one appears and chases the owner out of the house and then looks comfortably out of the window as if it would be his own. Since it is not an unconsciousness which takes place, a conscious self inhabits without any interruption the body, the spirit which is now in her knows very well—even better than before—what happens around him, but it is a different resident that lives in there. (Kerner, 1834, p. 42, cited in Peter, 2011, p. 91)

From the mid-nineteenth century onward, occurrences of multiple personalities began to be described objectively and discussed in writing by European physicians (e.g., Azam, 1887; Camuset, 1882; Flournoy, 1900; Moreau de Tours, 1845; Myers, 1887). The most influential early contributions to modern understanding of pathological dissociation came from France (Jean-Martin Charcot and Pierre Janet) and the United States (Morton Prince):

- Some of Jean-Martin Charcot's most famous lectures at the Salpêtrière Hospital in Paris focused on cases involving alterations of identity and loss of the sense of agency and amnesia (Charcot, 1889). For example: a fifty-four-year-old midwife was on her way to assist with a delivery one night in 1885. She fell on the staircase and lost her conscious awareness briefly, came to, proceeded to the patient's apartment, delivered the baby and went back home and fell asleep. Hours later, after she had been called by the mother, the midwife reacted with violent shivers and then regained her former identity, only to be deeply perplexed as to how the baby had been delivered, recalling nothing about the complex procedure she had performed only hours earlier.
- Pierre Janet is considered to be the first to explicitly conceptualise dissociation and dissociative disorders of identity and to describe them as psychological defences against overwhelming trauma (Van der Hart & Horst, 1989). Janet claimed that the integrative capacity of the mind can be challenged by stress and lead to the splitting off (*dédoublement*) of nuclei of consciousness which can continue to lead lives of their own, as demonstrated by his famous patient Lucie/ Adrienne (Janet, 1886).
- Morton Prince (1906), an American neurologist with an interest in abnormal psychology is best known for his classical description of the case of the traumatised twenty-three-year-old Miss Beauchamp. In his report he identified four alternating personalities. Prince pointed out that all conscious states, "belong to, take part in, or help to make up a self" (ibid., p. 76) and coined the term "co-consciousness".

The rich history of documented cases displaying disordered senses of agency and identity suggests that Western healers had been aware of these mental aberrations and the associated suffering, long before the modern era debate on the validity of DID surfaced. These very similar cross-temporal descriptions of dissociative phenomena were presented with divergent meanings reflecting the prevailing zeitgeist and contemporary knowledge. An examination of historical and current non-Western manifestations of DID-related phenomena can help determine the extent to which dissociative disorders of identity are specific to present-day North America and the West, as the detractors of this field would argue.

Cross-cultural perspectives on dissociative disorders of identity

Dissociative disorders — not just Western phenomena

My approach in writing this chapter is both universalist and relativist, or time- and culture-specific. In line with Kim and Berry (1993), I maintain that it is possible to reach a universalist formulation of similar illness expressions (derived etic) described from a medical anthropology (emic) point of view. As posited earlier in this chapter, the universal existence of DID and other forms of mental health are clearly influenced by social and cultural forces which determine the specific local idioms of distress and their behavioural manifestations. This realisation and the unfortunate, yet understandable, defensive stance against it is concisely reflected in the title of a book published a decade ago: *Trauma and Dissociation in a Cross-cultural Perspective: Not Just a North-American Phenomenon* (Rhodes & Şar, 2005). This section of the chapter will present data on the universal validity of dissociative psychopathology by demonstrating cross-cultural occurrences of dissociative disorders of agency and identity, primarily as manifested in various forms of dissociative trance disorder (DTD).

The epidemiology and phenomenology of dissociative disorders have been documented in non-clinical populations in Canada (Ross, 1991), Turkey (Akyüz, Doğan, Şar, Yargic, & Tutkun, 1999; Tutkun et al., 1998), and the USA (Murphy, 1994; Ross, Duffy, & Ellason, 2002), and in clinical populations in Australia (Middleton & Butler, 1998), Canada (Ellason, Ross, Sainton, & Mayran, 1996), China (Fan et al., 2011; Xiao et al., 2006), Germany (Gast, Rodewald, Nickel, & Emrich, 2001), India (Adityanjee & Khandelwal, 1989; Chaturvedi, Desai, & Shaligram, 2010); Israel (Ginzburg, Somer, Tamarkin, & Kramer, 2010; Somer, Ross, Kirshberg, Shawahday Bakri, & Ismail, in press), Japan (Uchinuma & Sekine, 2000); Norway (Knudsen, Draijer, Haselrud, Boe, & Boon, 1995), Puerto Rico (Martínez-Taboas, 1989), South Africa (Gangdev & Matjave, 1996); Switzerland (Modestin, 1992), and the Netherlands (Friedl & Draijer, 2000).

In contrast to the above-presented evidence on the occurrence of dissociative disorders internationally, some scepticism about the validity and universality of these disorders persists. According to the socio-cognitive model of dissociation, dissociative disorders are a product of a popular Western psychological discourse. According to this model dissociative disorders are rare and typically emerge in response to cultural influences and role demands made by therapists (e.g., Piper & Merskey, 2004a, 2004b). The socio-cognitive model excludes, of course, the trauma model for dissociative disorders. An elegant refutation of the social contamination model of dissociative psychopathology was demonstrated with data collected in China (Ross, et al., 2008). The authors compared two samples with similar rates of reported childhood physical and sexual abuse: one from Canada and one from China, where no popular or professional knowledge about DID exists, precluding iatrogenesis and social persuasion processes from contaminating the clinical phenomena. The results were inconsistent with the socio-cognitive model for pathological dissociation as both samples reported similar levels of pathological dissociation.

The occurrence of dissociative experiences and the belief in possession by "non-me" entities has been widely documented in the anthropological literature. For example, in 488 societies studied, Bourguignon (1970, 1973) identified various forms of institutionalised altered states of consciousness in 90%, possession beliefs in 74%, and possession trance in 52% of societies. Lewis-Fernandez (1992) argued that most non-Western cultures, which make up 80% of the world's total, exhibit culturally patterned dissociative syndromes, typically manifesting major discontinuities of consciousness, memory, identity, and behaviour. In fact, possession trance disorder has actually been part of the DSM-IV-TR Dissociative Disorder Not Otherwise Specified (American Psychiatric Association, 2000) and defined ("where the dissociative or trance disorder is not a normal part of a broadly accepted collective cultural or religious practice.") as a:

> single or episodic disturbances in the state of consciousness, identity, or memory that are indigenous to particular locations and cultures. Dissociative trance involves narrowing of awareness of immediate surroundings or stereotyped behaviors or movements that are experienced as being beyond one's control. Possession trance involves replacement of the customary sense of personal identity by a new identity, attributed to the influence of a spirit, power, deity, or other

person, and associated with stereotyped "involuntary" movements
or amnesia and is perhaps the most common Dissociative Disorder
in Asia. (APA, 2000, p. 301)

Although experiences of pathological possession are very common
expressions of DID in cultures around the world, they were not included
in the DSM-IV-TR diagnostic criteria. The dissociative disorders work
group recommended including language that encompasses possession disorders, to assist diagnosis in cultures where the "diagnostic
niche" of dissociative disorders related to identity alteration is filled
by possession-related symptoms (Spiegel et al., 2011). In the DSM-5
(American Psychiatric Association, 2013) the APA formally incorporated possession as part of the theoretical framework of the dissociative
paradigm to state that dissociative identity disorder is a:

> Disruption of identity characterized by two or more distinct
> personality states or an experience of possession, as evidenced
> by discontinuities in sense of self, cognition, behavior, affect,
> perceptions, and/or memories. (APA, 2013, p. 292)

This accomplishment for the field of dissociative disorders was under-
scored by recent data published showing that possession trance disorder (PTD) symptoms measured in Uganda meet DSM-5 criteria for
DID (Van Duijl, Kleijn, & de Jong, 2013). The authors expressed their
reservation, however, about APA's colonial stance by arguing that "ranking PTD (described in over 360 societies) under DID (described in con-
siderably fewer societies) expresses a Western ethnocentric approach"
(ibid., p. 1428).

A comprehensive survey of reported dissociative disorders of
identity in non-Western cultures is beyond the scope of this chapter. For
the sake of conciseness, I will focus on select reports on PTD from Asia
and Africa to illustrate non-Western ("culture-bound") manifestations
of dissociative psychopathology involving alterations of identity.

Possession Trance Disorder (PTD)

Goodman (1988) suggested that we might think of possession trance
as representing a range of experience spanning from the socially sanctioned, construed, learned, and ritually controllable possession by

revered deities at one end of the spectrum, to the unauthorised, unruly, and threatening occurrences of demonic possession, representing PTD, at the other.

PTD in a Hindu context

The world's third largest religion with an estimated one billion followers, Hinduism promotes belief in reincarnation, the continuity of life from one birth to the next until the soul is realised and reaches nirvana (Juthani, 2001). Illness and misfortune are frequently regarded in India as the result of possession by a spirit, or *bhut bhada*. Brockman (2000) reported that, in India, to be possessed is to be the victim of a chance event and not about failures or conflicts that arise from within. It serves as explanations for sudden changes in behaviour such as "voices" heard suddenly, these being understood as the voice of a spirit which has entered the body by pushing out the spirit which usually resides and "talks" within. Despite the purported chance causality in PTD among Hindus, evidence suggests a strong link between PTD and stress. For example, at the time of a smallpox epidemic in India, 400 admissions to a psychiatric hospital presented with disowned identity due to possession (Varma, Srivastava, & Shahay, 1970). Treatment from a traditional healer is usually sought first when a demon or a harmful spirit is the possessing agent (Castillo, 1994; Varma, Bouri, & Wig, 1981). Practitioners of the ancient Hindu system of medicine, the Ayurveda, often use their own possession states for diagnosis and confrontation with their patients' possessing spirits (Gadit, 2003). It was reported that 75% of psychiatric patients in India consulted religious healers about possession (Campion & Bhugra, 1994). The unique clinical pictures presented by Indian psychiatric patients renders many of them unclassifiable by the DSM or the ICD manuals (Alexander & Das, 1997). Recently, however, anthropological research reported a homogenisation of the identities of spirits and the use of psychological idioms, a change interpreted as signaling an erosion of context and the ascendance of universal categories (Hallibrun, 2005). A description of PTD in India was offered by Akhtar (1988):

> A woman in her twenties and faced with an affect-laden situation, starts having periods of altered states of consciousness. During these spells, she behaves as if she is a different person, as if a religious deity, or the spirit of a dead relative or neighbor has taken

over her mind and body. Her demeanor changes markedly and her face acquires an entirely new repertoire of expressions. Body movements of various kinds occur and she starts talking. The possessing spirit then, through her, makes various demands on the surroundings, usually from near relatives who humbly comply with them. This sometimes brings a single episode of possession to an end … Often at this stage, the patient is taken to a faith-healer believed to be capable of conversing with and driving away the spirit in question. (ibid., p. 71)

This account portrays how in a culture alien to Western psychotherapy, the stressed woman expresses her suffering in a disowned manner which is adaptive, in the sense that it signals the support system to appease her.

PTD in a Confucian context

In China, Taiwan, and Korea, religious beliefs are mostly influenced by Confucianism, an obedience- and conformity-promoting faith, and by Taoism, a creed that embraces the principles of dual energies (yin and yang) and of a spirit world of immortal creatures that could intercede for devotees. Reports from rural areas in these parts of the world, where people cling to their religious convictions, describe possession agents representing spirits of deceased individuals, deities, animals, and devils, and describe possession as developing abruptly and manifested particularly among distressed women (Gaw, Ding, Levine, & Gaw, 1988). In Japan, most of the nation's many horticulturalist-, Shinto-, and Buddhist-derivative religions are said to attract individuals who have stress-related illness. Believers often consider illness as caused by dojo possession: evil spirits, unhappy ghosts, or dangerous spirits of animals (Davis, 1980). A description of divine possession presented by a twenty-seven-year-old Korean immigrant in the USA was presented by Yongmi Yi (2000):

Following a stressful acculturation period and a prolonged conflict with her sister the woman suffered from waist bending, nightmares and olfactory hallucinations. She had difficulty breathing, and felt that some kind of ki (energy or spirit) had entered her body. When these symptoms continued for several weeks with no sign of abatement, her older sister ventured an observation that these symptoms happened to other people when a shin (god) was trying to enter them. The two women then arranged to visit a Korean shaman in the city. The shaman explained that Anna's symptoms were caused by haan-laden dead ancestors trying to enter into her. (Haan is a Korean word describing accumulated and unresolved feelings of resentment, anger, and grief over experiences of victimisation or oppression.) The shaman told Anna that the ancestral spirits chose her to be their carrier because other members of the family either were too stubborn or were otherwise unsuitable. In order to be rid of her symptoms, the shaman instructed her to receive the spirits and become a shaman. Anna was frightened of this prospect and protested against it. The shaman then suggested a way out of this fate by prescribing a goot (shamanic ritual) to comfort the spirits. Anna was convinced that during this ritual her dead relatives entered the shaman's body and spoke out their haan through the shaman's mouth. The stories these dead relatives told via the shaman seemed to Anna to be very real and convincing. At the end of the ritual, Anna was told that the spirit of one of her dead uncles was her protector and that with his protection she now would not be required to become a shaman. Anna did not have new severe bouts of the symptom following the goot. (ibid., pp. 472–473)

This PTD account describes dissociative alterations of agency and identity that allowed for disowned feelings of anger to be expressed within animistic and Confucian paradigms. The shaman provided the patient with a corrective reparative relationship with her ancestral caregivers while addressing issues that were psychologically pertinent to the dissociating patient. The relationship between PTD and psychological stress and trauma was also demonstrated in a wider study in Singapore (Ng & Chan, 2004). All the participants with PTD from a sample of ethnic Chinese patients (adhering to a blend of Confucianism, Buddhism, and Taoism) described at least one overwhelming psycho-social precipitator, primarily: conflicts over religious and cultural issues, military life, and domestic disharmony.

PTD in a Muslim context

The model for understanding illness or personal problems in the Muslim context is jinn possession. The Qur'an and Sunnah indicate that jinn exist and that there is a purpose for their existence in this life, which is to worship Allah. However, jinn invading humans are essentially bad because they tend to inflict maladies. Often spirits are thought to physically strike or possess a person incidentally with the person ignorant of the reason for the affliction in the first instance (Crapanzano, 1973). The word jinn comes from an Arabic root meaning "hidden from sight". The ability to possess and take over the minds and bodies of other creatures is one of the powers attributed to the jinn.

Muslim tradition dictates that the individual expresses only love and positive regard for his or her parents. Expression of frustration, anger, or hatred is forbidden, even if the children are neglected or maltreated. The individual can expect to enjoy familial support and to have his or her needs met by the family. In return, one relinquishes needs pertaining to actualisation of the self. Aggressive feelings towards members of the immediate and extended family are functionally repressed. The conformist choice actually condones intra-psychic dissociation and repression as a means of circumventing conflict between the person and society (Somer, 2001). Traditions in these societies allow for dissociated and somatised distress to be expressed in ways that reinforce the supremacy of male-dominated society and validate religion. The solution is for a religious healer to exorcise the spirit, or to appease God or the possessing agents, which then frees the person from the affliction (Abdullah, 2007).

Below are excerpts from a case study of Sheila, an Urdu-speaking twenty-four-year-old married woman possessed by djinnati in Iran (Kianpoor & Rhoades, 2006):

> She presented with the chief complaints of irritability, apprehension, impaired memory and episodes of compromised consciousness and change of identity. The problem had developed gradually six months after her obligatory marriage at age thirteen to an age fourty wealthy widower (father of two). The attacks, as her brother explained, would start with a trance state after staring for a while. The patient would exhibit escape-like behavior, accompanied by screaming ... The patient would calm down after three to five minutes (with the help of her family, ES) and would begin to speak in a different voice in fluent English. During the attacks, the patient would introduce herself as a female djinni named Flora. Flora noted that she lived in England, but liked Sheila and her beautiful features and so would sometimes capture Sheila's body. When

possessed, Sheila behaved and spoke in a disinhibited way with the family, especially the son and daughter of her husband. The attacks would last up to an hour. The family would usually take the patient to the local healers to "push out" the djinn ... She had no memory of the attacks or of Flora, but was aware that there are many episodes of amnesia when she didn't know what had happened. (ibid., pp. 151–152)

This case description illustrates the universal features of this dissociative disorder: potentially traumatic circumstances in the life of a member of an oppressed group; Schneiderian first-rank symptoms such as made feelings and actions, alteration of identity, amnesia; as well as its shaping by the specific cultural milieu in which it is expressed. This case demonstrates how PTD can allow a child-wife the expression of otherwise self-endangering behaviours (challenging her stepchildren, symbols of her oppression, in a disinhibited way) in a socially condoned manner that preserves the local male-dominated social structure (she is brought to religious male healers by her brother).

PTD in the African syncretist context

Traumatic stress resulting from civil conflicts, poverty, and epidemics may be manifested in Africa through symptoms that are locally understood to originate from spirits or witchcraft. Reis (2013), for example, has argued that in Northern Uganda, "Children's externalization of evil in the notion of contagious revengeful spirits, and their internalization of evil in the notion of child-witches exemplify their problems in dealing with the grief, guilt, anger, and anxiety which result from a severely damaged moral fabric which can no longer sustain and nurture them" (ibid., p. 635). Contemporary literature on the phenomenology and treatment of African PTD includes descriptions of possession by Zar spirits among Ethiopians. These spirits are said to favour victims subjected to psychosocial stressors. Zar possession is often perceived as a situation in which the spirit has a sexual relationship with the victim who is of the opposite sex; often a woman sleeping alone at night is attacked by a male Zar spirit (Witztum & Grisaru, 1996) and exorcism ceremonies involve chanting, drumming and dancing (e.g., Somer & Saadon, 2000). Another source of information on indigenous African forms of PTS emanates from South Africa (e.g., Swartz, 1998).

Amafufunyana (literally, "the evil spirits") can be contracted by chance or through witchcraft.

Following are excerpts from a description of *amafufunyana* presented by a Xhosa girl in a rural village in the Eastern Cape of South Africa (Krüger, Sokudela, Motlana, Mataboge, & Dikobe, 2007):

> Nomthandazo fell ill and became confused for a few days ... Her family consulted a traditional healer but this did not help. Her symptoms of restlessness, fever, and confused speech worsened. Her behaviour became odd. She started walking on all fours. Her voice changed to that of a young man, and she called herself by this young man's name. Her family recognised the name and voice as those of a young man known to have passed away two years earlier. The girl described the events that had led to his death. He alleged that one of their neighbours had bewitched him and was using him as a slave. He said that he was not quite dead but could not come back to life as he had been bewitched. As a means of healing and resolution the family decided to take Nomthandazo to the neighbour that the male voice had reported to have bewitched him. A crowd gathered in the house. The alleged witch was confronted with the information gathered and the girl, through the male voice, openly accused the neighbour of witchcraft. As they all stood inside, the house suddenly caught fire, starting at the top of the thatched roof ... The girl and her family returned home, at which time her symptoms resolved and her voice returned to normal. She was, however, amnesic regarding these events. She was subsequently able to return to school and remained well. (ibid., pp. 14–15)

Ensink & Robertson (1996) report that stress was the feature most commonly mentioned as associated with *amafufunyana* by healer respondents. The authors identified support for the notion that *amafufunyana* is a dissociative disorder, in which abusive or traumatic experiences are regarded as causal. In line with observations in other cultural contexts of PTD, Zar possession and *amafufunyana* can provide meaningful explanations which are consistent with a broader religious belief system and social structure, ensures continued social support for the disenfranchised patient, provides an acceptable explanatory framework for the patient as to why his or her condition arose, offers a means of minimising stigma for the oppressed patient, and an apportioning of blame for the condition elsewhere (Lundt, 1994; Somer & Saadon, 2000).

Conclusion

The evidence presented in this chapter does not support claims that dissociative disorders of identity are iatrogenic, cultural artifacts due to transient social influences, rare or simulated (Spanos, 1996). The consistency of core elements in documented cases of pathological conversion and possession trance throughout history and across cultures speaks volumes to the stable validity of dissociative psychopathology and its traumatic genesis. In fact, the core elements of "culture-bound" syndromes are not unique to non-Western societies. For example, by administering the Dissociative Trance Disorder Interview Schedule to 100 predominantly Caucasian, American, English-speaking trauma programme inpatients at a hospital in the United States, Ross, Schroeder, and Ness (2013) found a wide range of possession experiences and exorcism rituals, as well as the classical culture-bound syndromes of *latah*, *bebainan*, *amok*, and *pibloktoq*, suggesting that the classical culture-bound syndromes are not really culture bound but rather universal. At the same time, I acknowledge in this chapter the emic perspectives on emotional distress and illness and its unique manifestation in dissociative disorders of identity, such as DID and PTD. The data reviewed in this section of the book weakens attempts to polarise the trauma versus the socio-cognitive models of DID (Boysen & VanBergen, 2013) because it supports previous assertions that post-traumatic and dissociative disorders, as indeed all psychopathological phenomena, are always coloured by cultural and societal processes (Şar, Krüger, Martínez-Taboas, Middelton, & Dorhay, 2013; Swartz, 1998).

References

Abdullah, S. (2007). Islam and counseling: models of practice in Muslim communal life. *Journal of Pastoral Counseling, 42*: 42–55.

Adityanjee, R. G. S., & Khandelwal, S. K. (1989). Current status of multiple personality disorder in India. *The American Journal of Psychiatry, 146*(12): 1607–1610.

Akhtar, S. (1988). Four culture-bound psychiatric syndromes in India. *The International Journal of Social Psychiatry, 34*(1): 70–74.

Akyüz, G., Doğan, O., Şar, V., Yargic, L. I., & Tutkun, H. (1999). Frequency of dissociative identity disorder in the general population in Turkey. *Comprehensive Psychiatry, 40*: 151–159.

Alexander, P. J., & Das, J. A. (1997). Limited utility of ICD-10 and DSM-IV classification of dissociative and conversion disorders in India. *Acta Psychiatrica Scandinavica, 95*: 177–182.

American Psychiatric Association. (2000). *Diagnostic and Statistical Manual of Mental Disorders: DSM-IV-TR.* Washington, DC: APA.

American Psychiatric Association. (2013). *Diagnostic and Statistical Manual of Mental Disorders* (5th edn). Washington, DC: APA.

Azam, E. E. (1887). *Hypnotisme, Double Conscience et Altérations de la Personnalité: le Cas Félida X (Hypnotism, Double Consciousness, and Personality Changes: the Case Félida X).* Paris: Baillière.

Boysen, G. A., & VanBergen, A. (2013). A review of published research on adult dissociative identity disorder. *Journal of Nervous and Mental Disease, 201*: 5–11.

Brockman, R. (2000). Possession and Medicine in South Central India. *Journal of Applied Psychoanalytic Studies, 2*(3): 299–312.

Brown, J. C. (1986). *Immodest Acts: The Life of a Lesbian Nun in Renaissance Italy.* New York: Oxford University.

Bourguignon, E. (1970). *Possession.* San Francisco, CA: Chandler & Sharp.

Bourguignon, E. (Ed.) (1973). *Religion, Altered States of Consciousness, and Social Change.* Columbus, OH: Ohio State University.

Campion, J., & Bhugra, D. (1994). *Religious Healing in South India.* Presented at the World Association of Social Psychiatry Meeting. Hamburg, Germany.

Camuset, L. (1882). Un cas de dédoublement de la personnalité; piriode amnésique d'une annie chez un jeune homme. *Annales Medico-Psychologgues, 40*: 75–86.

Castillo, R. J. (1994). Spirit possession in South Asia, dissociation or hysteria? I. Theoretical background. *Culture, Medicine and Psychiatry, 8*(1): 1–21.

Charcot, J. M. (1889). *Leçons du Mardi à la Salpêtrière.* Paris: Bureau du Progrès Mèdical.

Chaturvedi, S. K., Desai, G., & Shaligram, D. (2010). Dissociative disorders in a psychiatric institute in India—a selected review and patterns over a decade. *International Journal of Social Psychiatry, 56*(5): 533–539.

Crapanzano, V. (1973). *The Hamadsha. A study in Moroccan Ethnopsychiatry.* Berkeley, CA: University of California.

Davis, W. (1980). *Dojo: Magic and Exorcism in Modern Japan.* Stanford, CA: Stanford University Press.

Dell, P. F. (2006). A new model of dissociative identity disorder. *Psychiatric Clinics of North America, 29*: 1–26.

Despine, C. A. (1840). *De l'emploi du Magnétisme Animal et des Eaux minérales dans le Traitement des Malades Nerveuses, Suivi d'une Observation très Curieuse de Guérison de Nécropathie* [A study of the uses of animal magnetism in the treatment of disorders of the nervous system followed by a case of a highly unusual cure of neuropathy]. Paris: Germer, Bailière [reprinted Annecy: 1938].

Ellason, J. W., Ross, C. A., Sainton, K., & Mayran, L. W. (1996). Axis I and II co-morbidity and childhood trauma history in chemical dependency. *Bulletin of the Menninger Clinic, 60*: 39–51.

Ellenberger, H. F. (1970). *The Discovery of the Unconscious: The History and Evolution of Dynamic Psychiatry*. New York: Basic.

Ensink, K., & Robertson, B. (1996). Indigenous categories of distress and dysfunction in South African Xhosa children and adolescents as described by indigenous healers. *Transcultural Psychiatric Research Review—Psychiatry in Africa, 33*(2): 137–172.

Fan, Q., Yu, J., Ross, C. A., Keyes, B. B., Dai, Y., Zhang, T., Wang, L., & Xiao, Z. (2011). Teaching Chinese psychiatrists to make reliable dissociative disorder diagnoses. *Transcultural Psychiatry, 48*(4): 473–483.

Flournoy, T. (1900). *Des Indes a la Planete Mars*. Geneva: Atar [reprinted: *From India to the Planet Mars: A Case of Multiple Personality with Imaginary Languages*. Princeton, NJ: Princeton University Press, 1994].

Friedl, M. C., & Draijer, N. (2000). Dissociative disorders in a Dutch psychiatric inpatient population. *American Journal of Psychiatry, 157*: 1012–1013.

Gadit, A. A. (2003). Ethnopsychiatry review. *Journal of the Pakistani Medical Association, 53*(10): 1–6.

Gangdev, P. S., & Matjave, M. (1996). Dissociative disorders in black South Africans: a report on five cases. *Dissociation, 9*(3): 176–181.

Gast, U., Rodewald, F., Nickel, V., & Emrich, H. M. (2001). Prevalence of dissociative disorders among psychiatric inpatients in a German university clinic. *Journal of Nervous and Mental Disease, 189*: 249–257.

Gaw, A. C., Ding, Q., Levine, R. E., & Gaw, H. (1988). The clinical characteristics of possession disorder among 20 Chinese patients in the Hebei province of China. *Psychiatric Services, 49*: 360–365.

Ginzburg, K., Somer, E., Tamarkin, G., & Kramer, L. (2010). Clandestine psychopathology: Unrecognized dissociative disorders in inpatient psychiatry. *Journal of Nervous and Mental Disease, 198*: 378–381.

Gleaves, D. H. (1996). The socio-cognitive model of dissociative identity disorder: a reexamination of the evidence. *Psychological Bulletin, 120*: 42–59.

Gmelin, E. (1791). *Materialien für die Anthropologie*. Tübingen: Verlag der Cottaischen Buchhandlung.

Goodman, F. D. (1988). *How About Demons? Possession and Exorcism in the Modern World*. Bloomington, IN: Indiana University.

Hallibrun, M. (2005). "Just some spirits": the erosion of spirit possession and the rise of "tension" in South India. *Medical Anthropology, 24*: 111–144.

Janet, P. (1886). Les actes inconscients et le dédoublement de la personnalité pendant le somnambulisme provoqué. *Revue Philosophique de la France et de l'Etranger, 22*: 577–592.

Juthani, N. V. (2001). Psychiatric treatment of Hindus. *International Review of Psychiatry, 13*(2): 125–130.

Kerner, J. (1834). *Geschichten Besessener neuerer Zeit* [Stories of possessed ones in recent times]. Karlsruhe: Braun.

Kianpoor, M., & Rhoades G. F. Jr. (2006). Djinnati: a possession state in Baloochistan, Iran. *Journal of Trauma Practice, 4*(1/2): 147–155.

Kim, U., & Berry, J. (Eds.) (1993). *Indigenous Cultural Psychologies: Research and Experience in Cultural Context*. Newbury Park, CA: Sage.

Knudsen, H., Draijer, N., Haselrud, J., Boe, T., & Boon, S. (1995). *Dissociative Disorders in Norwegian Psychiatric Inpatients*. Paper presented at the spring meeting of the International Society for the Study of Dissociation, Amsterdam, Netherlands.

Krüger, C., Sokudela, B. F., Motlana, L. M., Mataboge, C. K., & Dikobe, A. M. (2007). Dissociation: a preliminary contextual model. *South African Journal of Psychiatry, 13*(1): 13–21.

Lewis-Fernandez, R. (1992). The proposed DSM-IV trance and possession disorder category: potential benefits and risks. *Transcultural Psychiatry Research Review, 29*: 301–317.

Lilienfeld, S. O., & Lynn, S. J. (2003). Dissociative identity disorder: multiple personalities, multiple controversies. In: S. O. Lilienfeld, S. J. Lynn, & J. M. Lohr (Eds.), *Science and Pseudoscience in Clinical Psychology* (pp. 109–142). New York: Guilford.

Lilienfeld, S. O., Lynn, S. L., Kirsch, I., Chaves, J. F., Sarbin, T. R., Ganaway, G. K., & Powell, R. A. (1999). Dissociative identity disorder and the socio-cognitive model: recalling the lessons from the past. *Psychological Bulletin, 125*(5): 507–523.

Lundt, C. (1994). *Xhosa Speaking Schizophrenic Patient's Experience of their Condition: Psychosis or Amafufunyana?* Unpublished psychology honours thesis, University of Cape Town.

Lynn, S. J., Rhue, J. W., & Green, J. P. (1988). Multiple personality and fantasy proneness: is there an association or dissociation? *British Journal of Experimental and Clinical Hypnosis, 5*: 138–142.

Martínez-Taboas, A. (1989). Multiple personality disorder in Puerto Rico: analysis of fifteen cases. *Dissociation, 2*: 128–131.

Martínez-Taboas, A., Dorahy, M., Şar, V., Middelton, W., & Kruger, C. (2013). Growing not dwindling: international research on the worldwide phenomenon of dissociative disorders. *The Journal of Nervous and Mental Disease, 201*: 353–354.

Middleton, W., & Butler, J. (1998). Dissociative identity disorder: an Australian series. *Australia and New Zealand Journal of Psychiatry, 32*: 794–804.

Modestin, J. (1992). Multiple personality disorder in Switzerland. *American Journal of Psychiatry, 149*: 88–92.

Moffatt, J. (2013). *The Parallel New Testament* (pp. 108–109). London: Forgotten Books.

Moreau de Tours, J. J. (1845). *Du Hachisch et de l' aliénation Mentale: Études Psychologiques*. Paris: Fortin, Masson [*Hashish and Mental Illness*. New York: Raven, 1973].

Murphy, P. E. (1994). Dissociative experiences and disorders in a non-clinical university group. *Dissociation, 7*: 28–34.

Myers, F. W. H. (1887). Multiplex personality. *Proceeding of the Society of Psychical Research, 4*: 496–514.

Ng, B. Y., & Chan, Y. H. (2004). Psychosocial stressors that precipitate disso- ciative trance disorder in Singapore. *Australian and New Zealand Journal of Psychiatry, 38*: 426–432.

Paris, J. (2013). Response to dissociative identity disorder letters from Matínez-Taboas et al. and Brand et al. *The Journal of Nervous and Mental Disease, 201*: 356–357.

Peter, B. (2011). On the history of dissociative identity disorders in Germany: the doctor Justinus Kerner and the girl from Orlach, or possession as an "exchange of the self". *International Journal of Clinical and Experimental Hypnosis, 59*(1): 82–102.

Piper, A., & Merskey, H. (2004a). The persistence of folly: a critical examina- tion of dissociative identity disorder. Part I. The excesses of an improb- able concept. *Canadian Journal of Psychiatry, 49*: 592–600.

Piper, A., & Merskey, H. (2004b). The persistence of folly: critical examina- tion of dissociative identity disorder. Part II. The defense and decline of multiple personality or dissociative identity disorder. *Canadian Journal of Psychiatry, 49*: 678–83.

Prince, M. (1906). *The Dissociation of a Personality*. New York: Longmans, Green.

Putnam, F. W. (1997). *Dissociation in Children and Adolescents: A Developmen- tal Perspective*. New York: Guilford.

Reis, R. (2013). Children enacting idioms of witchcraft and spirit possession as a response to trauma: therapeutically beneficial, and for whom? *Tran- scultural Psychiatry, 50*(5): 622–643.

Rhodes, G. F., & Şar, V. (Eds.) (2005). *Trauma and Dissociation in a Cross-cultural Perspective: Not Just a North-American Phenomenon*. Binghamton, NY: Haworth.

Ross, C. A. (1989). *Multiple Personality Disorder. Diagnosis, Clinical Features, and Treatment*. New York: Wiley.

Ross, C. A. (1991). Epidemiology of multiple personality and dissociation. *Psychiatric Clinics of North America, 14*: 503–517.

Ross, C. A., Duffy, C. M. M., & Ellason, J. W. (2002). Prevalence, reliability and validity of dissociative disorders in an inpatient setting. *Journal of Trauma & Dissociation, 3*: 7–17.

Ross, C. A., Keyes, B. B., Yan, H. Q., Wang, Z., Zou, Z., Xu, Y., Chen, J., Zhang, H., & Xiao, Z. (2008). A cross-cultural test of the trauma model of dissociation. *Journal of Trauma and Dissociation, 9*: 35–50.

Ross, C. A., Schroeder, E., & Ness, L. (2013). Dissociation and symptoms of culture-bound syndromes in North America: a preliminary study. *Journal of Trauma and Dissociation, 14*: 224–235.

Şar, V., Akyüz, G., & Doğan, O. (2007) Prevalence of dissociative disorders among women in the general population. *Psychiatry Research, 149*: 169–176.

Şar, V., Krüger, C., Martínez-Taboas, A., Middelton, W., & Dorhay, M. (2013). Sociocognitive and posttraumatic models of dissociation are not opposed (Letter to the editor). *The Journal of Nervous and Mental Disease, 5*: 439.

Somer, E. (2001). *Between Exorcism and Psychotherapy: Dissociation and Trauma in Middle Eastern Societies*. Mini-workshop presented in the 18th conference of the International Society for the Study of Dissociation, New Orleans, LA, 2–4 December.

Somer, E. (2004). Trance possession disorder in Judaism: sixteenth-century dybbuks in the near east. *Journal of Trauma and Dissociation, 5*(2): 131–146.

Somer, E. (2006). Culture-bound dissociation: a comparative analysis. *Psychiatric Clinics of North America, 29*: 213–226.

Somer, E., Ross, C., Kirshberg, A., Shawahday Bakri, R., & Ismail, S. (in press). Dissociative disorders and possession experiences in Israel: a comparison of opiate use disorder patients, Arab women subjected to domestic violence and a non-clinical group. *Transcultural Psychiatry*.

Somer, E., & Saadon, M. (2000). Stambali: dissociative possession and trance in a Tunisian healing dance. *Transcultural Psychiatry, 37*(4): 579–609.

Spanos, N. P. (1996). *Multiple Identities and False Memories: A Socio-cognitive Perspective*. Washington, DC: APA.

Spiegel, D., Loewenstein, R. J., Lewis-Fernández, R., Şar, V., Simeon, D., Vermetten, E., Cardeña, E., & Dell, P. F. (2011). Dissociative disorders in DSM-5. *Depression and Anxiety, 28*: 824–852.

Swartz, L. (1998). *Culture and Mental Health: A South African View*. Oxford: Oxford University.

Tutkun, H., Şar, V., Yargic, L. I., Ozpulat, T., Yanik, M., & Kiziltan, E. (1998). Frequency of dissociative disorders among psychiatric inpatients in a Turkish university clinic. *American Journal of Psychiatry, 155*: 800–805.

Uchinuma, Y., & Sekine, Y. (2000). Dissociative identity disorder (DID) in Japan: a forensic case report and the recent increase in reports of DID. *International Journal of Psychiatry in Clinical Practice*, 4: 155–160.

Van der Hart, O., & Horst, R. (1989). The dissociation theory of Pierre Janet. *Journal of Traumatic Stress*, 2(4): 397–411.

Van der Hart, O., Lierens, R., & Goodwin, J. (1996). Jeanne Fery: a sixteenth-century case of dissociative identity disorder. *Journal of Psychohistory*, 24(1): 18–35.

Van Duijl, M., Kleijn, W. I., & de Jong, J. (2013). Are symptoms of spirit possessed patients covered by the DSM-IV or DSM-5 criteria for possession trance disorder? A mixed-method explorative study in Uganda. *Social Psychiatry and Psychiatric Epidemiology*, 48(9): 1417–1430.

Varma, L. P., Bouri, M., & Wig, N. N. (1981). Multiple personality in India: comparison with hysterical possession state. *American Journal of Psychiatry*, 35(1): 113–120.

Varma, L. P., Srivastava, D. K., & Shahay, R. N. (1970). Possession syndrome. *Indian Journal of Psychiatry*, 12: 58–62.

Witztum, E., & Grisaru, N. (1996). The "Zar" possession syndrome among Ethiopian immigrants to Israel: cultural and clinical aspects. *British Journal of Medical Psychology*, 69(3): 207–225.

Yongmi Yi, K. (2000). Shin-byung (divine illness) in a Korean woman. *Culture, Medicine and Psychiatry*, 24(4): 471–486.

Xiao, Z., Yan, H., Wang, Z., Zou, Z., Xu, Y., Chen, J., Zhang, H., Ross, C. A., & Keyes, B. B. (2006). Trauma and Dissociation in China. *American Journal of Psychiatry*, 163: 1388–1391.

CHAPTER FIVE

"Dissociating dissociation"*—debates and controversies

Amelia van der Merwe

A brief history

Despite a long history of categorisation in the Diagnostic and Statistical Manual, controversy and debate continue to surround dissociative identity disorder (DID). In this chapter, I shall provide compelling evidence in favour of the existence of DID in response to some of the continued arguments that the disorder, and its antecedents, do not exist.

Debates and controversies

There has been a long history of debates and controversy surrounding dissociation and DID in particular. Traub (2009, p. 347) points out that although DID now appears in the DSM system which gives it some "stamp of respectability from the American Psychological Association", many clinicians continue not to believe in the existence of the disorder (e.g., Piper & Merskey, 2004). Its existence has been vehemently debated, particularly in the earlier literature (e.g., Mulhern, 1991; Young, 1991). Some of the most common reasons for doubting its existence is that the

---

*Freyd, cited in Goldsmith et al., 2009, p. 249.

diagnosis seems to wax and wane with changing diagnostic fashions, or psychiatric "fads" (Boor, 1982), that it captures the imagination of a sensationalist media (Traub, 2009), and that it is used as a dubious defence in criminal cases concerning culpability (Allison, 1984; Thigpen & Cleckley, 1984). Books and films such as *Sybil* and *Michelle Remembers* were followed by a radical increase in reported cases of satanic ritual abuse (Traub, 2009). Some have argued that the fluctuating prevalence of DID is the result of an unrefined diagnostic protocol, which has led to numerous misdiagnoses (Traub, 2009). Others have argued that research indicates the over-diagnoses of DID by a small number of clinicians (Lilienfeld et al., 1999). It has been suggested that DID is an invention of popular present-day North America, similar to popular religious constructions of demonology, possession, and exorcism in the past (Spanos, 1994).

Coons (1994) has argued, on the basis of a small-scale study of patients who presented at a dissociative disorders clinic, that satanic ritual abuse memories in particular are the product of suggestion, social contagion, hypnosis, misdiagnosis, and the misapplication of hypnosis, dreamwork, or regressive therapies. There are also those who question the existence of alternate or alter personalities as separate entities, and whether the disorder can be ameliorated through the integration of these personalities, and still others who believe that DID is a culture-bound syndrome—what this raises is whether DID is simply a manifestation of our time, or whether it is a reliably identifiable syndrome; a valid or perhaps so-called universal diagnostic category (Traub, 2009).

Sceptics who do not believe in the existence of DID mention the use of self-report measures of childhood trauma, and that memory about the past tends to be constructed long after the abuse occurred, which has implications for the accuracy of recall (Good, 1994; Offer, Kaiz, Howard, & Bennett, 2000). It has also been argued that memory may be the product of the imagination (Mazzoni & Memon, 2003) and that some psychotherapists may subtly entrench or encourage these kinds of memories (Lindsay & Read, 1995).

While there is cross-sectional evidence of extreme trauma during childhood, usually of a sexual nature in people living with DID, there is a lack of longitudinal studies making a link between trauma and DID (Traub, 2009).

It has been argued that the diagnosis of DID is improbable because of the overwhelming severity of abuse and torture suggested in the aetiology of the disorder (Traub, 2009). For this reason, some have argued that these trauma memories are pseudo- or false memories (Young, Sachs, Braun, & Watkins, 1991).

Aldridge-Morris (1989) also argues that patients may "fake" DID to gain attention, maintain an acceptable self-image, accrue financial gain, or to escape responsibility for actions. This is both insulting to DID patients who have suffered horrendous abuse, and to clinicians who are skilled enough to determine an accurate diagnosis.

Aldridge-Morris (1989) further suggests that in some instances, strabismus (the deviation of one eye from the axis of the other), visual evoked potentials, electrocardiograms, galvanic skin response, or blood pressure did not change from one personality to the other. However, it can equally be said that in some studies, they did. The findings are mixed; for example, IQ scores are roughly the same across personalities, while the Rorschach indicated distinct personalities in a single patient (Aldridge-Morris, 1989).

Evidence in favour of DID as a valid disorder

Corroboration

To establish a relationship between childhood trauma and DID, verification of the occurrence of the abuse needs to be presented (Traub, 2009). External sources may become necessary, including corroboration from medical records, photographic illustrations, recent eyewitness accounts, and even information from perpetrators themselves, given that there has been no coercion (ibid.). Corroboration does exist, and provides evidence for the validity of the disorder. In fact, Chu, Frey, Ganzel, and Matthews (1999) found that more than half of a sample of ninety female patients admitted to a unit specialising in the treatment of trauma-related disorders found physical evidence of the abuse (e.g., scars from physical injury, medical records), and the rates of verbal confirmation for those with complete amnesia who attempted corroboration were significant: 93% for physical abuse and 89% for sexual abuse (Chu, Frey, Ganzel, & Matthews, 1999). Herman and Schatzow (1987) also found that the majority of participants in their study who remembered experiences of sexual abuse in childhood were able to find corroboration for their abuse from other information sources. The majority of participants who did not find corroborating evidence were those who did not attempt to find such evidence (ibid.).

Belief in the severity of the abuse

That the degree of abuse is severe does not make it impossible. As Traub (2009) suggests, history bears witness to unthinkable violence and acts of genocide, thus why would it not be possible for a single person to inflict similar atrocities on another person or group of people? In my view, people do not want to believe in DID because they do not want to believe that an individual may be capable of such repugnance against a child or group of children; such a belief would shake the defensive view of the world as an essentially benevolent and safe place. There is a deep-seated blindness when it comes to child abuse, and especially ritual child abuse (Kordackie, 1991). For example, 69% of a large sample of Massachusetts-registered psychiatrists endorsed the following statement: "The numbers of false accusations of childhood sexual abuse, appearing to emerge from the psychotherapy of adults, constitute a real problem needing public acknowledgment as such by the mental health professions" (Feigon & de Rivera, 1998). Interestingly, in a survey to investigate the extent to which claims of recovered memory, satanic/ritualistic abuse, DID, and cases of suspected false memory are encountered by chartered clinical psychologists and hypnotherapists, the authors found that twice as many hypnotherapists reported having seen such a case compared with chartered clinical psychologists (Ost, Wright, Easton, Hope, & French, 2013). The authors do not explore why this may be, but perhaps it has to do with how memories are retrieved. Sceptics might say that during hypnosis, the patient is susceptible to suggestion, which might have influenced these findings. Ross and Norton (1989) found that DID patients who had been hypnotised reported significantly higher rates of sexual and physical abuse than DID patients who had not been hypnotised. However, research has shown that childhood abuse memories are predominantly not pseudomemories, and that neither psychotherapy nor hypnosis is an intervention that encourages pseudomemories (Chu et al., 1999). It is worth remarking that participants who reported recovering memories of abuse did not generally do so while in treatment, but rather at home, alone, or with family or friends; very few were in therapy sessions when they recovered their first memory (Chu et al., 1999). It is also worth noting that in general, allegations of false memories seem to be declining (Rosik, 2004).

False memory syndrome

The False Memory Syndrome Foundation (FMSF) has been instrumental in eroding the belief that sexual abuse is a major antecedent of DID. There is much support for false memory syndrome in the literature (e.g., de Rivera, 1997; Gardner, 2004; Goldstein, 1997). However, scholars such as Pope (1996) have developed arguments that question the validity of false memory syndrome, and it is perhaps arguments such as his that are responsible for the decline in allegations of false memories. Essentially, Pope (ibid.) argues that psychology is a science, and that any discovery needs to be backed up by empirical evidence. He asks:

> If there are validation studies for false memory syndrome and the epidemic that do not reflexively judge all reports of recovered memories of abuse to be objectively false, what was the research methodology for determining whether the reports were objectively true or false: Does the methodology yield an acceptable rate of false positives and false negatives? Assuming more than one person made each judgment, what was the interrater reliability? How was the methodology itself validated? (ibid., pp. 959–960)

It is argued that claims about valid, reliable identification of false memories of child abuse or of false accusations based on these false memories should lead to thorough evaluation accompanied by evidence and logic (ibid.). This is clearly not the case with the FMSF. Two ways were presented as demonstrating that memories forming the basis of accusations against members were false:

> There are two ways that we will address this concern. The first has to do with who we are. If I had taken a camera to any of the three meetings held here in Philadelphia, I would have been hard put to know whom to photograph. We were a good looking bunch of people: graying hair, well-dressed, healthy, smiling. The similarity of the stories is astounding, so script-like and formulaic that doubts

> dissolve after chats with a few families. Just about every person who has attended is someone you would likely find interesting and want to count a friend.
>
> The second way that we will address this concern involves lie detector tests ... If all members of the FMS Foundation either have had or express a willingness to be polygraphed, we will have a powerful statement that we are not in the business of representing pedophiles. (Pamela Freyd, in Pope, 1996, p. 960)

It is interesting that clothing, attractive appearance, smiling, and chatting can be assessed as a reliable basis for innocence, yet the FMSF argues that presenting symptoms cannot lead anyone to suspect that a person may have been sexually abused (Pope, 1996). A member of FMSF writes, "it is not permissible to infer, or frankly even to suspect, a history of abuse in people who present symptoms of abuse". He similarly argued, "You can never, never, never, never, never, never infer a history of sexual abuse from the patient's presenting symptoms. Nevernevernevernevernevernevernevernevernevernever." (Kihlstrom in Pope, 1996, p. 960)

It would be helpful for the FSMF and its Scientific and Professional Advisory Board to describe the research protocol and other research procedures involved by which false memory syndrome was adequately validated as a syndrome and by which it was determined that it affected the documented tens of thousands of individuals and their families (Pope, 1996). As Pope (ibid.) argues, any study that reports the widespread nature of false memory syndrome requires independent analysis, verification, and replication, processes which are at the heart of scientific empiricism. He further questions how the FMSF could possibly "diagnose" people without ever meeting them; without interviewing, evaluating, or knowing them. Pope (ibid.) believes that it is possible that the impressive names, prestige, offices, and affiliations of the Scientific and Professional Advisory Board may have unintentionally influenced fellow scientists, the courts, the popular media, and others to accept without routine scepticism, attention, and consideration of other hypotheses the methodology and ranges of primary data relevant to the notion of false memory syndrome and other FMSF proclamations as scientifically validated (ibid.).

Pope's (1996) concluding message to the FMSF, is that scientists are responsible for examining primary data, research methodology, assumptions, and inferences. He argues that science works at its best when claims and hypotheses can be habitually questioned. That which prevents doubt and disgraces anyone who disagrees is not likely to develop the scientific venture or to encourage public policies and clinical practices based on scientific principles (ibid.). Each scientific claim should triumph or collapse on the basis of its research validation and logic (ibid.).

Other authors agree with Pope, and call for a stop to the misapplications of published research by the FMSF (Gleaves & Freyd, 1997). They demonstrate the unscientific manner in which this foundation has gone about producing "evidence" for "false" allegations and the alleged nonexistence of repression and amnesia (ibid.). Gold (1997) concedes that the FMSF was founded during a time of moral panic about the continued rise in sexual abuse cases, a time when therapists were more interested in uncovering hidden truths than in enhancing safety and improving individual functionality. Gold (ibid.) stresses the dangers inherent in this approach: that the retrieval of memories can strip away an essential form of protection, which is accompanied by intrusive and emotionally overwhelming recollection, leading to dramatic deterioration. He argues that more than two decades later, we are moving away from the emphasis on memory retrieval towards focusing on coping skills as a priority, and on making treatment an empirical issue. Gold (ibid.) argues: "Although they present themselves in the roles of sceptic and scientist and tend to depict those who treat survivors as gullible and antiempirical, proponents of the validity of false memory syndrome have failed to generate data which would permit empirical evaluation of their claims" (ibid., p. 989). He concludes that survivors will be best served by clinicians who reject the polarised view of empirical practice and empirical research as mutually exclusive initiatives, and consider them instead as interdependent features of professional functioning (ibid.).

It is interesting to note that trauma accuracy scholars such as Schacter emphasise that there is no hard scientific evidence that false memories of child sexual abuse can be implanted during psychotherapy, and that "only a minority of healthy children and adults are prone to producing extensive false memories" (in Brown, Scheflin, & Hammond, 1998, p. 45). There are currently no studies that provide evidence of therapists suggesting false memories to susceptible clients (ibid.).

Other authors who have, with good intention, done harm to the cause of DID, are those who have suggested the widespread simulation of DID due to contagion, or iatrogenesis, or both (Draijer & Boon, 1999). These authors argue that clinicians have to be highly skilled and experienced to differentiate between "true" DID cases and those which imitate DID to avoid responsibility for negative behaviour, as is typically found in patients with borderline or antisocial personality disorder, or in those who are compensating for an overwhelming feeling of not being seen (ibid.). The last, "hysterical" personality is typically characterised by identity disturbances that may range in severity depending on the underlying borderline structure (ibid.). It is considered very challenging to differentiate between flamboyant "true" DID with coexisting histrionic personality disorder (which is seen as a rarity) and imitations (ibid.).

The neurobiological basis of DID

Neurobiological studies provide a great deal of evidence for the existence of trauma-related dissociation and DID. They also provide strong arguments against "false memory syndrome" (e.g., Bremner, Krystal, Charney, & Southwick, 1996). These studies demonstrate that there is evidence of dissociation, and DID in particular, in studies other than self-report studies. In defence of the validity of the diagnosis, EEG studies have demonstrated the disparity between alternate personalities, and studies using brain imaging found a difference in cerebral blood flow between the alternate personalities (Traub, 2009). Further studies demonstrated differences in visual capacities between alternate personalities (ibid.). This is highly suggestive of DID being a valid disorder (ibid.).

Further evidence is provided by Reinders et al. (2003) who investigated the anatomical localisation of self-awareness and the brain mechanisms involved in consciousness using functional neuroimaging in patients with DID. These authors provide neurological evidence for two distinct personality states. They show that specific changes in localised brain activity were consistent with their ability to generate two distinct mental states of self-awareness, each with its own access to autobiographical trauma-related memory (ibid.). Their findings demonstrate that there are different regional cerebral blood flow patterns for different senses of self (ibid.). From these results, it seems that the medial prefrontal cortex (MPFC) and the posterior associative cortices play an integral role in conscious experience (ibid.). For example,

Reinders et al. (ibid.) found that the neutral personality state (NPS), compared to the traumatic personality state (TPS), displayed disturbances of parietal and occipital blood flow, suggesting a fairly low level of somatosensory awareness and integration, by suppression of the reactivation of these areas (ibid.). This is consistent with the clinical and depersonalised features of the NPS (ibid.). By contrast, it seems as if the right prefrontal cortex plays a role in autobiographical, self-referential information processing which is particular to the TPS (ibid.). In addition, it appears that the most notable increase of activation relevant to the TPS is in the area known as the PO, including the region known as the IG, both of which play an important role in the emotional and behavioural response to pain and other distressing somatosensory cues (ibid.). Activation of these areas in patients with DID, in reaction to trauma-related cues, is accompanied by dissociation (ibid.). The right pre-frontal activation has previously been related to self-referential processing (Craik et al., 1999).

Nijenhuis, Van der Hart, and Steele (2004) make an interesting proposition. They suggest that traumatic experiences, especially when they are severe and occur early in life, cause the emergence of psychobiological action systems that developed during evolution. Specifically, they explore the trauma-related and evolutionary origins of the structural dissociation between two action systems known as the apparently normal part of the personality (ANP) and the emotional part of the personality (EP), as well as the reasons for their continued dividedness. The EP is designed to defend against threats, and it also controls attachment to caregivers (ibid.). Although they are determined to some extent by genetic potentials, they are also shaped by environmental factors, and so, by traumatic experiences, especially those which happened in early childhood, and subsequent external and internal contextual circumstances (e.g., social support, repetition of trauma, degree of dissociation between EP and ANP) (ibid.). By contrast, the ANP is committed to managing daily life and survival of the species (ibid.). The operation systems associated with the ANP ensure that the individual is able to explore the environment, manage energy levels through rest, sleep, eating, and drinking, interpersonal cooperation, and reproduction and caretaking (ibid.). This theory of the divided personality has received considerable empirical support. There are significant neuroendocrine differences between both psychobiological systems, for example, more prominent norepinephrine levels in EPs (leading to the activation of the sympathetic nervous system) compared to the ANPs upon exposure to perceived threat (ibid.). Differences in cortisol levels could also be detected (ibid.). Finally, ANPs and EPs responded differently in experiments with trauma memories and masked angry faces (ibid.).

Nijenhuis, Van der Hart, and Steele (2004) also explain the increasing complexity of structural dissociation which leads to secondary and tertiary dissociation which may occur when the trauma is chronic and severe, especially when the violence and/or neglect is interpersonal, the perpetrator is a caregiver, and the survivor is a child (ibid.). According to the theory, the authors suggest three levels of structural dissociation which mark a range of trauma-related disorders: simple PTSD (primary dissociation), complex PTSD, DES and DDNOS (secondary dissociation), and DID (tertiary dissociation) (ibid.). It is clear from this proposition that these disorders are situated on a continuum of complexity of structural dissociation, and that DID is not a manifestation of suggestion and role-playing as some authors have argued (ibid.).

The link between trauma and dissociation

There is a great deal of overlap between post-traumatic stress disorder (PTSD) and dissociation, particularly DID, probably because of a shared history of trauma. Lindemann's (1944) (cited in Koopman, Classen, & Spiegel, 1996) classic observation that survivors of acute trauma who dissociate are at risk of longer-term psychiatric symptoms, permeates current research. Shalev, Peri, Canetti, and Schreiber (1996) also argue in favour of heightened dissociability in PTSD and frequent dissociative reactions during stressful events. A relationship has been demonstrated between trauma severity, dissociative symptoms, and post-traumatic stress in Cambodian refugees (Carlson & Rosser-Hogan, 1991). Bremner, Krystal, Charney, and Southwick (1996) found that Vietnam veterans with PTSD had higher levels of dissociation than those who did not have PTSD. Tichenor, Marmar, Weiss, Metler, and Ronfeldt (1996) demonstrated a relationship between peri-traumatic dissociation and post-traumatic stress symptoms in a group of seventy-seven Vietnam theatre veterans. Peri-traumatic dissociation was also positively related to level of stress exposure and general dissociative tendencies (ibid.). Peri-traumatic dissociation was predictive of post-traumatic symptoms over and above the contributions of level of stress exposure and general dissociative tendencies (ibid.). Another example of the co-occurrence of post-traumatic symptoms and dissociation is a study conducted by Weiss, Marmar, Metzler, and Ronfeldt (1995) who found that after emergency services personnel members' exposure to a critical traumatic incident, and their emotional adjustment, social support, years of experience on the job, and locus of control were controlled, two dissociative variables (depersonalisation, derealisation) were still strongly predictive of post-traumatic symptomatic response. Koopman, Classen, and Spiegel (1996) found that individuals with a high level of exposure to a traumatic event (a firestorm) experienced on average eight dissociative symptoms (of thirty-three) during and immediately after the firestorm, and that these symptoms, as well as anxiety symptoms, significantly increased with increased exposure to the firestorm. In addition, previous stressful events and gender (female) was found to be associated to dissociative and anxiety symptoms (ibid.). It is interesting to note that dissociative symptoms were also significantly associated with engaging in irrelevant passive activities, or dangerous activities, such as trying to get closer to the fire and going into blocked-off areas, and crossing barricades (ibid.). Finally, Shalev, Peri, Canetti, and Schreiber (1996) found that early dissociation was highly predictive of the development of later PTSD. These authors' prospective research demonstrated that participants (who were individuals recruited at a general hospital after sustaining a traumatic injury) were significantly more likely to have PTSD at the six month assessment point if they had scored higher on depression, anxiety, intrusive symptoms and peri-traumatic dissociation measures at the one-week post trauma assessment point. Peri-traumatic dissociation predicted a diagnosis of PTSD at six months beyond the contribution of any other factor and accounted for 29.4% of the variance of PTSD symptom intensity (ibid.).

Patients with dissociative PTSD have abnormally high activation in brain regions involved in arousal modulation and emotional regulation, including the dorsal anterior cingulate cortex and the medial prefrontal cortex (Lanius et al., 2010). These patients can be understood as experiencing emotional overmodulation as a reaction to exposure to traumatic memories (ibid.). This can involve subjective disengagement from the emotional content of the traumatic memory through depersonalisation or derealisation, mediated my midline prefrontal inhibition of limbic regions (ibid.). Interestingly, recent research that these authors report on showed that participants who had experienced early onset violence had

much higher levels of clinical symptoms associated with the dissociative subtype than those with later-onset abuse (ibid.).

A strong neurological link between trauma and dissociative amnesia has been found. Although not all trauma survivors forget their
trauma/s, many do sustain amnesia after severe stress or emotional
trauma. This is because prolonged and severe stress, fear, and arousal
induce learning deficits and memory loss of varying levels that are as
a result of hippocampal activation and arousal and the corticosteroid
secretion (Joseph, 1999). This suppresses neural activity associated
with learning and memory that results in hippocampal atrophy (ibid.).
Risk factors include a history of previous trauma or neurological injury
involving the hippocampus or temporal lobe, how repetitive and prolonged the trauma was, and the age and the individual differences in
baseline arousal and cortisol levels (ibid.). Smaller right hippocampal
volume in PTSD has also been linked specifically to functional deficits
in verbal memory (Bremner et al., 1995).

Trauma and memory

There is a long history of literature that attests to trauma-related amnesia (see for example, Freyd, 1994; Mechanic, Resick, & Griffin, 1998;
Van der Hart, Brown, & Graafland, 1999). As we have seen above, it is
mostly the supporters of the FMSF who continue to dispute the reality
of post-traumatic amnesia. I have already addressed this topic, so I will
not address it again in this section. Suffice it to say that research has
indicated that the frontal and parietal cortex are known to be involved
in distributed networks for working memory processes, interacting
with medial temporal areas during episodic memory processes, and are
known to be areas which are smaller in individuals with PTSD (Weber
et al., 2005). Abnormal functioning in these brain networks explains difficulties in concentration and memory in individuals with PTSD (ibid.).

Brewin (2001) argues in favour of distinct types of memory, which
have different neural bases that behave in different ways, accounting
for different kinds of symptoms, and responding to different kinds of
treatments. Specifically, he suggests that according to dual representation theory, memories of a personally traumatic experience can be of two
distinct types, stored in different representational formats. One type of
format is verbally accessible memory (VAM), which includes ordinary
autobiographical memories which are recalled either automatically or

using purposeful strategic processes (ibid.). The other type is situation-ally accessible memory (SAM), which refers to specific trauma-related dreams and "flashbacks" which are significant features of PTSD. SAM includes information that has been retrieved from lower level perceptual processing of the traumatic event (e.g., visuospatial information which has received limited conscious processing) and of the person's bodily or autonomic/motor response to it (ibid.). As a result, these memories are more detailed and emotion-laden than ordinary memories (ibid.). They are difficult to control because their exposure to sights, sounds, smells, and so on, which are reminders of the trauma, are difficult to control (ibid.). The emotions that the person feels when reminded of the trauma are restricted to what she felt during the experience or subse-quent moments of arousal, and primarily include fear, helplessness, and horror, but may less frequently involve states such as shame (ibid.).

A key structure in the neural basis of memory for fear is the amygdala (Brewin, 2001). Relevant information about threatening stimuli pro-cessed at the level of individual perceptual features reach the amygdala and activates defensive responses very rapidly (ibid.). Other pathways are slower, but include more sophisticated processing, and involve cor-tical structures such as the unimodal sensory cortex, association cor-tex, and the hippocampus, all of which project independently to the amygdala (ibid.). Projection from the prefrontal cortex to the amygdala is required for extinction of conditioned fear to take place (ibid.). The hippocampus also plays an important role in the extinction of condi-tioned fear (ibid.). The hippocampus may play an inhibitory role over the amygdala through direct associations between the two structures or, more likely, via the projection of the hippocampus to prefrontal cortex (ibid.). The importance of the amygdaloid complex in memory storage has previously been outlined (McGaugh, 1990).

As we have seen, at a neural level, PTSD is linked to irregulari-ties in parts of the neural system which process threatening informa-tion, including the amygdala and medial-prefrontal cortex, as well as areas involved in episodic memory, such as the hippocampus (Dickie, Brunet, Akerib, & Armony, 2011). However, there is limited knowledge about how these areas function once the individual recovers from the trauma. In this study, PTSD patients undertook two functional magnetic resonance imaging (fMRI) scans, six to nine months apart, while watch-ing fearful and neutral faces in preparation for a memory test (ibid.). At the second measurement point, 65% of patients were in remission.

Present symptom levels were associated with memory-related fMRI activity in the amygdala and ventral-medial prefrontal cortex (vmPFC) (ibid.). The change in activity within the hippocampus and the subgenual anterior cingulate cortex (sgACC) was positively related to the level of symptom improvement (ibid.). The authors argue that the results demonstrate that the differential involvement of structures within the fear network in symptom appearance and in recovery from PTSD: whereas activity within the amygdala and vmPFC seem to demonstrate present symptom severity, functional changes in the hippocampus and sgACC were indicative of recovery (ibid.). The authors stress that their results emphasise the importance of longitudinal studies for the identification of the differential neural structures related to the manifestation and remission of anxiety disorders (ibid.).

Longitudinal studies

In agreement with Traub (2009) there is a lack of longitudinal studies on dissociation, and DID in particular. However, one important longitudinal study of high-risk children was conducted by Ogawa, Sroufe, Weinfield, Carlson, and Egeland (1997). This study was conducted over nineteen years, and dissociative pathology was measured at four points among 168 participants (ibid.). These authors found that onset, chronicity and severity of trauma overlapped a great deal and predicted dissociation; dissociation during childhood was considered a more normative response pattern to disruption and stress, while dissociation in adolescence was considered a more pathological response pattern; preliminary support was found for G. Liotti's assertion that disorganised attachment, later trauma, and dissociation in adulthood, are connected; and finally, strong support was found for N. Waller, F. W. Putnam, and E. B. Carlson's assertion that psychopathological dissociation is not one end of a continuum of dissociative symptomatology, but rather a separate taxon which represents an extreme deviation from normal development (ibid.).

The socio-cognitive model

The socio-cognitive model (SCM) is quite different to the post-traumatic model (PTM) in its theories about the causation of DID. The models differ most sharply in their explanations for the emergence of alters

(Lilienfeld et al., 1999). In particular, the PTM argues that alters are the result of severe child abuse and other trauma, while the SCM suggests that alters are the result of therapist influences, media portrayals and socio-cultural expectations (ibid.). However, Lilienfeld et al. (ibid.) argue that fantasy proneness might place an individual at heightened risk for enacting imaginary identities as a reaction to therapeutic and sociocultural cues. Supporters of the SCM do not argue that DID does not exist, but rather about its origins and its maintenance (ibid.). What they ask is whether DID is best understood as a response to trauma or as a manifestation of therapeutic practices, culturally based scripts, and societal expectations (ibid.). Supporters of the SCM concede two points however; one, that memory implantation is more likely to occur when the event being implanted is plausible and accords with existent memory; and two, that individuals with DID do not seem to maintain symptoms for social reinforcement, such as attention from others. DID patients were described as "chronically disturbed, unhappy, polysymptomatic ... people who are emotionally needy" (Spanos in Lilienfeld et al., 1999, p. 516).

Reinders, Willemsen, Vos, den Boer, and Nijenhuis (2012) conducted a study with twenty-nine participants (eleven patients with DID, ten high fantasy prone DID simulating controls, and eight low fantasy prone DID simulating controls) and found that low fantasy prone controls simulated the performance of DID patients better than high fantasy prone controls. This is the opposite result than one would expect if one was a supporter of the sociocognitive and fantasy based model of DID (ibid.). In addition, these authors found that the activated areas of the brain were subdivided into two distinct neural networks: the neutral identity system (NIS) activated the areas in the cerebral cortex, while the trauma identity system (TIS) largely activated the subcortical areas (ibid.). Finally, Reinders, Willemsen, Vos, den Boer, and Nijenhuis (ibid.) also found sympathetic nervous system differences (e.g., higher heart rate and systolic blood pressure) between NIS and TIS in DID patients, and for TIS in DID, and hyperactivation of the cortical multimodal posterior association areas (e.g., the intraparietal sulcus and precuneus) for NIS in DID when listening to personal trauma scripts.

In another neuroimaging study, where thirteen DID patients were matched with fifteen healthy controls, results also disproved the SCM (Schlumpf et al., 2013). According to the Theory of Structural Dissociation of the Personality (TSDP), DID patients have fixed traumatic memories stored as emotional parts (EP), but mentally avoid these as apparently normal parts of the personality (ANP) (ibid.). The authors tested the hypotheses that ANP and EP have different biopsychosocial reactions to subliminally presented angry and neutral faces, and that actors (control group), when instructed as such, could simulate ANP and EP (ibid.). Interestingly, results showed that controls showed a tendency to inverse response times and neural activation patterns for EPs and ANPs. In other words, as ANP, the actors tended to react like EP in DID patients, and as EP, like ANP in these patients (ibid.). The actors were thus unable to simulate DID with respect to behavioural and neural reactivity, which opposes the sociocognitive model of DID (ibid.). Specifically, compared to DID patients in the EP condition, as ANP, controls had amygdala activity in the neutral face condition but neither brainstem activity nor a longer response time (ibid.). Whereas the neutral faces were thus salient for the DID EP condition, it was salient for ANP-simulating controls (ibid.). This study provides psychobiological evidence that DID is neither an effect of suggestion and fantasy, nor of role-playing (ibid.).

Conclusion

Merskey (1995) sees DID as a product of shaping in therapy, of hypnotic suggestion, as stimulation, and as an extension of characteristics found in normal personalities. He analyses leading nineteenth-century cases of DID, and argues that they are in fact cases of bipolar disorder, depression, anorexia, alcoholism, organic cerebral disorder, or hypnotic induction. He further argues other historic cases of DID emerged where there was prior knowledge of DID, and where the patient adopted symptoms in order to achieve a deliberate or unfair benefit at the expense of others or society (ibid.). Thus, according to Merskey (ibid.), no historic case of DID emerged through unconscious processes without any shaping or preparation by external factors such as by therapists (the few specialists in the field) or the media. Merskey (ibid.) argues that four suggestions explain how DID is created: first, there is the misinterpretation of organic and bipolar illness; second, there is the conscious development of fantasies as a solution to psychological problems; third, is the development of hysterical amnesia which is followed by retraining; and fourth, is the creation by implicit demand under hypnosis or repeated interviews.

Merskey (1995) also argues that most of the diagnoses are being made by a very small number of therapists. This is not supported by the evidence. Using the figures from the time that Merskey's book was printed, there were approximately 10,000 psychiatrists in North American who had made independent DID diagnoses (Ross, 1995).

It is difficult to understand what secondary gain there is for patient and therapist in the iatrogenic creation of DID (Chande, 1994). As Chande (ibid.) notes, there is nothing desirable or titillating about the disorder, rather it is a sign that the patient has creatively used dissociation as a child to navigate severe and prolonged abuse. The therapist knows that therapy will involve the recovery of brutal memories, which will be painful for therapist and patient alike (ibid.).

Putnam (1991) queries why asking a patient whether she has ever felt that there was another part or side to her is more likely to produce an alter personality than, for example, creating hallucinations or ruminations by asking if she has ever heard voices talking to her when no one else was present or had thoughts which occurred repeatedly which she could not stop. He argues that the suggestion that DID is produced by simply reading the book *Sybil* or seeing the film, *The Three Faces of Eve* is similarly flawed. A number of dramatic disorders, such as anorexia, bulimia, obsessive-compulsive disorder, and bipolar disorder are commonly written about in books, magazines, and newspapers, and appear in films, on radio and television (ibid.). Putnam (ibid.) asks whether these disorders are understood to be produced by the media, which they are not, and so asks why DID is singled out as uniquely susceptible to media contamination.

A further argument that is mounted against DID is that the existence of a reported history of childhood trauma is used tautologically to support the diagnosis (Ross, 1995). This is not logically possible since there are no trauma items in the DSM-IV criteria for the disorder (ibid.). This argument would, however, apply to adjustment and post-traumatic stress disorder but would not be used against them because the tautology would most likely be argued against by the majority of psychiatrists. It is interesting that the same argument is acceptable against DID, but ridiculed against another disorder.

Another debate about the reality of DID is that disbelievers typically cannot distinguish between a hypothesis and an argument (Ross, 1995). As Ross (ibid.) argues, in a scientific debate, when one makes a hypothesis, you gather evidence and arguments to support the hypothesis. In the "debate" about the reality of DID, hypotheses are simply insisted upon, as if they were in fact arguments (ibid.). For example, the suggestion that DID is a cultural artefact influenced by the media is a hypothesis, not an argument, because there are no data, no arguments, to support the hypothesis (ibid.).

Dissociation is associated with a range of other disorders, including borderline personality disorder, conversion disorder, substance use disorder, and obsessive compulsive disorder (Şar, Akyz, & Doğan, 2007). Further evidence for the existence of dissociative disorders such as DID is that childhood trauma and dissociation are independently related to other indicators of mental health problems such as self-harming and suicidality (ibid.). Other indicators that are common to both include pseudoseizures, somatisation disorder, and conversion disorder (ibid.).

Despite substantial evidence that dissociation, and DID in particular, is systematically associated with particular disorders, and a particular emotional and behavioural profile associated with early abuse of a severe nature, it continues to be surrounded by controversy. DID is considered a valid diagnostic category in the DSM-5. It is time we accepted it as such. The research evidence shows us that although there is a lack of longitudinal studies, and an over-representation of self-report studies, there is a recent emergence of neurobiological studies that provide sufficient evidence of the existence of dissociation, and DID. As the critics of Merskey have suggested, no one wants to believe in the dreadful antecedents of DID, the reality of heinous forms of abuse. No one wants their belief in an essentially benevolent world to be shattered. It is a reality too awful and too shameful to contemplate. But in not believing we betray these child survivors. It is time to stop "dissociating dissociation" and take cognisance of the empirical evidence that has been presented.

References

Aldridge-Morris, R. (1989). *Multiple Personality: An Exercise in Deception.* Hillsdale: Erlbaum.

Allison, R. B. (1984). Difficulties diagnosing the multiple personality syndrome in a death penalty case. *The International Journal of Clinical and Experimental Hypnosis, 32*: 102–117.

Boor, M. (1982). The multiple personality epidemic: additional cases and inferences regarding diagnosis, etiology, dynamics, and treatment. *Journal of Nervous and Mental Disease, 170*: 302–304.

Bremner, J., Krystal, J., Charney, D. S., & Southwick, S. M. (1996). Neural mechanisms in dissociative amnesia for childhood abuse. *The American Journal of Psychiatry, 153*(7): 71–83.

Bremner, J. D., Randall, P., Scott, T., Bronen, R. A., Seibyl, J. P., Southwick, S. M., Delayney, R. C., McCarthy, G., Charney D. S., & Innis, R. B. (1995). MRI-based measurement of hippocampal volume in patients with combat-related posttraumatic stress disorder. *The American Journal of Psychiatry, 152*(7): 973–981.

Brewin, C. R. (2001). A cognitive neuroscience account of posttraumatic stress disorder and its treatment. *Behaviour Research and Therapy, 39*: 373–393.

Brown, D., Scheflin, A. W., & Hammond, D. C. (1998). *Memory, Trauma Treatment, and the Law.* New York: Norton.

Carlson, E. B., & Rosser-Hogan, R. (1991). Trauma experiences, posttraumatic stress, dissociation, and depression in Cambodian refugees. *American Journal of Psychiatry, 148*: 1548–1551.

Chande, A. (1994). Reactions to four cases of supposed multiple personality disorder: evidence of unjustified diagnoses. *Canadian Journal of Psychiatry, 39*(4): 245–246.

Chu, J. A., Frey, L. M., Ganzel, B. L., & Matthews, J. A. (1999). Memories of childhood abuse: Dissociation, amnesia and corroboration. *American Journal of Psychiatry, 156*(5): 749–755.

Coons, P. M. (1994). Reports of satanic ritual abuse: further implications about pseudomemories. *Perceptual & Motor Skills, 78*(3): 1376–1378.

Craik, F. I. M., Moroz, T. M., Moscovitch, M., Stuss, D. T., Winocur, G., Tulving, E., & Kapur, S. (1999). In search of self: a positron emission tomography study. *Psychological Science, 10*(1): 26–34.

de Rivera, J. (1997). Estimating the number of false memory syndrome cases. *American Psychologist, 52*(9): 996–997.

Dickie, E. W., Brunet, A., Akerib, V., & Armony, J. L. (2011). Neural correlates of recovery from post-traumatic stress disorder: a longitudinal fMRI investigation of memory encoding. *Neuropsychologia, 49*(7): 1771–1778.

Draijer, N., & Boon, S. (1999). The imitation of dissociative identity disorder: patients at risk, therapists at risk. *The Journal of Psychiatry & Law, 27*: 423–458.

Feigon, E. A., & de Rivera, J. (1998). "Recovered-memory" therapy: profession at a turning point. *Comprehensive Psychiatry, 39*(6): 338–344.

Freyd, J. J. (1994). Betrayal trauma: traumatic amnesia as an adaptive response to childhood abuse. *Ethics & Behavior, 4*(4): 307–330.

Gardner, R. A. (2004). The psychodynamics of patients with false memory syndrome (FMS). *The Journal of the American Academy of Psychoanalysis and Dynamic Psychiatry, 32*(1): 77–90.

Gleaves, D. H., & Freyd, J. J. (1997). Questioning additional claims about the false memory syndrome epidemic. *American Psychologist, 52*(9): 993–994.

Gold, S. N. (1997). False memory syndrome: a false dichotomy between science and practice. *American Psychologist, 52*(9): 988–989.

Goldsmith, R. E., Cheit, R. E., & Wood, M. E. (2009). Evidence of Dissociative Amnesia in science and literature: Culture-bound approaches to trauma in Pope, Poliakoff, Parker, Boynes, and Hudson (2007). *Journal of Trauma & Dissociation, 10*(3): 237–253.

Goldstein, E. (1997). False memory syndrome: Why would they believe such terrible things if they weren't true? *American Journal of Family Therapy, 25*(4): 307–317.

Good, M. I. (1994). The reconstruction of early childhood trauma: Fantasy, reality, and verification. *Journal of the American Psychoanalytic Association, 42*: 79–101.

Herman, J. L., & Schatzow, E. (1987). Recovery and verification of memories of childhood sexual trauma. *Psychoanalytic Psychology, 4*(1): 1–14.

Joseph, R. (1999). The neurology of traumatic "dissociative" amnesia: commentary and literature review. *Child Abuse & Neglect, 23*(8): 715–727.

Koopman, C., Classen, C., & Spiegel, D. (1996). Dissociative responses in the immediate aftermath of the Oakland/Berkeley firestorm. *Journal of Traumatic Stress, 9*(3): 521–540.

Kordackie, J. (1991). Blindness to child abuse in Poland. *Child Abuse & Neglect, 15*: 616–617.

Lanius, R. A., Vermetten, E., Loewenstein, R. J., Brand, B., Schmahl, C., Bremner, J. D., & Spiegel, D. (2010). Emotion modulation in PTSD: clinical and neurobiological evidence for a dissociative subtype. *The American Journal of Psychiatry, 167*(6): 640–647.

Lilienfeld, S. O., Lynn, S. J., Kirsch, I., Chaves, J. F., Sarbin, T. R., Ganaway, G. K., & Powell, R. A. (1999). Dissociative identity disorder and the sociocognitive model: recalling lessons from the past. *Psychological Bulletin, 125*(5): 507–523.

Lindsay, D. S., & Read, J. D. (1995). "Memory work" and recovered memories of childhood sexual abuse: scientific evidence and public, professional, and personal issues. *Psychology, Public Policy, and the Law, 1*: 849–908.

Mazzoni, G., & Memon, A. (2003). Imagination can create false autobiographical memories. *Psychological Science, 14*: 186–188.

McGaugh, J. L. (1990). Significance and remembrance: the role of neuromodulatory systems. *Psychological Science, 1*(1): 15–25.

Mechanic, M. B., Resick, P. A., & Griffin, M. G. (1998). A comparison of normal forgetting, psychopathology, and information-processing models of reported amnesia for recent sexual trauma. *Journal of Consulting and Clinical Psychology, 66*(6): 948–957.

Merskey, H. (1995). The manufacture of personalities: the production of multiple personality disorder. In: L. M. Cohen, J. N. Berzoff, & M. R. Elin (Eds.), *Dissociative Identity Disorder: Theoretical and Treatment Controversies* (pp. 3–33). Northvale, NJ: Aronson.

Mulhern, S. (1991). Embodied alternative identities. Bearing witness to a world that might have been. *The Psychiatric Clinics of North America, 14*(3): 769–86.

Nijenhuis, E. R. S., Van der Hart, O., & Steele, K. (2004). *Trauma-related Structural Dissociation of the Personality*. Trauma Information Pages website: www.trauma-pages.com/a/nijenhuis-2004.php [last accessed 13 November, 2015].

Offer, D., Kaiz, M., Howard, K. I., & Bennett, E. S. (2000). The altering of reported experiences. *Journal of the American Academy of Child and Adolescent Psychiatry, 39*: 735–742.

Ogawa, J. R., Sroufe, A., Weinfield, N. S., Carlson, E. A., & Egeland, B. (1997). Development and the fragmented self: longitudinal study of dissociative and symptomatology in a nonclinical sample. *Development and Psychopathology, 9*: 855–879.

Ost, J., Wright, D. B., Easton, S., Hope, L., & French, C. C. (2013). Recovered memories, satanic abuse, dissociative identity disorder and false memories in the UK: a survey of clinical psychologists and hypnotherapists. *Psychology, Crime & Law, 19*(1): 1–19.

Piper, A., & Merskey, H. (2004). The persistence of folly: critical examination of dissociative identity disorder. Part II. The defence and decline of multiple personality or dissociative identity disorder. *Canadian Journal of Psychiatry, 49*: 678–683.

Pope, K. S. (1996). Memory, abuse and science: questioning claims about the false memory syndrome epidemic. *American Psychologist, 51*(9): 957–974.

Putnam, F. W. (1991). The satanic ritual abuse controversy. *Child Abuse and Neglect, 15*: 175–179.

Reinders, A. A. T. S., Nijenhuis, E. R. S., Paans, A. M. J., Korf, J., Willemsen, A. T. M., & den Boer, J. A. (2003). One brain, two selves. *NeuroImage, 20*: 2119–2125.

Reinders, A. A. R. S., Willemsen, A. T. M., Vos, H. P. J., den Boer, J. A., & Nijenhuis, E. R. S. (2012). Fact or factitious? A psychobiological study of authentic and simulated dissociative identity states. *Plos One, 7*(6): 1–17.

Rosik, C. H. (2004). Possession phenomena in North America: a case study with ethnographic, psychodynamic, religious and clinical implications. *Journal of Trauma & Dissociation, 5*(1): 49–76.

Ross, C. (1995). Diagnosis of dissociative identity disorder. In: L. M. Cohen, J. N. Berzoff, & M. R. Elin (Eds.), *Dissociative Identity Disorder: Theoretical and Treatment Controversies* (pp. 261–285). Northvale, NJ: Aronson.

Ross, C. A., & Norton, G. R. (1989). Effects of hypnosis on the features of multiple personality disorder. *Dissociation, 3:* 99–106.

Şar, V., Akyüz, G., & Doğan, O. (2007). Prevalence of dissociative disorders among women in the general population. *Psychiatry Research, 149:* 169–176.

Schlumpf, Y. R., Nijenhuis, E. R. S., Chalavi, S., Weder, E. V., Zimmermann, E., Luechinger, R., La Marca, R., Reinders, A. A. A. T. S., & Jäncke, L. (2013). Dissociative part-dependent biopsychosocial reactions to backward masked angry and neutral faces: an fMRI study of dissociative identity disorder. *NeuroImage: Clinical, 3:* 54–64.

Shalev, A. Y., Peri, T., Canetti. L., & Schreiber, S. (1996). Predictors of PTSD in injured trauma survivors: a prospective study. *American Journal of Psychiatry, 153*(2): 219–225.

Spanos, N. P. (1994). Multiple identity enactments and multiple personality disorder: a sociocognitive perspective. *Psychological Bulletin, 116:* 143–165.

Thigpen, C. H., & Cleckley, H. M. (1984). On the incidence of multiple personality disorder: a brief communication. *International Journal of Clinical and Experimental Hypnosis, 32:* 63–66.

Tichenor, V., Marmar, C. R., Weiss, D. S., Metzler, R. J., & Ronfeldt, H. M. (1996). *Journal of Consulting and Clinical Psychology, 64*(5): 1054–1059.

Traub, C. M. (2009). Defending a diagnostic pariah: validating the categorisation of dissociative identity disorder. *South African Journal of Psychology, 39*(3): 347–356.

Van der Hart, O., Brown, P., & Graafland, M. (1999). Trauma-induced dissociative amnesia in World War I combat soldiers. *Australian & New Zealand Journal of Psychiatry, 33*(1): 37–46.

Weber, D. L., Clark, C. R., McFarlane, A. C., Moores, K. A., Morris, P., & Egan, G. F. (2005). Abnormal frontal and parietal activity during working memory updating in post-traumatic stress disorder. *Psychiatry Research: Neuroimaging Section, 140*(1): 27–44.

Weiss, D. S., Marmar, C. R., Metzler, T. J., & Ronfeldt, H. M. (1995). Predicting symptomatic distress in emergency services personnel. *Journal of Consulting and Clinical Psychology, 63*(3): 361–368.

Young, W. C. (1991). Letters to the editor. *Child Abuse & Neglect, 15:* 609–618.

Young, W. C., Sachs, R. G., Braun, B. G., & Watkins, R. T. (1991). Patients reporting ritual abuse in childhood: a clinical syndrome. Report of 37 cases. *Child Abuse & Neglect, 15*(3): 181–189.

CHAPTER SIX

Variations in identity alteration—a qualitative study of experiences of psychiatric patients with dissociative identity disorder

Christa Krüger

Introduction

The old norm of distinct-personality-state dissociative identity disorder (DID) does not apply universally, as was recently recognised in the DSM-5's inclusion of possession experiences in the main diagnostic criterion for DID (see below) (APA, 2013). This new nosological development around possession reflects underlying questions about identity, how a person's identity is constituted, how or from where identity is controlled, how rigidly it is controlled, and how it may be altered.

What was previously called possession trance—which involves replacement of the customary sense of personal identity by a new identity, attributed to the influence of a spirit, power, deity, or other person, and associated with stereotyped "involuntary" movements or amnesia, and which was classified as an example of dissociative disorder not otherwise specified (DDNOS) in the DSM-IV (APA, 1994)—was recently incorporated in the main diagnostic criterion for DID in DSM-5 (APA, 2013) as a cultural variant of DID, and an alternative to distinct-personality-state DID. The A-criterion of DID in DSM-5 now reads:

> Disruption of identity characterised by two or more distinct personality states, which may be described in some cultures as an

experience of possession. The disruption in identity involves marked discontinuity in sense of self and sense of agency, accompanied by related alterations in affect, behavior, consciousness, memory, perception, cognition, and/or sensory-motor functioning. These signs and symptoms may be observed by others or reported by the individual. (APA, 2013, p. 292)

The incorporation of possession trance in the main diagnostic criterion of DID means that a person does not necessarily have to have two or more distinct personality states or alter personalities with accompanying switches to be diagnosed with DID, but might instead have possession experiences (reported by the person herself or observed by others). Such possession experiences must fall outside of what is considered normal, broadly accepted cultural or religious practice, and must cause clinically significant distress or disability in social, occupational, or other important activities to be regarded as pathological (APA, 2013).

The DSM-5's inclusion of possession experiences in the criteria for DID might assist diagnosis of DID in cultures where a pathological disruption of identity might show itself as possession states rather than as overtly multiple personality states. As possession experiences have been found in numerous cultures, the inclusion of possession will likely increase the global utility and cross-cultural applicability of the DID diagnostic category (Cardeña, Van Duijl, Weiner, & Terhune, 2009).

The purpose of this chapter is to describe some of the clinical variations in identity alteration including possession experiences and identity confusion in a group of psychiatric patients who suffer from DID or from DSM-5's other specified dissociative disorder (OSDD). Steinberg (1994a) describes identity alteration as the objective behaviours that are observable manifestations of different identities; and identity confusion as the subjective sense of conflict or uncertainty about one's identity due to non-integrated or fragmented self-states, with the confusion resulting from intrusions from these fragmented and dissociated self-states. The descriptions that follow come from a qualitative study of in-depth individual interviews with fourteen psychiatric patients.

This qualitative study formed a part of a broader mixed-methods research project (Creswell & Plano Clark, 2011). The objectives of the broader project include screening for patients with dissociative disorders among psychiatric inpatients; exploring differences between patients with and without dissociative disorders; describing local variations in the clinical picture of the dissociative disorders; monitoring treatment progress and outcome in patients with dissociative disorders; evaluating available local non-public mental health services for patients with dissociative disorders; and generating hypotheses for future research.

Within the broader project, this specific qualitative study was designed as a collective instrumental case study, and an explorative descriptive approach was followed, where the rich experiences of a defined group of patients suffering from DID or OSDD were used to inform an analysis of the concepts which are the focus of this study, namely identity alteration and possession (Creswell, 2013; Fouché & Schurink, 2011; Nieuwenhuis, 2007).

The contributions of this work include a qualitative evaluation of the merits of DSM-5's inclusion of possession experiences in the criteria for DID, as well as a suggestion for a more relaxed understanding of fluid shifts and transitions on a continuum between unitary personal identity and multiplicity—which might be tested in future research.

The scope of this chapter will be limited to the reporting of the methodology and findings of this qualitative research study, along with a few preliminary interpretations of the findings. Further phases of analysis and their detailed interpretation will follow. For a more detailed exploration of the concept of possession and its varied presentation in different cultures and at the interface between the fields of psychiatry, psychology, religious studies, anthropology, ethnography, and cultural studies, see for example, Cardeña, Van Duijl, Weiner, and Terhune (2009), During, Elahi, Taieb, Moro, and Baubet (2011), Espi Forcen and Espi Forcen (2014), Ferracuti, Sacco, and Lazzari (1996), Halliburton (2005), Harley (1996), Hegeman (2013), Henley (2006), Islam and Campbell (2014), Levack (2014), Lund and Swartz (1998), Martínez-Taboas (1999; 2005), Mercer (2013), Reis (2013), Ross (2011), Ross, Schroeder, and Ness (2013), Sapkota et al. (2014), Şar (2014), Şar, Alioğlu, and Akyüz (2014), Seligman and Kirmayer (2008), Spiegel et al. (2011), Swartz (1998), Taves (2006), Van Duijl, Nijenhuis, Komproe, Gernaat, and De Jong (2010), and Van Duijl, Kleijn, and De Jong (2013, 2014).

Notwithstanding fascinating research by many authors on culture-specific possession-type syndromes, for the purposes of this chapter I will work on the assumption that possession represents a universal phenomenon of which an individual's specific presentation is coloured by that person's cultural, religious, and societal background (APA, 2013; Dorahy, 2001; Eshun & Gurung, 2009).

The methods, analysis, findings and interpretation of the findings of this study are given below according to widely accepted guidelines for qualitative research reporting, with the addition of some elements of quantitative research reporting to account for the situatedness of this qualitative study within a broader mixed-methods research project (Creswell & Plano Clark, 2011; Delport & Fouché, 2011; Wolcott, 2002). Although the section on the setting and sampling below might sound very "quantitative" in its approach, I believe that it assists the reader to appreciate how and why this collective instrumental bounded case of fourteen patients came to be defined in the way that it was.

Research methodology

Setting and sampling

The fourteen patients who participated in this qualitative study were identified from 116 psychiatric inpatients who participated in the broader project, that is, fifty-eight patients from each of two hospitals: Weskoppies Hospital (WKH) (a specialised state psychiatric hospital in Pretoria, and one of the academic training hospitals for the University of Pretoria) and Tshwane District Hospital (TDH) (a regional hospital that also provides primary level psychiatric care).

The 116 patients of the broader project represented consecutive psychiatric admissions who fulfilled the set inclusion and exclusion criteria—as far as was physically possible to be evaluated by three research assistants appointed during overlapping periods in 2013 and 2014. The inclusion criteria were an age of eighteen or older and the ability to read and write English sufficiently to complete self-report questionnaires (even though some of the scale measures were interviewer-administered). The exclusion criteria were severe neurological or general medical conditions, or severe psychiatric impairment that precluded the patient's ability to complete self-report questionnaires.

The 116 patients had completed the questionnaire scales listed in Figure 1 during 2013 (at WKH) and 2014 (at TDH) with the assistance of the research assistants. Demographic and clinical data were also collected. The fourteen patients with DID or OSDD were subsequently diagnosed using a combination of the following: scores of >30 on both the Dissociative Experiences Scale (DES) (Bernstein & Putnam, 1986; Carlson & Putnam, 1993) and the Multidimensional Inventory of Dissociation (MID) (Dell, 2006), my discussion with the relevant multidisciplinary treating team, consulting the clinical records, my conducting

Abbreviation	Scale name	Reference	What it measures
1. DES	Dissociative Experiences Scale	Bernstein & Putnam (1986); Carlson & Putnam (1993)	Usual frequency of dissociative experiences
2. MID	Multidimensional Inventory of Dissociation	Dell (2006)	Presence and severity of pathological dissociation and dissociative disorders
3. SDQ-20	Somatoform Dissociation Questionnaire	Nijenhuis, Spinhoven, Van Dyck, Van der Hart, & Vanderlinden (1996)	Presence of somatoform dissociative symptoms
4. TSI-2	Trauma Symptom Inventory—2	Briere, Elliott, Harris, & Cotman (1995)	Current acute and chronic post-traumatic symptomatology
5. PCL-C	Post-traumatic Stress Checklist—Civilian	Weathers, Litz, Huska, & Keane (1994)	PTSD symptomatology and its severity
6. TEC	Traumatic Experiences Checklist	Nijenhuis (1999)	Past history of traumatic events, when they occurred, and the impact on the patient
7. SCL-90-R	Symptom Checklist 90—Revised	Derogatis (1975); Derogatis & Lazarus (1994)	Psychological symptom patterns and general psychological distress

Figure 1. Scales administered in the broader project.

Abbreviation	Scale name	Reference	What it measures
8. BDI	Beck Depression Inventory	Beck (1987); Beck & Steer (1993); Beck, Ward, Mendelson, Mock, & Erbaugh (1961)	Severity of depressive symptoms
9. BAI	Beck Anxiety Inventory	Beck (1990); Beck, Epstein, Brown, & Steer (1988)	Severity of anxiety symptoms
10. DTDIS	Dissociative Trance Disorder Interview Schedule	Ross (2011)	Presence of possession trance symptoms and related dissociative symptoms
11. SCID-D-R	Structured Clinical Interview for DSM-IV Dissociative Disorders— Revised	Steinberg (1994a, 1994b)	Diagnostic interview for the dissociative disorders

Figure 1. Continued.

clinical psychiatric interviews, and administering the Structured Clinical Interview for DSM-IV Dissociative Disorders—Revised (SCID-D-R) (Steinberg, 1994b). The SCID-D-R was administered in nine cases to confirm the clinical diagnosis. Diagnosed using these procedures, the proportion of patients with DID or OSDD was 12.1% of the 116 original patients.

Despite being a joint appointee of Weskoppies Hospital and the University of Pretoria, I was only very briefly and indirectly involved in the multidisciplinary treating team of two of the identified fourteen patients until the team decided on discharge from the hospital and outpatient follow-up. I was not involved in the treatment of any of the other patients.

Twelve of the fifty-eight TDH patients who had scores of >30 on both the DES and MID were lost to follow-up after their discharge from TDH, either because of non-functional mobile phone numbers or moving to different provinces, and a further two patients declined future contact after the questionnaire scales. In other words, these patients who might have suffered from DID or OSDD based on their DES and MID scores, were not fully assessed subsequently and therefore not diagnosed. Hence the diagnosed proportion of 12.1% for DID or OSDD patients for this study may be lower than what might have been found if these other lost-to-follow-up patients had been fully assessed.

The fourteen identified patients who participated in this study had a mean age of thirty-four, a female-to-male ratio of 3.7:1 and racial distribution of white:coloured:black of 9:3:2 (Figure 2). (The racial distribution is given in the standardised way in which it is usually given in formal South African governmental statistics. There were no Indian participants in this study.) Ten patients were unemployed, with three of them receiving a disability grant. Six patients came from the sample of fifty-eight WKH patients (10.4%), and eight from the sample of fifty-eight TDH patients (13.8%), giving a proportion of 12.1% of the sample of 116 patients. As primary psychiatric diagnoses, eleven patients had DID (three of them primarily of the possession type), three patients had OSDD (chronic or recurrent mixed dissociative symptoms which approach, but fall short of, the diagnostic criteria for DID), and four patients had comorbid conversion disorder (with seizures).

Data collection

I conducted the in-depth interviews between May 2013 and January 2015, using a semi-structured interview guide which covered the events leading up to this hospital admission, current life circumstances and problems, specific psychiatric symptoms, dissociative symptoms, symptoms relating to possession and trance, experiences relating to identity, roles and conflict, spiritual experiences, and experiences around information processing. The interview guide was adapted in subsequent interviews, depending on what themes emerged in the previous interviews, resulting in an iterative, reflexive process.

The interviews varied in length depending on the patient's tolerance, and in some cases were split into two parts. In some cases there was only a short break between the two interviews, and in others the two interviews were conducted on different days. A few of the patients opted for a single long interview of around ninety to one hundred minutes because of transport problems which made it difficult to arrange

Pt No.	Age	Gender	Race	Occupation	Hospital where recruited	Primary psychiatric diagnosis	No. of interviews	Language of interview
1	26	F	C	Personal assistant	WKH	DID	1	E
2	35	F	W	Unemployed	WKH	DID	1	A
3	33	F	B	Security guard	WKH	DID (with possession)	2	E
4	23	F	W	Unemployed	WKH	DID	2	A
5	41	F	C	Unemployed, receiving disability grant	WKH	DID, and conversion disorder (with seizures)	4	A (mixed with E)
6	30	F	W	Unemployed	WKH	DID (with possession), and conversion disorder (with seizures)	1	A
7	54	F	W	Unemployed, receiving disability grant	TDH	DID	2	E
8	41	F	W	Unemployed	TDH	DID, and conversion disorder (with seizures)	1	A
9	45	F	W	Unemployed, receiving disability grant (fine artist)	TDH	OSDD	2	A
10	19	F	C	Unemployed	TDH	OSDD, and conversion disorder (with seizures)	1	E

11	39	M	W	Unemployed (piece jobs as manual labourer)	TDH	DID	2	E (mixed with A)
12	33	M	B	Unemployed (previously IT consultant)	TDH	OSDD	1	E
13	42	M	W	Land surveyor	TDH	DID	2	A (mixed with E)
14	21	F	W	Administrator	TDH	DID (with possession)	1	E

Figure 2. Demographic and clinical characteristics of study participants.
Abbreviations: Pt=patient; F=female; M=male; C=Coloured; W=White; B=Black; WKH=Weskoppies Hospital; TDH=Tshwane District Hospital; DID=dissociative identity disorder; OSDD=other specified dissociative disorder; E=English; A=Afrikaans.

a follow-up interview. One patient was interviewed four times, partly because of ward programme limitations and partly because of her request to have more time to share her experiences.

In summary, I conducted single interviews with seven patients; two interviews with each of six patients; and four interviews with one patient (Figure 2). The language used in the interviews was English for six patients, Afrikaans for five patients, and a mixture of the two for three patients. I opted for not using an interpreter where the home language of the patient was not English or Afrikaans because of the risk of losing some of the meaning through an interpreter, and also to preserve confidentiality for the patients. The home language of one of the black African patients (patient 3) was isiZulu, and those of the other patient (patient 12) were siSwati and isiNdebele (with siSwati being his primary language, i.e., that of his father's family with whom he grew up).

For the WKH patients the interviews were held either in the hospital ward where they were admitted at that stage, or if discharged between their initial recruitment and the date of the in-depth interview, at the central admissions unit (as a specially arranged outpatient study visit). For the TDH patients whose hospital admissions tended to be shorter than those of the WKH patients, the interviews were held mostly as specially arranged outpatient study visits at the WKH central admissions unit, or in the WKH ward to which some of them were transferred following their TDH admission, or in one case as a specially arranged study visit at the TDH ward where she was previously admitted. In all cases the interviews were held in privacy in a consultation room setting. The costs of the patients' transportation to the study visits were reimbursed to them as per the study protocol.

One of the problems relating to all of these settings was the unpredictable noise levels in the respective buildings, which intermittently caused some degree of disturbance during the audio recordings. Fortunately none of this was severe enough to jeopardise successful recordings.

All interviews were audiotaped and fully transcribed professionally. Field notes taken of all interviews also formed a part of the data that was analysed.

Analysis

I analysed the qualitative data using thematic analysis (Braun & Clarke, 2006; Creswell, 2013; Schurink, Fouché, & De Vos, 2011). The computer software programme ATLAS.ti was used to aid electronic data management. Open coding of transcriptions was followed by axial and selective coding, using a combination of inductive and deductive techniques through several iterations.

I pursued trustworthiness of the research process by maintaining my own researcher reflexivity, collaborating with the participants, gathering thick, rich descriptions, searching for disconfirming evidence, and maintaining an audit trail (Creswell, 2013).

Ethical considerations

All study participants signed written informed consent prior to participating in the study—separately for both the broader project and for this specific qualitative study which included audio recordings. Their data was handled anonymously to maintain confidentiality. The original research protocol received approval by the Research Ethics Committee of the Faculty of Health Sciences, University of Pretoria (protocol 121/2012) and minor amendments were approved by the same committee in April 2013, August 2013, and January 2014. All research data is stored securely according to the Policy for the Preservation and Retention of Research Data of the University of Pretoria.

Results

The three most grounded themes which emerged from my preliminary analyses of the data were possession of unknown external origin; identity alteration which took the form of variable and fluid shifts between singularity and multiplicity; and the struggle associated with inner identity confusion.

Possession of unknown external origin

Three of the patients interviewed had experienced possession as the determining symptom of their DID. Contrary to what I expected, two of these patients were white. Other DID patients interviewed also experienced some possession, although their diagnosis of DID was not primarily dependant on possession.

None of the patients could give first-person accounts of their possession experiences. They could only recount what witnesses had told them.

All of the patients who had experienced possession felt unsure of its origin, but placed the origin outside of themselves. They had all also been told by others who or what might have possessed them.

One patient (patient 3), a thirty-three-year-old black African woman, experienced recurrent possession experiences in church or healing contexts, which included fainting, seizures, and aggressive and out-of-character behaviour since a young age. These experiences were given different interpretations, depending on the context. Some sangomas (traditional healers) said her behaviour of asking for cannabis during her possession experiences resembled that of her late grandfather and that the incidents represented the calling by her ancestors to become a traditional healer. Church leaders, on the other hand, said her aggressive behaviour was evidence that a demon possessed her and that it was a sign that she should become a prophet. Still others said that she had been bewitched.

She gave the following rich and touching account with minimal interruption from my side. I provide a slightly abbreviated version, below, in which I have removed my clarifying sentences and interjections to make it a more readable whole, but all of the following account is her exact words. I felt that too much would be sacrificed by abbreviating it any further.

> Sometimes I get sick and when they take me to a traditional healer, the, the, I faint. When I faint, when I wake up, they would tell me that there was a, um, my grand, what do they call it, grandfather ... Father's father, I don't know, and then they will say he was saying he wants this and this and this and this and this. So but I didn't take it serious until now when I found myself everything was blocking. Nothing which I do is going alright so when I got there to the sangoma and then they tell me the same story which I have heard since before. It's many times. Since from I was young.
>
> Yes, but sometimes when I go to church they will say it's the demons at church. Yes, they will say it's demons and then, mm, the other prophet will say it's the ancestors calling and the sangomas, other sangomas, will say it's the ancestors calling. So I'm not sure which is which.
>
> I don't know, just because sometimes when I'm at church, sometimes I collapse. I collapsed and when I wake up I wake up when they have tied me ... It's a calling. That's because you, when, at

the church they don't ask question, they just pray and pray and pray and when it happens when I'm at the sangoma they, they, they kneel down and they will be doing like this [she claps] and they will be talking and they, the people who are around will tell me when I wake up that it was not my voice, it was someone else's voice and it like maybe a grandfather, grandfather's voice.

My mother sometimes is there and my father when he was still alive he was also there many times when we go and this thing will start and then sometime they say I smoke cigarettes but me, I don't remember smoking cigarette but I, I sometimes dream smoking cigarette but I didn't see myself smoking. But when I wake up they will tell me that the grandfather said he wants to smoke ganja [i.e., cannabis], you know ganja, it's what do they call, something which the people sometimes they take it. I don't know what can I call it. What they say it's ganja, eh, yes they will say the grandfather say it like that and then they will say we, we, we asked the grandfather that he must not ask for that just because the, the, the, the law doesn't allow that so at least we give cigarette. So they say it was not me smoking it was that grandfather who wanted to smoke. Yes, they will say that.

Me, I don't remember anything. They will tell me when I wake up that one, two, three it was happening but me I, I see nothing. Maybe it takes sometimes even an hour.

Yes, yes but me I, when it start, I feel dizzy. Like, I feel like I'm dizzy and I feel like uh, uh, uh, I'm falling down and then they will take me. And what I remember is sometimes I do like this, like I have, I have fits like. I do like that and that is the only thing I remember and then from there I, I don't remember anything and then I will just wake up, some people surrounding me and maybe sometimes I wake up I am tied just because they say I, I will be fighting but me, I don't see that. She [a friend] was saying she was seeing me mm, mm, I was beating all those people and they tied me up and they were praying for me.

Each and every time when I go to church, when they are praying it always happen. I don't go like every time in church, but that time, maybe I go twice or once a month at church. But always when I go to church it will happen. Like in the Easter holidays I was always going to church like every day on those Easter holidays and it was always happening.

I was worried, I was worried and I started confirming to the, and of the family, and they were telling me that yes, they know that I am supposed to take that job for my grandfather which he, he was doing and they told me that there, there, there are two people who want me to take their job. The other one is a man, the other one is a woman and the woman is using, mm, church, like it's praying for people and that is what I am supposed to do and the other one is using herbs, making traditional herbs and that one is a man. And they always tell me that that is why I don't have a, a boyfriend. It's because of, eh, I didn't do, oo, all those things which they were telling me to do. Just because they are the ones who are going to open my waist so that I can get married or what.

That they told me that just because when I got to the prophets or to the sangoma they always tell me since I was young that I must take the ... the calling, so I did it so that is why all the things are blocked. It is like I have to do all the things and then after all my things are going to be open. They said the one who is a man, the ancestors, is the one who is blocking my ways.

I'm not sure. Like they, they say in black people, the other people like they are witching and they can put something like a tokolosh, they call it tokolosh, so I ... my mind always think like it's true just because each and every day, each and every dream I have I'm always having a baby boy. I'm always having a baby boy with me on my back. Each and every time ...

They pray to me (at the church), yes. And then they will talk to the demon. They call it a demon. They will be talking to it and chasing it, "Go away, go away, we are putting fire on you. You must not come to stay with this. This one is the, is the mm, daughter of God so leave her alone." And then sometimes they will tell me that it said, "I will never leave her alone, I will never. I will never leave her alone." And, but one day they told me that it said, "I am tired, I'm going." But when I go again to church it will come again so it means it didn't go.

Another patient (patient 14), a twenty-one-year-old white woman with distinct alter personality states, also had experienced possession thrice, every time in association with alcohol use, and the first two of these incidents occurred in the context of occultist practices. As an occultist practitioner at the time of the first incident, she was performing an incantation under the influence of alcohol, and then allegedly went into a two-hour episode of possession of which she has no memory and received limited reports from witnesses. At the second incident, also under the influence of alcohol, according to eye witnesses she might have performed an occultist incantation, then allegedly spoke fluent Hebrew and picked up her ex-boyfriend—a very big, heavy man. She has no memory of this incident either. She said she might have ascribed the incident to an ordinary emotional "meltdown" (i.e., an emotional breakdown), but since she had had no connection with Hebrew prior to the incident, she interpreted the Hebrew speaking as a sure sign of external possession. At the third incident two weeks prior to our interview she had large amounts of alcohol, but it did not happen in a spiritual kind of context at all. She allegedly spontaneously entered a state of possession and tried to stab her boyfriend and his housemate, while apparently speaking fluent Russian (a language with which she had had no prior connection either). This episode apparently lasted several hours during the night.

She explained that as an occultist one opens oneself to the spiritual realm in which anything can happen, and that this might have made her vulnerable to external possession—which might explain the foreign languages which she allegedly spoke during the episodes of possession. She believed that the foreign languages must have arisen externally, because she had never had any prior exposure to or learning of these languages.

She explained the vulnerability like this:

> Because, um, the reason why I stopped becoming an occultist is because I experienced what people would generally call possession ... And then after that I was scared. And not that paganism necessarily has a direct link to possession, I just feel if I touch anything that sort of opens your subconscious, or whatever you wanna call to it, it's going to make me vulnerable and I had an experience two weeks ago.

Variable and fluid shifts in identity between singularity and multiplicity

A twenty-six-year-old coloured woman (patient 1) with DID based on distinct named alter personality states described the process of shifting between her different personality states, and in effect between singularity and multiplicity. She used two different analogies.

One analogy was of being partly and variably caught up in a bottle or jar on the table while one of her named alters is active. Although she did not name the alter in the quotation below, she referred to it by name at other stages in the interview. Her experience also appears to reflect co-consciousness between the alters. The history which she gives of the "bubble" suggests that it may have served a protective function.

Patient abbreviated as Pt. Interviewer abbreviated as Int.

Pt: Yes, … and then on Sunday it was like … it's like, like almost as if I'm … like I've been put in a little jar and the jar gets put on the table and then … and stuff's happening and then I'm … I know what's happening because I'm there but I'm in the jar and the other part, which I'm pushing away, is not in the jar, so that part is … is me.

Int: Behaving in your place.

Pt: I don't know if it's behaving in my place or if … I'm confused because I don't know if it is me, maybe it is me and I just feel disconnected from that part of me. And then … but it's like … yesterday I was with my friends, and we were going somewhere and, you know, crossing the road and as I got to the pavement it's like everything … I don't know it's … my feet was walking and … I looked up and … it's like my body just … I don't know, my body is … it's like it does its own thing, it's like it has its own mind, like … it's like I stopped breathing but I was breathing and I was … I was, like, trying to … I was trying to be me because I had a plan, the plan was to stay away, you tell me what can I do and then it's like everything, like, I went into the jar, my body was just there and then that part just wanted to, like … act …

Int: Your body, you talk about your body that was acting.

Pt: It's like … it's like … It's like, when I'm in the jar it's like I lose ninety per cent and I'm ten per cent and I know and can see and I feel but, yes, I'm just … but then … but I'm not there, it's like I'm … like I'm … it felt like I just couldn't get back to me again, it's like I couldn't come out of the jar and I was trying so hard to get out of the jar and I was stuck and I couldn't … it's like because I was trying to control my breathing and try-ing to come back, it was like … it was just awful.

Int: Do you know what part … which name was out there?

Pt: It was … it was definitely the sensual one …. It feels like I have no control, it feels like I'm put in the bottle, like I …

Int: Put in the jar and the other one is carrying on.

Pt: Yes, it's like I'm watching from the inside, like I can see, like … and everything but at the same as I'm seeing this other part of me that I'm going okay, there's just this, you know, like … I just decrease and they just increase and then it's just … it's like decreasing just puts me into the bottle, into the jar and then I'm just there.

Int: And then you decrease into the jar.

Pt: Yes. And the same time it's like, even when I am me. It's like I have … at least these times I feel like I've moved out of myself like … like I remember when I was still at [job], I was, like, constantly not doing my work because I was running away to try and get myself back because I was like …. Yes, and then at the same … it's like … almost like I'm going to wake up soon, like, I feel like I'm going to wake up, like wake up and be in a completely different place.

Int: Has that ever happened that you found yourself in a different place and you don't know how you got there?

Pt: No not really, I don't think so because I …

Int: And for example that the one that comes out, does things without the other parts knowing.

Pt: No I'm always in the jar, so I'm always somewhat there.

Int: Somewhat there.

Pt: Yes, even if … even if I don't remember afterwards, like how I'm saying, I don't remember but I, I know, like, you know what I mean. I don't remember properly, but I know okay, something like that.

Int: Yes, you have parts of the memory.

Pt: Yes …. and it's like … it's like when I was small I would see angels standing around me and as I grew older it turned into brick walls and as I got older it turned into this bubble … and then the bubble disappeared and then everything just flooded, it's like I couldn't keep these things away from me, I couldn't keep what I saw away from me. I couldn't … it's like I … it's like when I was small I was amazed by them …. I could see my father's boots walking around or I'd see people or like, just … I don't know I used to see these things and as I grew older they just changed, they got scarier, they're got closer whereas when I was small I could keep them, the distance because of the angels, because of the walls, because of the bubble and, I mean, now it's like I've got nothing and it's just … like, if someone talks, you respond but that's why there's still that ten per cent. I don't know it's like … it's weird because it's like … I don't know it's like being … I'm trying to find an example, it's like being a sweet with two flavours and the two flavours are both there and the one flavour is, I don't know, that's a bad example, because a sweet can't talk, but, like, it's like the one flavour is, you can mostly taste that flavour but the other flavour is there. It's like I'm ... it's like I was there, and I could speak, like, I was speaking, I was there but I was ... it's like they are me, I don't know, it's like as much as ... it's like maybe it is ... they are me and I just don't want them to be.

The same patient's second analogy was of a tug-of-war rope of which the flag moves slowly to and fro along the distance between the two pulling teams, indicating partial shifting into an alter personality state.

Pt: It's like, yes ... it's like ... it's like almost as if ... it's like if there was a tug of war rope and the flag was in the middle, it's not like I become fully that person, like, I can ... at times maybe I do but it's like ... it's like being pulled and then it becomes ... it's like just less of that part and more of that part. And then the other part tries to come back and it can't and then ...

Int: So it's more of a fluid shifting.

Pt: Yes. It's like ... it's ... but that's what I'm saying, it's like it is me but it's ... like, they are me but they're not me, it's like I can see them clearly as separate but they ... but they still are me.

The above analogies stand in sharp contrast to the image of a broken telephone as offered by another patient, a forty-two-year-old white man (patient 13), to explain his more "traditional" categorical switching into different alters and the total lack of awareness, communication and co-consciousness between his named alter personality states. He became aware of this broken internal communication around the age of twenty-two (translations from Afrikaans are in italics).

Int: *And you cannot remember what happens then?*

Pt: Absolutely not.

Int: *And can that .... Yes .... So, as you are sitting here you will not know if that one can remember what you do?*

Pt: *Everything is as I say,* "broken telephone syndrome", *I get information bit by bit from different people* ... I really don't remember about anything. It's a blank. Really, it's a blank ... It's confusing for me because I really don't know what is going on. *I try to sort it out but* ...

The struggle associated with inner identity confusion

The thirty-three-year-old black woman (patient 3) whose recurrent possession experiences were given different interpretations depending on the context, had endorsed questionnaire items about an "angry part" at the time that she completed the MID in the context of the broader project (Dell, 2006). The structured nature of the following quotation reflects my attempt to clarify her experience of an "angry part", as endorsed by her in the abovementioned questionnaire. I had two questions in my mind—whether she had understood the relevant MID item at the time of completing the questionnaire; and to what degree she experienced such an "angry part" as separate from her usual self. My aim was to understand how she experienced her own identity as opposed to being possessed by an external agent.

From her responses, it appeared to me that she found her own angry behaviour unacceptable and that she might ascribe such behaviour to something from outside which survives within her. She also said, "I am not one" and indicated that she did not understand what was happening (see the phrases in bold type in the quotation from her second interview, below). However, later she referred to herself in the first person, as the one who acts so unacceptably. I interpreted her explanation around the "angry part" as inner identity confusion, rather than as clear shifts into alter personality states or as possession experiences. She told me that she had experienced this problem since she was about twenty years old.

It appears then that she experiences varying degrees of identity alteration—not only does she suffer from episodes of external possession (see above section on Possession of unknown external origin), but also she is also aware of inner identity confusion (see the quotation below). Indeed, her different varieties of experience might illustrate the fluid multiplicity referred to above and again in the discussion below.

Int: … this came from the questionnaire, in the questions, remember there was a questionnaire scale and you had to circle one to ten.

Pt: Yes.

Int: Now some of those questions were about parts.

Pt: About?

Int: Different parts, like as if one consists of different parts. So some of the questions said there's an angry part inside me that wants to control things or something. Do you remember those questions?

Pt: Yes.

Int: And you answered quite highly on some of those questions of the angry part inside. So I wanted to ask you about that, you know, what did you mean and how does it feel to you, this thing about an angry part?

Pt: When I'm angry?

Int: Mmm, does it feel like it's not you, your usual self or does it feel like it's somebody else or does it feel like a little part of you that's separate, or how does it feel?

Pt: I don't just understand, sometimes I just get angry and when I get angry I can do anything, no one can control me and then after I will start to regret and **I can't believe it was me doing like that** but just ... it's like each and every time when I get angry, I don't care even for the things I want to protect. I don't care when by that time I'm angry, yes.

Int: And then when it happens, you know what's happening, you are quite aware of what you are doing ... you can see yourself?

Pt: Yes.

Int: But you don't care ...

Pt: Yes.

Int: Okay so does it feel that it's you doing it?

Pt: No.

Int: No .... Do you think it's a separate person? How do you think about it?

Pt: **I don't understand about it.**

Int: ... Mmm, do you think of yourself as one, or do you think there are many inside?

Pt: **I think there is something in me but I don't understand what is it but I don't think I am one but I think there is something which is surviving with me.**

Int: And let's talk again about that angry part. Does that part have a name?

Pt: No.

Int: Okay, and you think it's part of you? Do you see it as part of yourself?

Pt: ... like, when I'm angry the way I act it's not the way I think I must do.

Int: Okay, but it's still you ...

Pt: Yes.

Another patient, a twenty-three-year-old white woman with a diagnosis of DID (patient 4), said that people had told her she had a demon inside her. She then recounted one incident where she had an ego-alien experience in church, which included involuntary movements of her hands and fingers. The church incident had raised questions for her about her own identity, and she remarked that it was scary to think that there might be someone else inside her.

Although on the surface the church incident itself represents an example of external possession, I interpreted her reflections about the incident and its potential implications as inner identity confusion (translations from Afrikaans are in italics).

Int: *... perhaps we should just go back again over what you told me. Did I understand you correctly that it feels to you as if there are ... you have different parts within you?*

Pt: *Yes.*

Int: *You said you do not give them names.*

Pt: *No ...* **Because it's sometimes scary to think about it that there might be someone else inside me.** *So I don't even want to give it a name. There have been people who told me that I have a demon inside me because I, when I enter a church ... OK ... I cannot walk into a church ... and the day that I eventually decided I am going to go to church now to give it a try, then when the minister preached to me then my skin burned. It felt as if it was on fire and I could not look the minister in the eye and when I eventually looked him in the eye, I felt so much hatred in me that it just, I couldn't help it, I just had to sit down, because when the minister starts talking to you then you fall down as the Holy Spirit comes over you, but this did not happen to me, and when I sat down my hands and fingers made such weird movements, as if it was not my own ... myself who made them. That was very scary that time.*

Int: *Was this the first time that it happened?*

Pt: *Yes. This happened recently, a short while ago when we still lived in [area]. They have a church, I don't know where it is, I am still new in Pretoria, so I don't really know the place.*

Int: *So you felt as if your ... something was controlling you.*

Pt: *Yes.*

Int: *What kinds of movements did they make then.*

Pt: *It's like this ... and this ... something almost like this ...*

Int: *Almost like claws.*

Pt: *Yes. Like interlocked and the one over the other and everything, like as if you want to get out, or ...*

The twenty-six-year-old coloured woman (patient 1) who felt as if she was in the jar on the table gave the following explanation for how she made sense of some of her inner conflicts. Her explanation appears to demonstrate identity confusion.

> Like, at times it's like ... okay I'm going to use examples from before, like, when C ... [her one alter] was out ... because she's got hectic beliefs .... She's got some hectic beliefs, like ... it's like ... it's like knowing ... it's me going to church and knowing that ... and believing Christianity and then C ... saying, but you're the devil's wife, but you're not ... and then believing that I'm, like, a child of God and believing that I'm somehow changed into, like, at one stage it got so confusing, I started believing that maybe the devil isn't someone, that I am the devil, that maybe I'm not the devil so I think maybe, like, I was just meant to just be evil. And at the same time it's, like ... it's like I know that can't be true, and, yes ...

A nineteen-year-old coloured woman (patient 10) had the following to say when I asked her about identity confusion and an inner struggle—which she then called "zoom in".

Pt: I don't like really know who I am. Now that I have anxiety. I can't even, like when I look myself in the mirror, I can't, I just can't get hold of who I am inside. I don't know like, you know, what my abilities are, like you know what I'm good at, I don't like have anything. Nothing interests me so I just don't know who I am ...

Int: You just don't know who you are?

Pt: No, I don't know who I am.

Int: Does it sometimes feel as if there's a struggle going on inside of you?

Pt: Like what kind of struggle?

Int: Like about who you are.

Pt: Yes. It happens a lot.

Int: A lot.

Pt: And there are some times where I just zoom in like when I'm alone I just, you know, stare at faces and I just, like zoom in, like everything. I can't just like get a hold of myself.

Int: Can't get hold of yourself? And when you say you zoom in, what do you mean by zoom in?

Pt: Like trying to figure out, like you know, what's going on like, with me. Like just trying to figure out what kind of person I am. That kind of zoom in.

Int: Mmm.

Pt: And if things are going to get better and how my future's going to be like, and you know all that.

Another young patient, the twenty-one-year-old white woman (patient 14) who recounted three distinct episodes of possession (see above section on possession of unknown external origin), in addition to her usual instances of categorical identity alteration, also acknowledged frequent lesser episodes of inner identity confusion. Prior to the quote below, she had explained these lesser episodes of identity confusion to me as an inner struggle associated with very "vivid thoughts". These "vivid thoughts" did not amount to voices (auditory hallucinations) and were not associated with behaviour that was so different from her usual self that she would attribute them to one of her named alters or to external possession. However, even within these lesser episodes of inner identity confusion, she felt these "vivid thoughts" to be somewhat external to herself (see the quotation below). Her explanation appears to suggest that she experiences varying and progressive degrees of identity related problems.

Int: Normally when you get this struggle and the vivid thoughts, it's not as if you act like a different person?

Pt: Um.

Int: You feel these things and you isolate yourself?

Pt: Yes, I won't say act like a different person but, um, I wouldn't really be able to speak for myself in a very, um, clear way when that happens. But not a different person. Just an aggravated person with thoughts that feel external.

Discussion and conclusions

The most grounded themes which emerged from these preliminary analyses of the data, and which appeared to be at least partly linked to each other, were possession of unknown external origin; identity alteration which took the form of variable and fluid shifts between singularity and multiplicity; and the struggle associated with inner identity confusion.

These findings, although they represent only very preliminary analyses, do appear to yield a few hypotheses that might be tested in future empirical research.

First, the findings appear to suggest that identity alteration may be much more variable than is generally considered under the rubric of "switching to a different alter". Instead, identity alteration might sometimes take the form of fluid multiplicity. This is not a new idea, as a model of normal, flexible multiplicity has been described before—indeed, the nature of identity appears to vary across cultures, culture impacts on the construction of self, and identity *per se* might not be unified but rather dependent on the expectations and needs of others (Castillo, 1997; Howell, 2005; Krüger, 2009; Krüger, Sokudela, Motlana, Mataboge, & Dikobe, 2007; Markus & Kitayama, 2010).

Second, before reaching the stage of fragmentation found in identity alteration where the "other" or alter may be considered separate from oneself, there might be a large grey area of identity confusion where a person still regards himself or herself as being one person (i.e., as having a unitary identity), but also as being influenced by varying and progressive degrees of "otherness"—where the "otherness" may come from the inner conflict of having to find or construct one's self amidst disruption and fragmentation, or it may come from what are perceived as external forces.

Third, on the "other side" of identity alteration and the separateness that comes with it, possession experiences appear to occur on the far end of an internal-to-external continuum. Possession might represent instances of identity alteration where the characteristics of "the other" appear so foreign to the individual that these characteristics are considered to have arisen externally, often in the spiritual realm. This theme is also consistent with existing literature—in cultures where the self is constructed as more open to external influences, possession syndromes may be more prevalent (Cardeña, Van Duijl, Weiner, & Terhune, 2009).

What was interesting in this study sample is that in a number of cases possession experiences and inner identity confusion co-occurred in the same individual. One possible way to think about this might be that individuals are often unaware of their possession experiences—they are informed by others of such incidents and their presumed aetiology, namely possession. The affected individual then has to try and make sense of the experience, others' explanations for it, and the implications for his or her personal identity. The process of trying to make sense of it might manifest as inner identity confusion. An alternative interpretation might be that the hypothesised gradations of separateness discussed above might not be mutually exclusive and that an individual may experience bits of different grades at any one time.

In conclusion, unitary personal identity and multiplicity might be considered to occur on a continuum if one considers the above hypothesised relationships, the possible gradations of separateness of aspects of self as manifesting from identity confusion through identity alteration to possession, as well as the qualitative findings of this study which support these hypothesised relationships.

Testing of these hypotheses aside, in the light of the above-suggested relationships between identity confusion, identity alteration, and possession, this study appears to offer qualitative support for the DSM-5's inclusion of possession experiences in the main diagnostic criterion for DID (APA, 2013). In this regard, however, Van Duijl, Kleijn, & De Jong (2013) have demonstrated that there might be a few problems with the specific way of incorporating possession in the criteria of DID.

An exploration of how these preliminary findings might support the work of identity theorists, DID theorists, possession theorists, and others falls outside of the scope of this chapter. However, there appears to be sufficient grounds to justify pursuing such exploration in future research.

Methodologically, this study design allowed for rich descriptions and explanations by the psychiatric patients of their graded experiences of identity alteration. If these preliminary thematic analyses could be extended using methods of grounded theory, there is the potential for the development of a detailed model of variations in identity alteration, which in turn might have clinical implications.

References

American Psychiatric Association. (1994). *Diagnostic and Statistical Manual of Mental Disorders* (4th edn) *(DSM-IV)*. Washington, DC: APA.

American Psychiatric Association. (2013). *Diagnostic and Statistical Manual of Mental Disorders* (5th edn) *(DSM-5)*. Washington, DC: APA.

Beck, A. T. (1987). *Beck Depression Inventory*. Orlando, FL: Harcourt Brace.

Beck, A. T. (1990). *Beck Anxiety Inventory*. Orlando, FL: Harcourt Brace.

Beck, A. T., Epstein, N., Brown, G., & Steer, R. A. (1988). An inventory for measuring clinical anxiety: psychometric properties. *Journal of Consulting and Clinical Psychology, 56*: 893–897.

Beck, A. T., & Steer, R. A. (1993). *Beck Depression Inventory: Manual*. Orlando, FL: Harcourt Brace.

Beck, A. T., Ward, C. H., Mendelson, M., Mock, J., & Erbaugh, J. (1961). An inventory for measuring depression. *Archives of General Psychiatry,* 4: 561–571.

Bernstein, E. M., & Putnam, F. W. (1986). Development, reliability, and validity of a dissociation scale. *Journal of Nervous and Mental Disease, 174*(12): 727–735.

Braun, V., & Clarke, V. (2006). Using thematic analysis in psychology. *Qualitative Research in Psychology, 3*(2): 77–101.

Briere, J., Elliott, D. M., Harris, K., & Cotman, A. (1995). Trauma symptom inventory: psychometrics and association with childhood and adult trauma in clinical samples. *Journal of Interpersonal Violence, 10:* 387–401.

Cardeña, E., Van Duijl, M., Weiner, L. A., & Terhune, D. B. (2009). Possession/ trance phenomena. In: P. F. Dell & J. A. O'Neil (Eds.), *Dissociation and the Dissociative Disorders: DSM-V and Beyond* (pp. 171–181). New York: Routledge.

Carlson, E. B., & Putnam, F. W. (1993). An update on the Dissociative Experiences Scale. *Dissociation, VI*(1): 16–27.

Castillo, R. (1997). *Culture and Mental Illness.* Pacific Grove, CA: Brooks/ Cole.

Creswell, J. W. (2013). *Qualitative Inquiry & Research Design: Choosing among Five Approaches* (3rd edn). Los Angeles: Sage.

Creswell, J. W., & Plano Clark, V. L. (2011). *Designing and Conducting Mixed Methods Research* (2nd edn). Thousand Oaks, CA: Sage.

Dell, P. F. (2006). The Multidimensional Inventory of Dissociation (MID): a comprehensive measure of pathological dissociation. *Journal of Trauma & Dissociation, 7*(2): 77–106.

Delport, C. S. L., & Fouché, C. B. (2011). The qualitative research report. In: A. S. de Vos, H. Strydom, C. B. Fouché, & C. S. L. Delport (Eds.), *Research at Grass Roots: For the Social Sciences and Human Service Professions* (4th edn) (pp. 425–430). Pretoria: Van Schaik.

Derogatis, L. R. (1975). *SCL-90-R: Symptom Checklist-90-R.* Minneapolis, MN: National Computer Systems.

Derogatis, L. R., & Lazarus, L. (1994). SCL-90-R, Brief Symptom Inventory, and matching clinical rating scales. In: M. E. Maruish (Ed.), *The Use of Psychological Testing for Treatment Planning and Outcome Assessment* (pp. 217–248). Hillsdale, NJ: Erlbaum.

Dorahy, M. J. (2001). Culture, cognition and dissociative identity disorder. In: J. F. Schumaker & T. Ward (Eds.), *Culture, Cognition and Psychopathology* (pp.157–169). Westport, CT: Praeger.

During, E. H., Elahi, F. M., Taieb, O., Moro, M. R., & Baubet, T. (2011). A critical review of dissociative trance and possession disorders: etiological, diagnostic, therapeutic, and nosological issues. *Canadian Journal of Psychiatry—Revue Canadienne de Psychiatrie, 56*(4): 235–242.

Eshun, S., & Gurung, R. A. R. (Eds.) (2009). *Culture & Mental Health: Sociocultural Influences on Mental Health.* Malden, MA: Blackwell.

Espí Forcén, C., & Espí Forcén, F. (2014). Demonic possessions and mental illness: discussion of selected cases in late medieval hagiographical literature. *Early Science and Medicine, 19*(3): 258–279.

Ferracuti, S., Sacco, R., & Lazzari, R. (1996). Dissociative trance disorder: clinical and Rorschach findings in ten persons reporting demon possession and treated by exorcism. *Journal of Personality Assessment, 66*(3): 525–539.

Fouché, C. B., & Schurink, W. (2011). Qualitative research designs. In: A. S. de Vos, H. Strydom, C. B. Fouché, & C. S. L. Delport (Eds.), *Research at Grass Roots: For the Social Sciences and Human Service Professions* (4th edn) (pp. 307–327). Pretoria: Van Schaik.

Halliburton, M. (2005). "Just some spirits": the erosion of spirit possession and the rise of "tension" in South India. *Medical Anthropology, 24*(2): 111–144.

Harley, D. (1996). Explaining Salem: Calvinist psychology and the diagnosis of possession. *American Historical Review, 101*(2): 307–330.

Hegeman, E. (2013). Ethnic syndromes as disguise for protest against colonialism: three ethnographic examples. *Journal of Trauma & Dissociation, 14*(2): 138–146.

Henley, P. (2006). Spirit possession, power, and the absent presence of Islam: re-viewing les maîtres fous. *Journal of the Royal Anthropological Institute, 12*(4): 731–761.

Howell, E. F. (2005). *The Dissociative Mind.* New York: Routledge.

Islam, F., & Campbell, R. A. (2014). "Satan has afflicted me!" Jinn-possession and mental illness in the Qur'an. *Journal of Religion & Health, 53*(1): 229–243.

Krüger, C. (2009). The influence of conflicting medieval church and social discourses on individual consciousness: dissociation in the visions of Hadewijch of Brabant. *Studia Historiae Ecclesiasticae, XXXV*(2): 239–266. Available at: http://hdl.handle.net/10500/4598 [last accessed 16 November 2015].

Krüger, C., Sokudela, B. F., Motlana, L. M., Mataboge, C. K., & Dikobe, A. M. (2007). Dissociation: a preliminary contextual model. *South African Journal of Psychiatry, 13*(1): 13–21. Available at: http://hdl.handle.net/2263/4341 [last accessed 16 November 2015].

Levack, B. P. (2014). The horrors of witchcraft and demonic possession. *Social Research, 81*(4): 921–939, 980.

Lund, C., & Swartz, L. (1998). Xhosa-speaking schizophrenic patients' experience of their condition: Psychosis and amafufunyana. *South African Journal of Psychology, 28*(2): 62–70.

Markus, H. R., & Kitayama, S. (2010). Cultures and selves: a cycle of mutual constitution. *Perspectives on Psychological Science, 5*(4): 420–430.

Martínez-Taboas, A. (1999). A case of spirit possession and glossolalia. *Culture, Medicine & Psychiatry, 23*(3): 333–348.

Martínez-Taboas, A. (2005). Psychogenic seizures in an *espiritismo* context: the role of culturally sensitive psychotherapy. *Psychotherapy: Theory, Research, Practice, Training, 42*(1): 6–13.

Mercer, J. (2013). Deliverance, demonic possession, and mental illness: some considerations for mental health professionals. *Mental Health, Religion & Culture, 16*(6): 595–611.

Nieuwenhuis, J. (2007). Qualitative research designs and data gathering techniques. In: K. Maree (Ed.), *First Steps in Research* (pp. 69–97). Pretoria: Van Schaik.

Nijenhuis, E. R. S. (1999). *Somatoform Dissociation: Phenomena, Measurement, and Theoretical Issues.* New York: Norton.

Nijenhuis, E. R. S., Spinhoven, P., Van Dyck, R., Van der Hart, O., & Vanderlinden, J. (1996). The development and psychometric characteristics of the Somatoform Dissociation Questionnaire (SDQ-20). *Journal of Nervous and Mental Disease, 184*(11): 688–694.

Reis, R. (2013). Children enacting idioms of witchcraft and spirit possession as a response to trauma: therapeutically beneficial, and for whom? *Transcultural Psychiatry, 50*(5): 622–643.

Ross, C. A. (2011). Possession experiences in dissociative identity disorder: a preliminary study. *Journal of Trauma & Dissociation, 12*(4): 393–400.

Ross, C. A., Schroeder, E., & Ness, L. (2013). Dissociation and symptoms of culture-bound syndromes in North America: a preliminary study. *Journal of Trauma & Dissociation, 14*(2): 224–235.

Sapkota, R., Gurung, D., Neupane, D., Shah, S. K., Kienzler, H., & Kirmayer, L. (2014). A village possessed by "witches": a mixed-methods case-control study of possession and common mental disorders in rural Nepal. *Culture, Medicine and Psychiatry, 38*(4): 642–668.

Şar, V. (2014). The many faces of dissociation: opportunities for innovative research in psychiatry. *Clinical Psychopharmacology and Neuroscience, 12*(3): 171–179.

Şar, V., Alioğlu, F., & Akyüz, G. (2014). Experiences of possession and paranormal phenomena among women in the general population: are they related to traumatic stress and dissociation? *Journal of Trauma & Dissociation, 15*(3): 303–318.

Schurink, W., Fouché, C. B., & De Vos, A. S. (2011). Qualitative data analysis and interpretation. In: A. S. de Vos, H. Strydom, C. B. Fouché, & C. S. L. Delport (Eds.), *Research at Grass Roots: For the Social Sciences and Human Service Professions* (4th edn) (pp. 397–423). Pretoria: Van Schaik.

Seligman, R., & Kirmayer, L. J. (2008). Dissociative experience and cultural neuroscience: narrative, metaphor and mechanism. *Culture, Medicine & Psychiatry, 32*(1): 31–64.

Spiegel, D., Loewenstein, R. J., Lewis-Fernandez, R., Şar, V., Simeon, D., Vermetten, E., Cardena, E., & Dell, P. F. (2011). Dissociative disorders in DSM-5. *Depression & Anxiety, 28*(9): 824–852. [Erratum in *Depression & Anxiety, 28*(12):1119.]

Steinberg, M. (1994a). *Interviewer's guide to the Structured Clinical Interview for DSM-IV Dissociative Disorders—Revised (SCID-D-R)* (2nd edn). Washington, DC: APA.

Steinberg, M. (1994b). *Structured Clinical Interview for DSM-IV Dissociative Disorders—Revised (SCID-D-R)*. Washington, DC: APA.

Swartz, L. (1998). *Culture and Mental Health: A Southern African View*. Cape Town: Oxford University.

Taves, A. (2006). Where (fragmented) selves meet cultures: theorising spirit possession. *Culture and Religion, 7*(2): 123–138.

Van Duijl, M., Kleijn, W., & De Jong, J. (2013). Are symptoms of spirit possessed patients covered by the DSM-IV or DSM-5 criteria for possession trance disorder? A mixed-method explorative study in Uganda. *Social Psychiatry & Psychiatric Epidemiology, 48*(9): 1417–1430.

Van Duijl, M., Kleijn, W., & De Jong, J. (2014). Unravelling the spirits' message: a study of help-seeking steps and explanatory models among patients suffering from spirit possession in Uganda. *International Journal of Mental Health Systems, 8*(1): 24.

Van Duijl, M., Nijenhuis, E., Komproe, I. H., Gernaat, H. B., & De Jong, J. T. (2010). Dissociative symptoms and reported trauma among patients with spirit possession and matched healthy controls in Uganda. *Culture, Medicine & Psychiatry, 34*(2): 380–400.

Weathers, F. W., Litz, B. T., Huska, J. A., & Keane, T. M. (1994). *The PTSD Checklist—Civilian version (PCL–C)*. Boston, MA: National Center for PTSD.

Wolcott, H. F. (2002). Writing up qualitative research … better. *Qualitative Health Research, 12*(1): 91–103.

CHAPTER SEVEN

Dissociative identity disorder, culture, and memory

Lina Hartocollis

I am a clinician. I am also a researcher and an academic. These different parts of me created something of an internal tension as I approached the writing of this chapter. I was asked to contribute a piece on the cultural context and meanings of so-called dissociative identity disorder. I was also asked to discuss the attendant polemic surrounding recovered memories of abuse. These are topics that, if not handled with care, can feel to survivors of abuse, like further assaults. Although I have not had first-hand experience with ritual abuse I have worked as a clinician with women who suffered sexual abuse as children and I have heard stories and seen suffering which has kept me up at night. I am well aware of the pain and the shame that can haunt abuse survivors well into adulthood. I know how important it is to create a therapeutic relationship in which support and validation and acceptance are necessary, if not sufficient, conditions for helping and healing survivors of abuse. I also firmly believe that survivors should be supported in finding their voice and telling their story—the story of their suffering and also a new narrative of healing and strength and hope for a different future. As a clinician, my role is not to question the "truth" of these stories in the forensic sense, nor do I question the nature of my patients' suffering or the particular shape and form which their suffering takes. I applaud

Anna for the courage it took to speak out and tell her story and I trust that although the story was not published in this volume, the writing of it gave her strength and helped in her journey toward wellness.

Contextualising DID

Dissociative identity disorder (DID) is a controversial diagnosis. It has been called an example of: an hysterical epidemic (Showalter, 1997); "an exercise in deception" (Aldridge-Morris, 1989); an iatrogenically produced disorder (Merskey, 1992); a "role enactment" (Lynn, Lilienfeld, Merckelbach, Giesbrecht, & van der Kloet, 2012); an artifact of hypnosis (Orne & Bates, 1992); a modern form of hysteria—with all the attendant questions of suggestibility which hysteria raises (McHugh, 2008); a culture-bound "idiom of distress" (Kenny, 1986); a "structured narrative" which shapes vulnerable peoples' experiences, and which a subsection of mental health professionals identify and encourage (Horwitz, 2002); an often neglected form of post-traumatic stress disorder, resulting from repeated and perverse childhood abuse (Herman, 1997); and an explanatory "traumaterigic paradigm" (Loewenstein & Ross, 1992).

Seventy years ago, Taylor and Martin (1944) wrote that those who most readily accept the reality of multiple personality are: "(1) persons who are very naive and (2) persons who have worked with actual cases or near cases" (ibid., p. 293). Taylor and Martin went on to say:

> A psychotherapist who thinks nothing of multiple personality, and who undertakes to steady and strengthen his patients directly, must discover few if any multiple personalities; whereas a psychotherapist who is aware of multiple personality as a pattern, and who seeks out his patients' conflicting systems ... must meet relatively many multiple personalities. (ibid., p. 295)

Why is it that some very experienced clinicians say that they have never seen a single case of DID, while others claim to have seen hundreds? How do we account for different people viewing the same world so differently? Beliefs are not personal creations, springing sui generis from the mind of the individual. Rather, they are examples of situationally bound thinking which are highly dependent on social, historical, and ideological context. In other words, such beliefs are not individual but intersubjective. In order to explore competing understandings or constructions of a psychiatric disorder such as DID, both the disorder and its discursive origins must be located within the particular sociocultural and historical context from which they arise. As Gergen (1994) posited:

> Mental health professionals exist in a symbolic relationship with the culture, drawing sustenance from cultural beliefs, altering these beliefs in systematic ways, disseminating their views back to the culture, and relying on their incorporation into the culture for continued sustenance of the speech act and profound relationship to history. (ibid., p. 155)

I have previously offered an analysis of the historical and social context which contributed to prevailing popular and professional constructions of what at the time was known as multiple personality disorder (Hartocollis, 1998). I described how popularised, and some have argued sensationalised cases of multiple personality disorder provided what cultural anthropologist Byron Good refers to as "prototypical illness narratives" (Good, 1992) for the condition. Particularly influential was the case of Sybil about which a bestselling book was written in the early 1970s (Schreiber, 1973). *Sybil* found a cultural fit that earlier accounts of multiple personality such as *The Three Faces of Eve* (Thigpen & Cleckley, 1957) did not, because it dovetailed with the growing recognition of and preoccupation in the US with child abuse (Hartocollis, 1998; see also Hacking, 1995). Accounts of sexual abuse by survivors and the therapists who treated them became increasingly common in the years following *Sybil*, and they offered a compelling explanation for a variety of forms of psychological distress, including dissociative identity disorder.

In short, sexual abuse became politicised as women who were victims were encouraged to break the silence, and sexual abuse stories became paradigmatic stories of the domination and exploitation of women. The focus on sexual abuse also gave rise to the trauma-dissociation theory of dissociative identity disorder, in which the sexually abused child defends against the overwhelming experience of trauma by segregating or dissociating the memories of the abuse from consciousness and locating them within alter personalities. The trauma-dissociation model mirrored cultural preoccupation with trauma, power and control, a fear that the centre would not hold, and a wish to escape from overwhelming practical life circumstances and demands (Hartocollis, 1998).

As a primarily women's disorder, DID invokes hysteria—the quintessentially female malady of the early years of psychiatry, which feminists have cast as a form of protest against a patriarchal society (Showalter, 1985). DID discourses emerged at the interface of psychiatric discourses on hysteria, and feminist and other discourses which privilege and problematize childhood sexual abuse and trauma. The trauma-dissociation model of DID is culturally resonant but it is also transgressive, challenging traditional psychodynamic modes of explanation which privilege endogenous, sometimes unconscious, intrapsychic factors, in favour of etiological models which implicate exogenous psychic trauma. At the same time, DID stirs-up lightning conductor issues that have periodically emerged and sparked controversy in the history of psychiatry and in the culture at large.

These polarising issues can be viewed as subtexts, fueling the debate. They include: questions about the impact of influence and suggestion on psychiatric diagnosis and treatment; questions about the prevalence of child sexual abuse and the veracity of recovered memories of abuse; and struggles over theoretical commitments and over what should count as scientific evidence. Professional and scientific discourses are organised around patterns of exclusion, in that they delimit what knowledge is considered acceptable, scientific, legitimate, and what is not. At base, debates about psychiatric nosology, such as that exemplified by the DID controversy, are a way of asking questions about what is and is not considered official knowledge (Hartocollis, 1998).

Expert agreements, disagreements, and constructions of DID

In the late 1990s, I conducted research in which I interviewed mental health "experts" who represented different and often opposing sides of the controversy around what was then still referred to as multiple personality disorder. My aim was to understand the role of experts in the production of psychiatric knowledge in general and DID in particular. I analysed the relationship between professional experiences and ideology, personal and social meaning-making, and beliefs about DID (Hartocollis, 1999).

Roughly half of the experts I interviewed were DID specialists and the other half were experienced, knowledgeable and influential mental health professionals. Not unexpectedly, the twenty-three experts expressed widely varying beliefs about DID. The differences between

the respondents' experiences and beliefs were striking, and the following quotes from two participants exemplify this divide:

> I've seen thousands (of DID patients)—in consultation or overseeing
> their treatment on my unit.
>
> I know there are people who claim to have seen one hundred
> and sixty cases ... I've never come across such a thing. I wish some-
> body would present such a case to me. I have supervised so many
> people in all parts of the country ...

Although the nuanced and sometimes contradictory quality of the
respondents' beliefs made it difficult to develop a typology, their views
can be summarised as follows. Eight of the respondents were specialists
who had seen many cases of DID and tended to believe the condition
was a result of severe and repeated childhood trauma, most often sexual abuse. Four of the respondents had seen a few cases of DID but were
sceptical of the diagnosis and troubled by the recent increase in reported
cases. Two respondents and seen a few cases of DID and were uncertain
about whether or not the diagnosis was rare. Of the eight remaining
respondents, all were highly sceptical of the diagnosis, believing it to be
a rare condition that occurs in suggestible patients.

The DID specialists argued that clinicians who have never seen
DID are really just overlooking it—failing to ask the right questions or
blinded by their particular ideological commitments. As one respondent said, when I asked why some very seasoned clinicians had never
encountered a case of DID: "They have, they just don't know it." Similarly, another respondent remarked: "If some disorder does not fit in
with a person's theory, they're less likely to see it or elicit it and the
patient is less likely to respond to it."

For the sceptics, DID was profoundly disturbing. For some it was
the "irrationality" of the phenomenon that bothered them the most. For
others, it was the social contagion aspects, which led them to suspect
that DID was a diagnostic "fad." Very few of the sceptics went as far as
to say that DID did not exist. Rather, they tended to argue that it was a
rare condition whose prevalence had been vastly inflated.

Respondents came to their beliefs by way of a combination of individual and social experiences to which they attached particular personal meaning. Although most remembered scant attention to DID
in their early professional education and training, the DID specialists

described later formative experiences which led them to questions this lack of attention. Among these experiences, the influence of respected mentors and colleagues stood out as especially important. Respondents also ascribed significance to their direct experiences with DID, with "believers" tending to remember in great detail their first "eye opening" DID cases, and the "sceptics" tending to gloss over and de-emphasise their direct experiences with DID.

All of the DID specialists had "come of age" professionally in the 1970s or early 1980s, when childhood trauma and dissociation were becoming increasingly resonant explanatory themes in the popular culture and the psychiatric community for a widening range of psychiatric disorders, including DID. Moreover, respondents' beliefs about DID seemed linked to their beliefs about the importance of childhood sexual trauma and dissociation, with respondents who were DID "believers" tending to embrace this shift in attention to trauma and dissociation.

The respondents' beliefs about DID reflected tensions in the larger culture and in the psychiatric community, namely concerns about the impact of influence and suggestion on psychiatric diagnosis and treatment, and questions about the prevalence and etiological significance of childhood sexual abuse and dissociation. There were considerable differences in both the way that respondents defined and understood childhood trauma and dissociation, and the significance they attached to these experiences and concepts. Such differences led respondents to conceptualise DID differently.

While all the participants agreed that childhood sexual abuse is traumatic, they differed with respect to their perception of its prevalence, its definition, and its effects. The DID experts tended to emphasise the importance of childhood sexual abuse as a key etiological factor in the genesis of DID and other psychiatric symptoms and disorders. A striking difference between DID experts and other respondents was that none of the DID experts raised the issue of the reliability of memories of sexual abuse, whereas almost all of the other respondents did, saying things like: "With the concept of trauma, you have the whole problem of the reality of memory, the validity of memory ... it doesn't make a difference whether its fantasy or reality except when you're basing a theory on it or taking somebody to court to prosecute them", and "I have no idea of this whole recovered memories business, how much is exaggeration and how much not", and "memory changes over time according to the developing needs of the individual".

Respondents on both sides referred to the "politicised" nature of sexual abuse and recovered memories. However, while all the respondents acknowledged that abuse of children can have negative consequences, there was considerable variation in the extent to which the respondents viewed childhood abuse as causal in the development of DID and other psychiatric disorders. The respondents' views tended to fall into two general categories which are captured in the following quotes; the first cautioning against pushing the issue of child abuse underground, and the second warned against an over-reliance on child abuse as explanatory, to the exclusion of other factors:

> There is a kind of shaming and silencing that always attends trauma patients … They're upsetting us, they're making us feel things we don't want to feel and look at things we don't want to look at. Make them go away.
>
> It's an impossible scientific and epistemological question to reconstruct the degree to which childhood physical and sexual abuse is causal because there are so many confounding variables and it certainly can't be studied in a controlled way. The fact that a person has a history of [abuse] doesn't mean that event created their current problems. So you have to be respectful of the possible aetiology in childhood physical and sexual abuse and you certainly need to be respectful of the fact that patients come with a strong belief that this may be important. On the other hand it's a mistake to exaggerate it … It's also a mistake to suggest it.

One of the recurring criticisms of DID sceptics was their impression that DID patients tended to be unusually suggestible. These respondents were suspicious of the increase in cases:

> Such patients are suggestible. Because after all, in the course of one's life we meet so many people, we read about so many people and we imagine for a moment, if only I could have been so and so. We have a fantasy of what it would be like to be so and so. We do it all the time.
>
> My sense is that we've always had suggestible patients in the world and I've tended to disregard a fair amount of what is described as dissociation as being related to suggestion.
>
> Of course you always have to look at suggestion and susceptibility to suggestion in these sorts of patients—secondary gain.

I've sat in hospital units, in groups, and seen one patient talk
about how she was in a satanic cult, and then another patient in
the group says I think I was in that cult. So there is this contagion
because of high suggestibility.

I have a sense that there's a very strong iatrogenic effect of
suggestion.

A number of the DID experts resented the implication that DID was
iatrogenically produced. They pointed out that they did nothing out
of the ordinary in their diagnosis of these patients, for example, taking a careful history or using standardised psychological tests to measure such things as dissociation. However, several of the DID experts
did talk about using hypnosis as a diagnostic and/or therapeutic tool,
something which most of the other respondents denied using.

Ultimately most of the sceptics indicated that they did not view DID
as simply iatrogenic since they considered the patient's distress to be
"real". Rather than iatrogenic, several of these respondents referred to
DID as a "co-construction" between patient and therapist, wherein, as
one respondent put it, "the patient and therapist negotiate an understanding that pleases them". Respondents on both sides of the issue
highlighted how the nature of DID almost inevitably raises the question of suggestion. Almost all of the respondents agreed that people
diagnosed with dissociative identity disorder tend to be suggestible.
For sceptics, this lent credence to their argument that many cases of
DID were the product of suggestion. While for DID experts, the fact
that certain patients may be suggestible did not necessarily mean that
therapists were inducing DID through suggestion.

A number of the respondents also discussed the influence of culture
on psychiatric diagnosis. Sceptics spoke of the cultural exigencies that
led DID to become a resonant way for people to describe and experience
their distress, and coupled this with the argument that the diagnosis is
probably a passing fad. One sceptic went as far as to suggest that the
focus on trauma and feminist issues which fuel the proliferation of DID
are likewise "fads": "I suspect it's a fad and it links to other fads—the
trauma fad, for example, it also probably links to feminist things; most
of the patients are women ... and many of the therapists are men."

While DID experts also discussed cultural influences on psychiatric diagnoses, they tended to portray dissociative disorders as universal conditions with enduring structures which are interpreted and

shaped differently by different cultures and different historical periods. Psychiatry has long struggled with the notion of how valid, reliable, "scientific" it is, and there is much at stake in this effort. The public's sense of legitimacy of psychiatry, its authority and power, are at stake. As Gergen (1994) suggests:

> Sufficient segments of culture—including prospective clients, law-makers, the medical profession, and insurance companies—must come to share in the ontology of mental illness and the belief that the professions can and should provide cures. From the pragmatic perspective there is no pattern of illness to which the professions are responding; rather, the conception of illness functions in ways that link the professional and the cultural in an array of mutually supportive activities. (ibid., p. 155)

If we acknowledge that we are essentially social creatures, and as such, malleable—shaped by one another and by our particular location in history and culture, then we must also admit that our psychiatric disorders are culturally constructed and as such, not immutable and not reflective of some objective reality. Gergen (1994) argues that the language used to describe mental illness reifies individual states or behaviours, in that such states are not objective realities until they are made real by the very language used to describe them. Similarly, medical anthropologist Arthur Kleinman (1996) posits that psychiatric diagnoses are culturally shaped constructions that are themselves constitutive of that which they describe, rather than scientifically verifiable realities:

> A psychiatric diagnosis, after all, is an interpretation of an interpretation. Contrary to the positivism of most academic psychiatry … there can be no immediate grasping of the reality outside of historically derived categories. What the patient reports is itself an interpretation of experience based on his or her own cultural categories, words, images, and feelings for expressing (and thereby constituting) symptoms. The psychiatrist's interpretation occurs one remove further. (ibid., p. 19)

In short, the lightning conductor issues that I have identified as subtexts in the DID debate carry with them historical baggage, already heavy with controversy. They stir up discomfort about the limits of psychiatric knowledge and authority, and highlight the power of professional claims-making and theoretical commitments. In this sense, DID is the channel through which these subterranean struggles have been forced to the surface. This has led the controversy surrounding DID to be over-determined, taking on an especially contentious tone which reflects those underlying crosscurrents.

Memory, false memory, and iatrogenesis

Among the most contested of these crosscurrents is the question of whether memories of childhood sexual abuse can be forgotten and later remembered or recovered. In 1992, a US couple who believed their daughter had falsely accused them of sexual abuse started the False Memory Foundation. Since then, the so-called "memory wars" have embroiled the mental health community in a contentious debate about the reliability of recovered memories of sexual abuse (Farrants, 1998; Freyd, 1994; Gordon, 1995; Greaves, Smith, Butler, Spiegel, & Kihlstrom, 2010; Grossman & Pressley, 1994; Haaken, 1995; Loftus, 1994, 2003; Ofshe, 1996; Roediger & McDermott, 1995; Spanos, 1996).

A number of well-publicised cases implicated therapeutic techniques such as hypnosis and memory reconstruction in the production of false memories of abuse that were later recounted or found through forensic evidence not to have occurred. This reinforced arguments that recovered memories that arise during the course of therapy are less reliable than spontaneous memories that occur outside the therapy. In a similar vein, Connolly & Read (2006) investigated Canadian criminal court reports of historic sexual abuse and found that most court cases related to false memory involved memories which were reconstructed or retrieved in the course of therapy rather than spontaneous memories which emerged outside of therapy. Adding fuel to the fire, in 2001 a journalistic inquiry into the case of Sybil cast doubt on the original story. Sybil was recast as a vulnerable, troubled, and attention-seeking young woman who was manipulated and exploited, wittingly or unwittingly, by an overzealous therapist who was determined to see multiple personalities and uncover a history of extreme childhood abuse which likely did not occur (Nathan, 2011).

Challenging the charge that memory recovery is the product of psychotherapy, a study of ninety women in an inpatient trauma disorders unit found that dissociative symptoms were higher in those reporting abuse than in those without abuse histories, and the earlier the abuse the more dissociative symptoms and amnesia (Chu & Frey, 1999). Most of the recovered memories happened outside of the therapeutic context, alone or with friends or family. Limitations of the study were that the data came from self-reports without external corroboration of abuse, and participants were drawn from a patient population in a unit that specialised in trauma, a potentially biasing factor. More recently, in a retrospective study researchers (Geraerts et al., 2007) attempted to independently corroborate accounts of childhood sexual abuse that were both continuously remembered and forgotten and later remembered. They found that both continuous and discontinuous memories remembered outside of therapy were more likely to be corroborated than memories recovered in therapy. The researchers concluded that therapist expectation can lead to the creation of false memories.

There has been a proliferation of such empirical studies on memory, the results of which lend credence to both sides of the recovered memory debate (see for example, Aglan, Williams, Pickles, & Hill, 2010; Bremner, Shobe, & Kihlstrom, 2000; Chu & Frey, 1999; Eisen, Morgan, & Mickes, 2002; Goodman et al., 2003; Huntjens, Wessel, Hermans, & van Minnen, 2014; Milchman, 2008; Moore & Zoellner, 2007; McNally, 2003; Ogle et al., 2013; Rubin & Boals, 2010; Wager, 2012; Winograd, Peluso, & Glover, 1998). Overall, research has demonstrated that memory is fallible, susceptible to social influence and reconstruction, and affected by the age and developmental stage of the individual and by other endogenous and exogenous factors and processes which we only partially understand (Loftus, 2003). Early childhood memories, prior to age four, are likely to be inaccurate, which is referred to as "infantile amnesia" (Howe & Courage, 1997).

Some research studies have suggested that individuals who report recovered memories are more likely to engage in memory distortion than control groups (Clancy & Schacter, 2000; Geraerts, Merckelbach, Jelicic, Smeets, & van Heerden, 2006). Studies have linked susceptibility to the creation of false memories to dissociative symptoms (Clancy & Schacter, 2000; Winograd, Peluso, & Glover, 1998), and PTSD (Bremner, Shobe, & Kihlstrom, 2000). Clancy and Schacter (2000) recruited four groups of women: sexually abused as children who consistently remembered the abuse; sexually abused and no memory of the abuse; those who reported recovered memory of child sexual abuse (CSA); and a control group who reported no abuse history. In word retrieval tests, the recovered memory group scored higher than other groups on false remembering. The researchers replicated the study with individuals who claimed to have been abducted by aliens with similar results (Clancy, McNally, Schacter, Lenzenweger, & Pitman, 2002).

Researchers have explored the relationship between recovered memories of childhood sexual abuse and dissociation. Geraerts, Merckelbach, Jelicic, Smeets, and van Heerden (2006) studied the frequency of dissociative symptoms and fantasy proneness in women who were sexually abused as children. They recruited four groups of women: those with repressed memories of CSA; those with recovered memories of CSA; those with continuous (never forgotten) CSA memories; and a control group who reported no history of CSA. Women with repressed and recovered memories of CSA scored higher on measures of dissociation than women with continuous memory and the control group with no history of abuse. However, participants with childhood sexual abuse histories, whether repressed, recovered, or continuously remembered, all had increased fantasy proneness as compared to the control group. The researchers concluded that their results refuted claims that dissociative symptoms are the result of fantasy proneness (ibid.).

In addition to laboratory experiments that have used word recognition and recall tests, researchers have devised other studies in which false memories are created or implanted in the laboratory through suggestive techniques. Porter, Birt, Yuille, and Lehman (2000) had interviewers suggest or attempt to "implant" false memories of emotional childhood events (such as being attacked by a dog). Memory distortion was associated with high dissociation scores. The researchers also found that interviewer-interviewee pairs in which the interviewer scored high on extroversion and the interviewee scored high on introversion, were associated with a tendency for memory distortion on the part of the interviewee. The researchers concluded that false memories may be the result of a "social negotiation" between interviewers and rememberers, in which extroverted interviewers are particularly successful at persuading introverted participants of the veracity of experiences in their past which did not occur (ibid., p. 507). While the relevance of this conclusion for clinical practice or forensic interviewing is far from certain, it does raise questions for further exploration about factors which may contribute to the production of false memories in clinical or forensic encounters.

Using neuroimaging techniques, Kosslyn (2005) found that both actual visual images and imagined scenes activate the same areas of the brain, suggesting that there can be confusion about the source of images as real or imagined. Similarly, studies involving individuals who believe they have been abducted by aliens has shed light not only on the fallibility and malleability of memory but also on the inextricability of the mind-body relationship and the way which perceived trauma, whether real or imagined, can cause both psychological and physiological distress. In one such study, McNally et al. (2004) found that people who believe they were abducted by aliens display striking psychophysiological responses to the "memories of abduction". They concluded that researchers and clinicians are "remiss in ignoring the host of variables, including fantasy proneness, suggestibility, suggestion, co-occurring disorders, cognitive failure, neurological deficits, and yes, the potential repercussions of trauma in their quest to achieve a comprehensive account of dissociation and dissociative disorders" (ibid., p. 496).

Also calling into question the reliability of memories and the power even implanted memories can have over people, Bryant and Harvey (1996) studied individuals who were involved in serious car accidents during which they had been knocked unconscious. Even though it was not possible that they had "real" memories of the event, the participants in this study developed PTSD after reconstructing the accident by viewing news reports and listening to others' accounts of the accident. In effect they had imagined the accident so vividly that it triggered full-blown PTSD.

In an attempt to resolve the "memory wars" and provide treatment guidelines, the American Psychological Association and the British Psychological Society independently conducted systematic inquiries into recovered memories (American Psychological Association Working Group on Investigation of Memories of Childhood Abuse, 1996; British Psychological Society, 1995). In both instances considerable controversy ensued, with criticism about their methodology, agenda and biases from both sides. The reports that were produced came to strikingly similar conclusions. Recovered memories of childhood events that had been completely out of awareness do occur. However, memory is malleable and susceptible to suggestion, including through therapeutic techniques that encourage iatrogenesis.

Researchers searching for curative factors in psychotherapy with sexual abuse survivors (Spitzer & Avis, 2006) found that post-therapy, abuse survivors reported remembering and retelling graphic abuse details as having had a negative impact on their functioning during the therapy, while "finding greater acceptance, meaning and understanding of the abuse" (ibid., p. 182) were identified by participants as a key aspects of their healing.

Perhaps the emphasis on recovering memories is misplaced and, as Singer (1997) suggests, causal models of trauma and memory are simplistic and do not do justice to the complexity of humans. Such models mirror the social and cultural context in which they arise and find resonance, and should guard against reducing complex human behaviours and conditions into what Singer (ibid.) describes as "political caricatures of 'good' and 'bad'". Singer, a clinical psychologist, goes on to say: "Our job, and it is a critical one, is to report on the meanings individuals construct of their memories and the roles these meanings play in their lives" (ibid., p. 326). I agree with Singer that as therapists we should not approach our work as sleuths, but rather as co-authors in a narrative of understanding and healing. We should also understand that the narrative we create together is culturally and historically situated.

References

Aglan, A., Williams, J. M. G., Pickles, A., & Hill, J. (2010). Overgeneral autobiographical memory in women: association with childhood abuse and history of depression in a community sample. *British Journal of Clinical Psychology, 49*(3): 359–372.

Aldridge-Morris, R. (1989). *Multiple Personality: An Exercise in Deception.* Hove: Erlbaum.

American Psychological Association Working Group on Investigation of Memories of Childhood Abuse. (1996). *Working Group on Investigation of Memories of Childhood Abuse: Final Report.* Washington, DC: APA.

Bremner, J. D., Shobe, K. K., & Kihlstrom, J. F. (2000). False memories in women with self-reported childhood sexual abuse: an empirical study. *Psychological Science, 11*(4): 333–337.

British Psychological Society (1995). *Recovered memories: The report of the working party of the British Psychological Society.* Leicester: BPS.

Bryant, R. A., & Harvey, A. G. (1996). Visual imagery in posttraumatic stress disorder. *Journal of Traumatic Stress, 9*(3): 613–619.

Chu, J. A., & Frey, L. M. (1999). Memories of childhood abuse: dissociation, amnesia, and corroboration. *American Journal of Psychiatry, 156*(5): 749–755.

Clancy, S. A., McNally, R. J., Schacter, D. L., Lenzenweger, M. F., & Pitman, R. K. (2002). Memory distortion in people reporting abduction by aliens. *Journal of Abnormal Psychology, 111*(3): 455–461.

Clancy, S. A., & Schacter, D. L. (2000). False recognition in women reporting recovered memories of sexual abuse. *Psychological Science, 11*(1):
333–337.

Connolly, D. A., & Read, J. D. (2006). Delayed prosecutions of historic child
sexual abuse: analyses of 2064 Canadian criminal complaints. *Law and
Human Behavior, 30*(4): 409–434.

Eisen, M. L., Morgan, D. Y., & Mickes, L. (2002). Individual differences in
eyewitness memory and suggestibility: examining relations between
acquiescence, dissociation and resistance to misleading information.
Personality and Individual Differences, 33(4): 553–571.

Farrants, J. (1998). The "false memory" debate: a critical review of the
research on recovered memories of child sexual abuse. *Counselling Psychology Quarterly, 11*(3): 229–238.

Freyd, J. J. (1994). Betrayal trauma: traumatic amnesia as an adaptive
response to childhood abuse. *Ethics & Behavior, 4*(4): 307–329.

Geraerts, E., Arnold, M. M., Lindsay, D. S., Merckelbach, H., Jelicic, M., &
Hauer, B. (2006). Forgetting of prior remembering in persons reporting
recovered memories of childhood sexual abuse. *Psychological Science,
17*(11): 1002–1008.

Geraerts, E., Merckelbach, H., Jelicic, M., Smeets, E., & van Heerden, J.
(2006). Dissociative symptoms and how they relate to fantasy proneness
in women reporting repressed or recovered memories. *Personality &
Individual Differences, 40*(6): 1143–1151.

Geraerts, E., Schooler, J. W., Merckelbach, H., Jelicic, M., Hauer, B. J. A., &
Ambadar, Z. (2007). The reality of recovered memories: corroborating
continuous and discontinuous memories of childhood sexual abuse.
Psychological Science, 18(7): 564–568.

Gergen, K. (1994). *Realities and Relationships: Soundings in Social Construc-
tionism.* Cambridge, MA: Harvard University.

Good, B. J. (1992). Culture and psychopathology: directions for psychiatric
anthropology. In: T. Schwartz, M. White, & K. Lutz (Eds.), *New Directions in Psychological Anthropology* (pp. 181–205). Cambridge: Cambridge
University.

Goodman, G. S., Ghetti, S., Quas, J. A., Edelstein, R. S., Alexander, K. W.,
Redlich, A. D., Cordon, I. M., & Jones, D. P. H. (2003). A prospective
study of memory for child sexual abuse: nNew findings relevant to the
repressed–memory controversy. *Psychological Science, 14*(2): 113–118.

Gordon, B. (1995). The myth of repressed memory: false memories and
allegations of sexual abuse. *New England Journal of Medicine, 333*(2):
133–134.

Greaves, D. H., Smith, S. M., Butler, L. D., Spiegel, D., & Kihlstrom, J. E.
(2010). *Are the Recovered Memories of Psychological Trauma Valid?* New York:
McGraw-Hill.

Grossman, L. R., & Pressley, M. (1994). Introduction to the special issue on recovery of memories of childhood sexual abuse. *Applied Cognitive Psychology, 8*(4): 277–280.

Haaken, J. (1995). The debate over recovered memory of sexual abuse: a feminist-psychoanalytic perspective. *Psychiatry: Interpersonal & Biological Processes, 58*(2): 189–198.

Hacking, I. (1995). *Rewriting the Soul: Multiple Personality and the Sciences of Memory.* Princeton, NJ: Princeton University.

Hartocollis, L. (1998). The making of multiple personality disorder: a social constructionist view. *Clinical Social Work Journal, 26*(2): 159–176.

Hartocollis, L. (1999). The making of multiple personality disorder: the role of experts in the production of psychiatric knowledge. *Dissertation Abstracts International, A: The Humanities and Social Sciences, 60*: 1767.

Herman, J. L. (1997). *Trauma and Recovery* (revised edn). New York: Basic.

Horwitz, A. V. (2002). *Creating Mental Illness.* Chicago, IL: University of Chicago.

Howe, M. L., & Courage, M. L. (1997). The emergence and early development of autobiographical memory. *Psychological Review, 104*(3): 499–523.

Huntjens, R. J. C., Wessel, I., Hermans, D., & van Minnen, A. (2014). Autobiographical memory specificity in dissociative identity disorder. *Journal of Abnormal Psychology, 123*(2): 419–428.

Kenny, M. G. (1986). *The Passion of Ansel Bourne: Multiple Personality in American Culture.* Washington, DC: Smithsonian Institution.

Kleinman, A. (1996). How is culture important for the DSM-IV? In: J. E. Mezzich, M. D. Kleinman, H. Fabrega, & D. L. Parron (Eds.), *Culture & Psychiatric Diagnosis: A DSM-IV Perspective* (pp. 15–26). Washington, DC: APA.

Kosslyn, S. M. (2005). Reflective thinking and mental imagery: a perspective on the development of posttraumatic stress disorder. *Development and Psychopathology, 17*(3): 851–863.

Loftus, E. F. (1994). *The Myth of Repressed Memory: False Memories and Allegations of Sexual Abuse.* New York: St. Martin's.

Loftus, E. F. (2003). Make-believe memories. *American Psychologist, 58*(11): 867–873.

Loewenstein, R. J., & Ross, D. R. (1992). Multiple personality and psychoanalysis: an introduction. *Psychoanalytic Inquiry, 12*(1): 3–48.

Lynn, S. J., Lilienfeld, S. O., Merckelbach, H., Giesbrecht, T., & van der Kloet, D. (2012). Dissociation and dissociative disorders: challenging conventional wisdom. *Current Directions in Psychological Science, 21*(1): 48–53.

McHugh, P. R. (2008). Hysteria in four acts. *Commentary, 126*(5): 18–24.

McNally, R. J. (2003). Recovering memories of trauma: a view from the laboratory. *Current Directions in Psychological Science, 12*(1): 32–35.

McNally, R. J., Lasko, N. B., Clancy, S. A., Macklin, M. L., Pitman, R. K., & Orr, S. P. (2004). Psychophysiological responding during script-driven imagery in people reporting abduction by space aliens. *Psychological Science, 15*(7): 493–497.

Merskey, H. (1992). The manufacture of personalities: the production of multiple personality disorder. *British Journal of Psychiatry, 160*: 327–340.

Milchman, M. S. (2008). Does psychotherapy recover or invent child sexual abuse memories? A case history. *Journal of Child Sexual Abuse, 17*(1): 20–37.

Moore, S. A., & Zoellner, L. A. (2007). Overgeneral autobiographical memory and traumatic events: an evaluative review. *Psychological Bulletin, 133*(3): 419–437.

Nathan, D. (2011). *Sybil Exposed: The Extraordinary Story Behind the Famous Multiple Personality Case.* New York: Free.

Ofshe, R. (1996). *Making Monsters: False Memories, Psychotherapy, and Sexual Hysteria.* Berkeley, CA: University of California.

Ogle, C. M., Block, S. D., Harris, L. S., Goodman, G. S., Pineda, A., Timmer, S., Urquiza, A., & Saywitz, K. J. (2013). Autobiographical memory specificity in child sexual abuse victims. *Development & Psychopathology, 25*(2): 321–332.

Orne, M. T., & Bates, B. L. (1992). Disorders of the self: myths, metaphors, and the looking glass of hypnosis past. In: A. Kales (Ed.), *Mosaic of Contemporary Psychiatry in Perspective,* (pp. 247–260). New York: Springer-Verlag.

Porter, S., Birt, A. R., Yuille, J. C., & Lehman, D. R. (2000). Negotiating false memories: interviewer and rememberer characteristics relate to memory distortion. *Psychological Science, 11*(6): 507–510.

Roediger, H. L., & McDermott, K. B. (1995). Creating false memories: remembering words not presented in lists. *Journal of Experimental Psychology: Learning, Memory, and Cognition, 21*(4): 803–814.

Rubin, D. C., & Boals, A. (2010). People who expect to enter psychotherapy are prone to believing that they have forgotten memories of childhood trauma and abuse. *Memory, 18*(5): 556–562.

Schreiber, F. R. (1973). *Sybil.* Chicago, IL: Regency.

Showalter, E. (1985). *The Female Malady: Women, Madness, and Culture in England, 1830–1980.* New York: Pantheon.

Showalter, E. (1997). *Hystories: Hysterical Epidemics and Modern Culture.* New York: Columbia University.

Singer, J. A. (1997). How recovered memory debates reduce the richness of human identity. *Psychological Inquiry, 8*(4): 325–329.

Spanos, N. P. (1996). *Multiple Identities & False Memories: A Sociocognitive Perspective.* Washington, DC: American Psychological Association.

Spitzer, B., & Avis, J. M. (2006). Recounting graphic sexual abuse memories in therapy: the impact on women's healing. *Journal of Family Violence,* 21(3): 173–184.

Taylor, W. S., & Martin, M. F. (1944). Multiple personality. *Journal of Abnormal and Social Psychology, 39*: 281–300.

Thigpen, C. H., & Cleckley, H. (1957). *The Three Faces of Eve.* New York: McGraw-Hill.

Wager, N. (2012). Psychogenic amnesia for childhood sexual abuse and risk for sexual revictimisation in both adolescence and adulthood. *Sex Education: Sexuality, Society and Learning, 12*(3): p. 331–349.

Winograd, E., Peluso, J. P., & Glover, T. A. (1998). Individual differences in susceptibility to memory illusions. *Applied Cognitive Psychology, 12*: S5–S27.

Further reading

Kihlstrom, J. F. (1994). One hundred years of hysteria. In: S. J. Lynn & J. W. Rhue (Eds.), *Dissociation: Clinical and Theoretical Perspectives* (pp. 365–394). New York: Guilford.

Kluft, R. P. (1997). *The Argument for the Reality of Delayed Recall of Trauma. Trauma and Memory: Clinical and Legal Controversies* (pp. 25–57). New York: Oxford University.

Spiegel, D. (1991). *Dissociation and Trauma. American Psychiatric Press Review of Psychiatry (Volume 10)* (pp. 261–275). Arlington, VA: American Psychiatric Association.

CHAPTER EIGHT

The psychiatric comorbidity of dissociative identity disorder: an integrated look

Vedat Şar

Introduction

Clinical psychopathology, as a discipline, is based on phenomenology (Jaspers, 1913). This has been helpful to avoid precocious inferences about possible pathogenesis of psychiatric disorders and to remain in contact with diverging theoretical stances despite differing diagnostic and therapeutic extrapolations originating from them. The DSM-III (American Psychiatric Association, 1980) and its subsequent versions have considered this as a motto while trying to represent a common ground for psychiatric nosology and classification viable in an index time period. Consequently, phenomenological diagnostic criteria have become a major tool of thinking in clinicians' and researchers' minds. Nevertheless, phenomenology should not be misunderstood as an approach looking merely "from outside" because it addresses subjectivities (one's "internal world") as well. Hence, it does not preclude looking from "inside out" and inquiring the common root of appearances that seem to be autonomous and separate at first sight.

The apparently fragmentary nature of dissociation and dissociative disorders constitutes a diagnostic challenge not only for clinicians and researchers, but also an enigma for laymen, including those who suffer

181

from the disorder. Unlike other psychiatric disorders such as depression and schizophrenia, dissociative disorders cannot be conceived as a unitary phenomenon in the community. Although everyone is conceptually familiar with some type of dissociative symptom or experience (e.g., estrangement, trance states, an experience of possession, or multiple personalities), it is difficult to relate each one to the other unless one has access to the knowledge making this possible.

Even patients with dissociative identity disorder (DID) and its subthreshold forms may claim only a subgroup of their symptoms that dominate their mental status during index admission or represent a particular individual pattern (Kluft, 1985, 1991). Alternatively, these patients may come up with such a broad range of symptoms that it would be hard to classify them. Beside the omission of the appropriate knowledge in the general psychiatric training, one particular obstacle for many clinicians to make the diagnosis of DID and its sub-threshold forms is the predominance of the so called secondary or associated symptoms (e.g., hallucinations, Schneiderian passive-influence experiences) which usually prevail in the frontline of the clinical picture (Steinberg, 1994). Moreover, while dissociation may be manifest in both chronic and acute conditions, any seemingly acute dissociative condition may be superimposed on a chronic one to eclipse the latter in the eyes of the clinician (Tutkun, Yargic, & Şar, 1996). A chronic dissociative disorder such as DID may have a fluctuating course over years, resembling a periodical episodic illness (Kluft, 1985) or merely a single acute response to a stressful event or to an internal conflict which may recur over time or may not.

To make the situation more complex, in addition to constituting disorders in their own right, dissociation may accompany almost every psychiatric disorder and may influence their phenomenology as well as response to treatment (Şar & Ross, 2006). Despite their universal character, the cultural sensitivity in perception of DID and its sub-threshold forms (Lewis-Fernandez, Martínez-Taboas, Şar, Patel, & Boatin, 2007; Şar, 2006) is represented even in eye-catching differences on the official diagnostic manuals of psychiatric disorders such as the DSM-5 (American Psychiatric Association, 2013) and the ICD-10 (World Health Organization, 1992) in a scope unusual for other clinical constructs. In sum, this fragmentary background has to be considered in any discussion on psychiatric comorbidities of DID, that is, an "in depth" and integrative look is required to catch the "true" situation.

Here is the key to avoid any confusion: dissociation is not a static condition but a dynamic one. One particular issue to be considered in understanding DID is that individuals suffering from dissociation do not experience only discontinuities and/or disruption of their mental functions, but they are simultaneously in an intense striving to achieve the normal integration of them to experience wholeness (Tagliavini, 2014). Many patients with DID unsuccessfully struggle with their condition to achieve an improvement (self-reparation or self-treatment) by themselves for several years before the appropriate diagnosis has been made by a clinician. On the other hand, dissociation is not only an intrapsychic but also an interpersonal phenomenon (Liotti, 2006). The latter factor contributes to the dynamism of dissociation in terms of the contextual factors affecting the condition of the individual. Hence both Liotti (ibid.) as well as Barach (1991) underlined the role of interpersonal attachment disturbances in DID.

Liotti (2006) proposes that pathological dissociation should be viewed as a "primarily intersubjective reality hindering the integrative processes of consciousness" (ibid., p. 55), rather than as an intrapsychic defence against mental pain. Additionally, early defences against attachment-related dissociation may lead to interpersonal controlling strategies that inhibit the attachment system further. Dissociative symptoms emerge as a consequence of the breakdown of these defensive strategies when exposed to events that activate the attachment system.

According to Liotti (2006), it was Bowlby (1973) who first hinted at the relationship between attachment processes and dissociative psychopathology. Namely, Bowlby proposed that inadequate care-seeking interactions with the primary caregivers could lead the infant to develop multiple internal representations of self and attachment figures which he called internal working models (IWM). One IWM becomes dominant in regulating interpersonal relationships in a certain context, while the other IWMs remain separated from mainstream conscious experience. The latter surface in stressful situations to regulate emotions and cognitions in a way that may, more or less, be alien to the person's usual sense of self. In addition, sense of agency is influenced by this alteration.

Liotti (2006) suggests that the shifts among the multiple IWMs fit the drama triangle (Karpman, 1968), namely the interactions between the main characters oscillate between the roles of the benevolent rescuer, the malevolent persecutor, and the helpless victim. The link between attachment theory and the drama triangle is represented in the model of attachment to the perpetrator (Ross, 1997), which serves the victim sub-jectively in achieving a sense of control in the abusive condition. Hence, according to Liotti (2006), psychotherapy of pathological dissociation should be a phase-oriented process focused primarily on achieving attachment security, and it should deal with trauma only secondarily. However, one should consider that the disavowal of the attachment to the perpetrator requires some type of trauma work.

Interestingly, in a recent study conducted on a large group of college students who had either a dissociative disorder (including DID and it sub-threshold forms) or borderline personality disorder (BPD), or both, there were significant differences between self-rating and clinician-rated dissociative amnesia scores (Şar, Akyüz, Kuğu, Öztürk, & Ertem-Vehid, 2006). Although both diagnoses were co-occurring in a subgroup of the participants, in a variance analysis looking at the main effects of the two diagnostic patterns, BPD was related to an awareness of dissociative amnesia in self-rating (in contrast to the observations in the clinical) assessment more readily compared with the dissociative disorder diag-nosis. Unlike that of BPD, the dissociative disorder diagnosis was related to significant dissociative amnesia in the presence of the clinician which the participants were not able to report in the self-report instrument, possibly due to diminished awareness because of "amnesia to amnesia" (Kluft, 1988). Hence, the discrepancies in dissociative amnesia in self-rating and clinician-assessment settings were associated with the two partly overlapping diagnostic categories. Two questions arise: Does the presence of the clinician (interpersonal situation) have a special effect on the status of the evaluated subject? If so, what is the relationship between this effect and the two diagnoses?

First of all, such fluctuations may pertain to the self-system of the individual with DID which may involve hidden influences of non-executive personality states, or which may cause covert switching during assessment contingent on perceptual alterations to traumatic memories (Beere, 2009a, 2009b). Beere (2009b) has demonstrated that individuals who are dissociative but do not have DID report more amnesia than non-dissociative individuals. As the dissociative psy-chopathology entered the DID range, reports of amnesia appeared to decrease (although it is known clinically that there is more amnesia among those manifesting DID than manifested in this particular sub-group). Such fluctuations seem to be induced both by the presence of an interviewer as well as by being invited to introspect when alone.

The presence of an interviewer represents clearly a situation that is the model setting of interpersonal attachment, which has a crucial importance for the studied population (Liotti, 2006).

Interestingly, Kaehler and Freyd (2009) found that higher "betrayal" traumas are associated with greater BPD characteristics, based on data collected from clinical and nonclinical subjects. Betrayal trauma theory suggests that dissociation is an adaptive response to childhood abuse, which allows survival by enabling the child to maintain attachment to a figure vital to her/his development (Freyd, 1994). Combining the perceptual (Beere, 2009a) and betrayal (Freyd, 1994) theories of dissociation, I would hypothesise that the origin of perceived threat differs in the two response patterns on this post-traumatic spectrum. Diagnosis of BPD seems to be related to a greater "interpersonal (external) phobia" and to increased vigilance against perceived threats in interpersonal situations which would lead to preponderance of memory continuity in self-system during clinical interview, for example by taking over of executive personality states. In accordance with this and interestingly, individuals with BPD were reported to have significantly better performances in the reading the mind in the eyes test (RMET), a measure of the capacity to discriminate the mental state of others from expressions in the eye region of the face (Fertuck et al., 2009). Antidepressant medication status, PTSD co-occurrence, current versus past depression, and childhood physical or sexual abuse did not predict this observation. DID and its sub-threshold forms, on the other hand, are characterised rather by internal "phobias" (Steele, van der Hart, & Nijenhuis, 2001) against traumatic memories and alter personalities which are complex derivatives of them, usually perceived as internal figures. The latter seem to trigger distance to the content of the "internal world" on the side of the subject making the dissociative amnesia noticeable to the observer (e.g., intra-interview trance or amnesia). However, this does not facilitate the "entrance" of the dialogue partner into the fearful "internal world" of the patient either.

Unfortunately, the interpersonal nature of dissociative disorders has been misinterpreted by some clinicians (Chodoff, 1997) and researchers as an alleged proof for their iatrogenesis, and somewhat strangely, in the name of an alleged "sociocognitive" model. In fact, DID does have sociocognitive origins, as do several psychiatric disorders and the psychological trauma itself; a truly sociocognitive etiology neither excludes the role of psychological trauma in the origin of dissociative disorders, nor does it constitute proof for the role of iatrogenesis (Şar, Krüger, Martínez-Taboas, Middleton, & Dorahy, 2013). On the other hand, the influence of the observer on the subject to be assessed is recognised even in exact sciences such as physics and computer programming and this cannot be expected to be different in clinical psychology and psychiatry, which work on subjectivities as well as objectivities. There are software bugs in computers which seem to disappear or alter their behaviour when one attempts to study them (Raymond, 1996); an effect called "Heisen bug" in remembrance of the thesis by Werner Heisenberg, the physicist who first asserted the observer effect of quantum mechanics, stating that the act of observing a system inevitably alters its state. Nevertheless, in the postmodern globalism era, the scope of potentially dissociogenic influence of systemic societal traumata (Şar & Öztürk, 2013) is still unknown, but should be considered for adolescent dissociation in particular (Şar, Önder, Kilinçaslan, Zoroglu, & Alyanak, 2014), namely a developmental period devoted to identity formation as an integrative task.

Trauma- and stressor-related disorders

Post-traumatic Stress Disorder (PTSD)

Identity alterations may be considered as an elaborated version of trauma-related mental intrusions and avoidance that represent the basic mechanism of PTSD. There are authors who claim that, in fact, PTSD is also a dissociative disorder (Nijenhuis, 2014). In DID, however, traumatic memories are decontextualised (Brewin, 2001) and processed to retain internal and external balance, which leads to formation of alter personality states each with their own sense of self and agency, personal history, and a mission. This elaboration is based on trauma-related cognitions, compensatory structures, and emotions assigned to the distinct personality states.

The prevalence of present or lifetime PTSD among patients with DID is between 46.7% and 79.2% (Ellason, Ross, & Fuchs, 1996; Kiziltan, Şar, Kundakçi, Yargic, & Tutkun, 1998). PTSD may be observed in a patient with DID in any stage of the latter, at the beginning or during later stages of treatment. A concurrent PTSD may lead the patient to further confusion about her clinical condition as seen in a patient suffering from repetitive assaultive behaviour because emerging traumatic material triggers uncontrolled behaviour in a vicious circle (Sakarya, Güneş, Öztürk, & Şar, 2012). This situation may benefit from gradual psycho-education of the patient in sorting out the diverse origin of symptoms that he or she can agree with the therapist on a working model. The therapist has the opportunity to intervene in a relatively paced man-ner in conditions where PTSD emerges due to increasing awareness about traumatic material as described by the "fractionated abreaction technique" (Kluft, 2013). Alongside several possible ways of interven-tion, eye movement desensitization and reprocessing (EMDR) is one of the options that may be of benefit at this stage. However, this should be adjusted to the requirements of ongoing dissociation to a greater or lesser degree (Twombly, 2000).

Mood disorders

Dissociative depression

Between 63.3% and 97.2% of patients with DID fit the diagnostic criteria for a major depressive episode and between 0.9% and 46.7% for a dys-thymic disorder (Ellason, Ross, & Fuchs, 1996; Kiziltan, Şar, Kundakçi, Targic, & Tutkun, 1998). While the large difference between two studies on the prevalence of dysthymic disorder remains unexplained, there are observations sufficient to conclude that most DID patients report chronic depression usually in the form of double depression, namely dysthymic disorder with repetitive major depressive episodes. The latter usually marks periods of collapse triggered by internal and/or external stressors throughout the life course of the dissociative patient. The chronic depression of DID patients is usually "treatment resistant" (i.e., it does not respond to antidepressant pharmacotherapy or "usual" methods of psychotherapy), while the depressive symptoms disap-pear instantly upon integration in psychotherapy on condition that the treatment is aimed at the latter. Şar (2011) has proposed the term "dissociative depression" to describe the distinct nature of this entity in pathogenesis, course, and treatment response compared to a pri-mary depressive disorder. In a study on a representative female sample recruited from the general population, 40.6% of the participants with a diagnosis of current major depression also had a lifetime diagnosis of dissociative disorder leading to a prevalence of 4.1% for "dissociative depression" (Şar, Akyüz, Öztürk, & Alioğlu, 2013).

Trauma-related (dissociative) depression (Şar, 2011) tends to have an earlier age of onset than primary depression and recurs more readily (Bülbül et al., 2013; Şar, Akyüz, Öztürk, & Alioğlu, 2013). In fact, many dissociative patients report onset of their depressive mood and even suicidal tendencies early in childhood. Women with dissociative depression report cognitive symptoms (such as thoughts of worthlessness and guilt, and diminished concentration and indecisiveness), suicidal ideas and attempts, experiences of possession, and appetite and weight changes, more frequently than those with primary depression (Şar, Akyüz, Öztürk, & Alioğlu, 2013). They reported childhood sexual abuse and neglect more frequently than the remaining participants.

In his famous study published in 1849, *Sickness Unto Death* (Kierkegaard, 1849), Danish existentialist philosopher Sören Kierkegaard (1813–1855) described "despair" as an experience of estrangement from oneself: "In despairing over something", the individual "really despair(s) over himself", and "wants to be rid of himself" (Marino, 2009, para. 7). In contrast of "despair", he formulated "unhappiness" (alias depression), as "a suffering which must have its basis in a mis-relation between ... mind and body, for it has no relation to (one's) spirit, which on the contrary, because of the tension between ... mind and body ... gain(s) an uncommon resiliency" (ibid., para. 9). According to these formulations, while despair and depression referred to different conditions, both seem to be related to dissociation. While the former describes an "escape from oneself" (psychological dissociation) and experiences of estrangement, the latter underlines a disruption between "psyche" and "soma" aggravating dissociative somatic symptoms or somatic dissociation.

In a study on a group of women with fibromyalgia or rheumatoid arthritis, there was a relationship between depression and post-traumatic anger (Kilic et al., 2014). In the same study, the diagnosis of lifetime depressive disorder (a trait measure) was predicted by "somatic dissociation" whereas "psychological dissociation" was related to current severity of depression (a state measure). In Kierkegaard's sense, while the former refers to "despair" (or estrangement) as a trait, the latter refers to "unhappiness" (depressive episode) as a state. Psychological dissociation in particular has its origin in "anger inside" which turns to "anger outside" during overt depression. Somatic dissociation, however, was predicted by childhood neglect and contributed to the tendency toward depression. Such depression was associated with identity fragmentation as well as a tendency toward loss of control due to potentially disruptive experiences such as anger outside, dissociative amnesias, and borderline phenomena.

Bipolar mood disorder

The bipolar mood disorder comorbidity of DID was between 6.7% and 9.3%, and this rate was between 0.0% and 7.5% for bipolar II (Ellason, Ross, & Fuchs, 1996; Kiziltan, Şar, Kundakçi, Yargic, & Tutkun, 1998). Patients with remitted bipolar mood disorder had higher dissociative experiences scale (DES) scores compared to healthy controls (Latalova et al., 2011). Among them, 51.2% had a DES score above thirty. On the other hand, trauma-related affect dysregulation and/or switching between personality states carrying distinct moods may resemble cyclothymia or bipolar (II) mood disorder. This can be differentiated from bipolar mood disorder by the abrupt nature of mood changes, which can happen several times in a day and may last very briefly (even minutes). Unlike those with a bipolar mood disorder, these patients perceive themselves estranged to their distinct mood states, namely their sense of self and agency is affected. In fact, these alterations do not respond to mood stabilisers but recover in integrative psychotherapy. Unfortunately, most of the clinicians are reluctant to attribute mood fluctuations to identity alterations although it represents one of the avenues to catch dissociative experiences in many patients who have DID, but do not report more eye-catching secondary symptoms of dissociation such as hallucinations (e.g., adolescents with sub-threshold DID).

Personality disorders

The possibility of making a personality disorder diagnosis in patients with DID is contentious because it may not be justified to attribute a clinical phenomenon to a personality disorder if it is already related to another disorder, such as DID. For instance, in a case of DID with the additional diagnoses of paranoid, passive aggressive, and borderline personality disorders in structured evaluation, the latter two diagnoses were dropped after integration in an eighteen-month treatment when assessed using the same methodology (Şar, Öztürk, & Kundakçi, 2002). However, alongside the still prevailing paranoid personality disorder, an additional diagnosis of narcissistic personality disorder emerged after integration.

In purely descriptive screening studies, the most frequently seen personality disorders in DID are borderline, paranoid, compulsive, avoidant, and dependent personality disorders (Ellason, Ross, & Fuchs, 1996; Kiziltan, Şar, Kundakçi, Yargic, & Tutkun, 1998). This somewhat contradictory combination of traits deriving from all the three DSM-5 personality disorder clusters (A, B, C) describes the situation of the traumatised person living in an alarmed "self-preservation" mode of security, rather than benefiting from a rather relaxed "self-regulation" mode (Ford, 2009). Compared to the non-dissociative depressive patients as a control group, patients with a dissociative disorder reported both preoccupied and fearful styles of attachment more likely which fits exactly the constellation of the "need-fear dilemma"; namely that a person has a simultaneous need for an event, object, or individual while also having a fear of it. This has once been proposed to describe the immense need of the "autistic" schizophrenic individual for interpersonal contact, but the simultaneous anxiety and the feeling of being threatened by close and intimate relationships (Burnham, Gladstone, & Gibson, 1969). Moreover, dissociative patients were living with both negative self and negative other models which undermined any hope and will for emancipation (Şar, İslam, & Öztürk, 2010). The "double bind" situation here represents a tendency to get entrapped in interpersonal relationships, which seems to be, in fact, a consequence of loss of basic trust to oneself and others due to the post-traumatic disillusionment (Fischer & Riedesser, 1999).

With its concept of "self-object", the psychoanalytic self-psychology emphasised attachment and underlined the problem of interpersonal boundaries as well as the disturbances of self-identity due to the rather "weak" self in conditions of pathological narcissism (Kohut, 1971). Battegay (1987) objected to conceptualisation of pathological narcissism as a "personality disorder" and proposed to classify it as a "neurosis" because it originated from adverse experiences of early childhood (neglect in particular). There are also attempts in the recent literature to explain pathological narcissism as a trauma-related condition and the interpersonal aspect of dissociation (Howell, 2003). For instance, the presence of overblown self-object representations in the internal world is a consequence of non-availability of appropriate relationships in the external world while this problem is also valid in the opposite direction; being attached to internal self-objects prevents healthy interchange with the external world and interferes with true intimacy in close relationships. In a further inquiry into the area between individual and society, Şar and Öztürk (2007) proposed an identity based model of dissociation which also covers pathological narcissism: "Functional dissociation of the self" into sociological and psychological selves with the symptomatic "trauma self" operating in between. The expansion of the sociological self due to traumatisation and additional factors does not facilitate better relationships with the external world. It becomes rather an obstacle due to the avoided and consequently frozen psychological self. The trauma-self remains in a perpetuating status of seeking help and becomes symptomatic clinically. This model has also implications for possession experiences among patients with DID as well as non-clinical populations which occur in the "transitional" area (sociological self) between individual and society (Winkelman, 2011). They are perceived as external entities controlling the person and, unlike the individual alter personalities, they can affect control, and even intrude on others as well; hence, they are "shared" entities in the community.

Borderline personality disorder

Many patients with a chronic dissociative disorder resemble borderline personality disorder (BPD) at the surface. Several studies have shown that this proportion is between 56.3% and 80.0% (Ellason, Ross, & Fuchs, 1996; Kiziltan et al., 1998). On the other hand, among subjects who fit the DSM-IV BPD criteria, 64.0% to 72.5% had a concurrent DSM-IV dissociative disorder in a descriptive evaluation (Şar et al., 2003; Şar, Akyüz, Kuğu, Öztürk, & Ertem-Vehid, 2006). These observations say little about the true nature of this phenomenological overlap (i.e., whether these subjects have BPD or dissociative disorder or both). In fact, DSM-IV BPD criteria describe interpersonal aspects of dissociation, and successfully catch many subjects who have a dissociative disorder. Hence, the DSM-IV criteria may not be sufficient to make a personality disorder diagnosis, as they do not exclude a chronic dissociative disorder. This has important consequences since it is likely to matter whether borderline patients are approached as having a severe (almost pre-psychotic) personality disorder or a disorder based on trauma-related dissociation as a central mechanism.

Interestingly, in a comparison of Turkish and Dutch patients with DID, there were large differences between two groups in BPD diagnostic criteria (Şar, Yargic, & Tutkun, 1996). Turkish dissociative disorder patients report intense anger and lack of control of this emotion, chronic feelings of emptiness and boredom, efforts to avoid abandonment, and intense but unstable relationships, more frequently than Dutch patients. In turn, Dutch patients report frequent mood swings, physically self-damaging acts, identity confusion, and impulsive and unpredictable behaviour, more frequently than Turkish patients. Some type of affect dysregulation was common to both groups. While Turkish patients had more symptoms in the interpersonal area inspiring attachment distur-bances (behaviour influenced by "external interpersonal phobias"), Dutch patients seemed to struggle in their internal world individually (behaviour influenced by "internal phobias"). Possibly, the BPD con-struct may not be stable across cultures. These differences in predomi-nant post-traumatic response types may stem from cultural factors affecting symptom presentation (e.g., overall lifestyle, drug abuse, family relationships), etiology of dissociative disorders, and last but not least, sanctions on disclosure of trauma histories in Dutch and Turkish patients. Some of the Turkish patients may have developed dissociative disorders as a result of developmental attachment difficulties and subtle transgenerational traumatisation rather than overt abuse and neglect predominantly (Öztürk & Şar, 2005).

In accordance with these observations, in a recent study on adolescents with DID and its sub-threshold forms in Turkey, there were no significant differences on childhood trauma histories and family dysfunctionality as assessed by self-report measures (Şar, Önder, Kilinçaslan, & Zoroglu, 2014). Unfortunately, the instrument used did not assess overprotection-overcontrol by parents which is relatively common in Turkey as a cul-turally accepted (normative) style (in fact, usually a self-compensatory behaviour of traumatised parents leading to intergenerational transition of subtle trauma) which may be threatening for interpersonal boundar-ies as well as private individual spheres, and in general overwhelming for the rising generation (Kogan, 2007). On the other hand, the group with DID or its sub-threshold forms had more comorbid separation anx-iety disorder compared to controls which underlined the possibility of attachment disturbances in the studied clinical sample.

Individuals who meet criteria for both BPD and DID have more comorbidity and trauma than individuals who meet criteria for only one (Ross, Ferrell, & Schroeder, 2014). In a Turkish study, while the pattern of BPD seemed to be related to childhood abuse in particular as the trauma of intrusive type leading to "external interpersonal phobias", the pattern of dissociative disorders was related to childhood emotional neglect as an omission type of trauma leading to "internal phobias" predominantly (Şar, Akyüz, Kuğu, Öztürk, & Ertem-Vehid, 2006). Nevertheless, childhood emotional neglect has been demonstrated as the main predictor of dissociation in a prospective study previously (Ogawa, Sroufe, Weinfield, Carlson, & Egeland, 1997). It is possible that both patterns represent two distinct types of dissociative response to developmental trauma, which may co-occur on an individual basis. Separate post-traumatic (omission versus intrusion types of childhood trauma) response tracks have also been observed among depressive women with fibromyalgia or rheumatoid arthritis in terms of somatic and psychological dissociation ("internal phobias") which may develop into borderline behavioural patterns ("external interpersonal phobias") and loss of control for a subgroup episodically (Kilic et al., 2014).

Somatic symptom and related disorders

Functional neurological (conversion) symptoms

According to a study conducted on a representative sample from the general population of a town in central-eastern Turkey, 26.5% of women who reported having experienced at least one conversion symptom in their life also had a dissociative disorder (Şar, Akyüz, Doğan, & Öztürk, 2009). This figure was between 30.1% among psychiatric inpatients (Tezcan et al., 2003) and 47.4% for outpatients (Şar, Akyüz, Kundakçi, Kiziltan, & Doğan, 2004) of both genders. The latter study demonstrated that when accompanied by a dissociative disorder, patients with a conversion symptom had more psychiatric comorbidity, childhood trauma history, suicide attempts, and non-suicidal self-injury. Functional somatic symptoms distinguish dissociative disorders from other psychiatric disorders (Şar, Kundakçi, Kiziltan, Bakim, & Bozkurt, 2000). In the latter study, among several somatic symptoms, only non-epileptic seizures ("pseudoseizures") were more prevalent among Turkish patients compared to a Dutch sample. Nevertheless, the prevalence of non-epileptic seizures seems to differ widely among different parts of the world which points to the strong cultural aspect of the disorder (Martínez-Taboas, Lewis-Fernandez, Şar, & Agrawal, 2010).

Functional neurological (conversion) symptoms may mark an acute crisis period superimposed on the chronic course of a dissociative disorder in these patients. With their seemingly life-threatening nature, the predominance of somatic symptoms such as non-epileptic seizures constitutes a medical emergency (Şar, Koyuncu, Öztürk, Yargic, Kundakçi, & Yazici, 2007). This necessarily leads to admission in neurological or emergency departments (rather than in psychiatric units), which may contribute to delayed awareness of the broader spectrum of dissociative symptomatology, unless a consultation and follow-up are considered in this direction. In Turkey, many patients with DID are admitted to psychiatric services because of treatment-resistant and dramatic conversion symptoms, including non-epileptic seizures. Functional neurological (conversion) symptoms (including non-epileptic seizures) may be considered as a specifier for DID in further revisions of DSM-5 on condition that further research documents differences between DID patients with and without conversion symptoms, including treatment response as external validators. One further area of interest is the documentation of differences between distinct personality states in terms of somatic symptoms as shown for "psychogenic" (dissociative) blindness in case examples (Bhuvaneswar & Spiegel, 2013; Waldvogel, Ulrich, & Strasburger, 2007).

Somatic symptom disorder

Patients with DID usually have a high number of somatic complaints that cannot be attributed to a bodily illness. Hence, almost half of the DID patients (41.1% to 53.3%) fit the diagnostic criteria of somatisation disorder (Ellason, Ross, & Fuchs, 1996; Kiziltan, Şar, Kundakçi, Yargic, & Tutkun, 1998). The term somatoform dissociation representing a broader spectrum than functional neurological (conversion) symptoms has been proposed to cover and explain the origin of somatic symptoms in dissociative disorders (Nijenhuis, Spinhoven, Van Dyck, Van der Hart, & Vanderlinden, 1998). In fact, somatic symptoms may go even beyond both of these spheres to become psychosomatic sequelae as seen in a case of DID with purpurae (Yücel, Kiziltan, & Aktan, 2000). In our view, rather than constituting merely a somato-"form" appearance on the surface, dissociation has deeper effects on "soma", possibly deserving the label "somatic dissociation".

For instance, in addition to non-specific forms of headache usually triggered by personality switching, many patients with DID suffer from genuine migraine. In a screening study conducted on a consecutive series of patients (N=103) with chronic headache (62.1% of them had migraine) who were admitted to an outpatient unit of a university neurology department, 6.8% (N=7) had a dissociative disorder. Three patients (2.9%) had DID, two (1.9%) had dissociative disorder not otherwise specified (DDNOS) type 1, and two (1.9%) had dissociative amnesia (Tutkun et al., 1996). The DID and DDNOS cases reported that their headache was related in some way to their distinct personality states; one patient was uncertain about this. In a naturalistic follow-up study conducted on patients with complex dissociative disorders who had been in treatment for periods of various length, somatic complaints increased in number despite an improvement in overall severity of the disorder, as shown by the scores on the dissociative experiences scale (DES) (Bakim, 1998). One reason for this rather surprising observation may be improving contact of these patients with their "soma" following psychotherapeutic treatment (R. Chefetz, personal communication, 1999) representing an improvement in "somatic self-detachment" as a component of depersonalisation.

Psychotic disorders

In descriptive evaluations, 74.3% to 80.0% of the patients with DID fit the diagnostic criteria of a psychotic disorder (Ellason, Ross, & Fuchs, 1996; Kiziltan, Şar, Kundakçi, Yargic, & Tutkun, 1998). The rate of schizophrenic disorder diagnosis was between 18.7% and 23.3%, which points to considerable overall deterioration due to DID rather than being based on schizophrenic disorder per se. Namely, in both of the studies, patients with psychotic disorders were excluded from study groups clinically. Hence, the psychotic disorder diagnoses including schizophrenic disorder were in fact false positives. This usually occurs due to the visual and acoustic hallucinations and Schneiderian passive influence experiences reported by the patients who have DID.

Acute dissociative reaction to stress (with psychotic features)

This condition has previously been well known as hysterical psychosis. To overcome the word hysteria, various names have been proposed such as reactive dissociative psychosis (Van der Hart, Witztum, & Friedman, 1993), or simply dissociative psychosis. Acute dissociative reaction stress has been listed in DSM-5 among other specific dissociative disorders (OSDD) without making a reference to the possibility of psychotic features (American Psychiatric Association, 2013). Dissociative conditions may constitute acute and transient responses to stressful life events as well as interpersonal problems. Such reactions may be as mild as a transient state of stupor; however, they may reach the severity of an acute psychosis. An acute dissociative disorder with psychotic features resembles a delirium, mania, or schizophrenic disorder (Şar & Öztürk, 2008, 2009). Both mild and severe types of acute dissociative disorders may represent a crisis condition superimposed on an underlying DID. Dissociative crises of patients with DID consist of trauma-related flashback experiences, non-suicidal self-injury, "revolving door crisis" of the alter personalities competing for control, and/or amnesia (Tutkun, Yargic, & Şar, 1996). These acute crises may serve as a "diagnostic window" for patients who have DID who may have only subtle symptoms between these acute decompensation periods.

Schizo-dissociative disorder and dissociative subtype of schizophrenic disorder

Ross (2004) proposed the possibility of a dissociative subtype of schizophrenia and documented a symptom pattern related to this concept. This pattern has been replicated by subsequent studies (Şar et al., 2010). Alongside concurrent symptoms of DID and schizophrenia, these patients report childhood traumas, BPD criteria and general psychiatric comorbidity more frequently than patients with non-dissociative schizophrenia (Şar et al., 2010). The differential diagnosis may be difficult in schizo-dissociative disorder in particular as the two psychopathologies are interwoven. The overlap between two psychopathologies is not important for differential diagnosis only, but it is also significant for future studies on schizophrenia in the context of neurobiology, drug treatment, and psychotherapy. There are authors who claim that there is an inherent relationship between the two psychopathologies (Moskowitz & Corstens, 2007; Ross, 2004), however, this point of view still remains speculative. Being close to the notion of comorbidity rather than continuity of psychopathologies, Şar and Öztürk (2008) propose an "interaction model" in further analysis of the relationship between dissociation and schizotypy: how do both psychopathologies interact if they are present in the same individual concurrently or subsequently? Typically, but in the short term, these patients respond to both anti-psychotic as well as psychotherapeutic treatment less positively than expected, and constitute a challenge to general psychiatry. However, studies are needed in particular about their potentials in responding to treatment in the long run which may be different.

Anxiety and substance use disorders

Among patients with DID, 83.3% to 89.7% had an anxiety disorder when PTSD was excluded (Ellason, Ross, & Fuchs, 1996; Kiziltan, Şar, Kundakçi, Yargic, & Tutkun, 1998). Panic disorder was the most prevalent one among them. The prevalence of alcohol and/or substance use was between 23.3% and 65.4% reflecting a cultural difference in the 1990s that may have diminished in the 2010s. Dissociative disorders were seen in 17.2% of a large inpatient group seeking treatment for substance abuse (Karadağ et al., 2005). Patients with a dissociative disorder utilised more types of substances, dropped out from treatment more frequently, had shorter remission duration, and tended to be younger. Dissociative symptoms started before substance use in the majority of cases (64.9%) and usually in adolescence (Karadağ et al., 2005). Suicide attempts, childhood emotional abuse, and female gender predicted dissociative disorder among substance users. The prevalence of dissociative disorders increased to 26.0% when probands with only alcohol dependency were excluded (Tamar-Gürol et al., 2008). These findings are alarming, because they demonstrate the importance of recognition of dissociative disorders for prevention and successful treatment of substance dependency among adolescents and young adults. The prevalence rate of dissociative disorders in alcohol-dependent inpatients was only 9.0% with none of them having DID (Evren, Şar, Karadag, Tamar-Gurol, & Karagoz, 2007).

The pathway of childhood trauma–dissociation–substance use typically represents possible self-treatment efforts of dissociative clients before they get an efficient psychotherapeutic intervention. Substance abuse may be seen as an "attachment disorder" resembling the "attachment to the perpetrator" (Ross, 1997) pattern that is common among traumatised dissociative individuals in their relationships, interpersonally and also in their internal world. Unfortunately, this is a very serious complication of dissociative disorders, which should and may be prevented by early intervention. A recent study on the prevalence of DID among adolescent psychiatric outpatients in a Turkish university in Istanbul revealed an alarming rate: 16.4% (Şar, Önder, Kilinçaslan, Zoroglu, & Alyanak, 2014). The DDNOS-1 (sub-threshold DID) cases added, the overall prevalence of dissociative disorders was 45.2%. Given the rapid increase in substance use in Turkey, this observation should be considered when implementing preventive measures in the community.

Impulsivity and compulsivity

Impulsivity and compulsivity are known to be the two sides of the same coin. Both child and adult forms of attention deficit hyperactivity disorder (ADHD) may resemble a dissociative disorder (Şar, Önder, Kilinçaslan, Zoroglu, & Alyanak, 2014). Among adolescents in particular, motor uneasiness and affect dysregulation due to a dissociative disorder may resemble an ADHD. True comorbidity is possible, however, so it is difficult to identify this among patients with a dissociative disorder due to the overlap of symptoms.

In clinical practice with adolescents in particular, a tetrad of comorbidity is relatively common: ADHD, DID, substance abuse, and a long-lasting enhanced affect dysregulation are sometimes impossible to distinguish from a bipolar mood disorder. These cases do not respond to treatment immediately and lead to several trials of drug prescription with the hope of a positive response. Immense family problems emerge; it is important to save the adolescent from further self-harm until the condition calms down after adolescence. The prognosis may be good despite a conspicuous and long-lasting symptomatic period depending on the availability of resiliency factors.

In two brain-imaging studies on patients with DID, diminished perfusion in orbitofrontal regions has been documented bilaterally (Şar, Ünal, Kiziltan, Kundakçi, & Öztürk, 2001; Şar, Ünal, & Öztürk, 2007). The orbitofrontal lobe has been known as a slow-maturating region sensitive to developmental traumata, which has integrative functions (Schore, 2003). Its diminished activity would lead to impulsivity, as shown among patients with BPD (Berlin, Rolls, & Iversen, 2005). Nevertheless, an orbitofrontal hypothesis of DID has been proposed already (Forrest, 2001).

Among patients with DID, 46.7% to 63.6% had obsessive compulsive disorder (OCD) (Ellason, Ross, & Fuchs, 1996; Kiziltan, Şar, Kundakçi, Yargic, & Tutkun, 1998). However, according to one study, only 15.8% of patients with OCD had DES scores of 30.0 or above (Lochner et al., 2004). Similarly, in a Turkish study, only 14.0% of the patients with OCD had a dissociative disorder, including 3.9% having DID (Belli, Ural,

Kanarya-Vardar, Yesilyurt, & Oncu, 2012). Significant positive correlations were found between DES scores and emotional, sexual, physical abuse and physical neglect scores (Lochner et al., 2004). Among children, instructions of a persecutory alter personality may resemble an OCD at the surface unless the patient is able to report the connection to dissociative symptoms.

Eating disorders have been reported in 6.7% to 38.3% of patients with DID (Ellason, Ross, & Fuchs, 1996; Kiziltan, Şar, Kundakçi, Yargic, & Tutkun, 1998). Some DID patients seek treatment for paraphilias which tend to occur repeatedly and may even lead to criminal acts (Ross, 2008). Among patients with DID, personality switching (e.g., to child or opposite-gender personalities) or flashback experiences may occur during a sexual relationship and mimic vaginismus due to emergence of an avoidant or fearful (e.g., male, child) personality state (Kuskonmaz, Şar, & Kundakçi, 2000). Unresolved trauma may lead the subject to repetitive assaultive behaviour in a vicious circle initiated by a persecutory alter personality leaving the "host personality" helplessly in an estranged situation, as seen in a case of "vampirism" where an alter used to become assaultive to obtain and drink blood periodically despite his desperate intention to get rid of this destructive urge (Sakarya, Güneş, Öztürk, & Şar, 2012).

The majority of patients with DID have suicidal ideas continuously; however, the prevalence of completed suicide is around 1% to 2% (Kluft, 1995). Although not constituting diagnostic categories *per se*, repetitive suicide attempts and non-suicidal self-injury are common in patients with DID and related conditions which appear as if impulsive and compulsive actions. Several studies have shown a relationship between childhood trauma, suicidality, and non-suicidal self-injury (Akyüz, Şar, Kuğu, & Doğan, 2005; Zoroglu et al., 2003). Many patients with DID inflict self-injuries during an acute dissociative crisis characterised by an internal struggle between personality states, depersonalisation, traumatic flashbacks, and functional neurological symptoms including non-epileptic seizures.

Conclusions: diagnostic and therapeutic considerations

The appearances of DID may be almost endless in number (Kluft, 1991; Şar, 2014a). Multiple personalities is only one of them. It would be wise to understand DID as a general category to look at their subtypes more closely. Introducing additional specifiers may also be helpful, for example DID with functional neurological symptoms (Şar, Akyüz, Doğan, & Öztürk, 2009), DID with possession experience (Şar, Alioğlu, & Akyüz, 2014), DID with chronic depressive mood (Şar, Akyüz, Öztürk, & Alioğlu, 2013), and so on. We also need a code of severity because DID may be mild or moderate, or may even reach a psychotic level (Şar & Öztürk, 2008, 2009). The latter may occur transiently in a disorganised manner or in relatively enduring "delusional" types such as believing that one remained alive while an alter personality was "killed"; clearly a dangerously suicidal status. This severity specification may also have important forensic implications. Not every DID is the same!

Overall, I propose considering DID as a larger spectrum than the concept of "multiple personality" which represent rather the "core". Such a development process of conceptualisation has occurred for many diagnostic categories in psychiatry over time that were defined in a rather narrow fashion at the beginning to become a "spectrum" covering many subtypes later. For instance, autism, mood disorders, anxiety disorders, and others followed this track. DID and dissociation, with their central role in human adaptation and maladaptation, deserve such detailed inquiry as much as every other psychiatric disorder and type of psychopathology.

Successful treatment of DID and its subthreshold forms require awareness and commitment not only on the side of the therapist, but also of the side of the patient. Hence, therapeutic alliance appears to be one of the main predictors of positive outcome (Cronin, Brand, & Mattanah, 2014). Psychiatric comorbidity interferes with comprehension of the therapeutic movements by the patient in the way of trauma resolution due to the interaction and confusing overlap between syndromes. In fact, comorbidity is never an advantage for any psychiatric disorder, as it is not for any somatic illness. It is always a marker of overall severity of the disorder. Hence, every comorbidity needs to be addressed early in treatment. This would allow the clinician to keep on track when striving to make progress in the main road of treatment and avoid complications interfering with this. There are no reasons not to consider these common principles for dissociative disorders as well.

Special remarks: a new era in learning and teaching

Description of human experience inside of the diagnostic schemes of the medical system as well as clinical psychopathology can be complete only by implementation of it into individual clinical histories of clients.

Working on the interface between diagnostic constructs and individual experience is a fascinating intellectual and professional task. However, it is always an acrimonious task for the author of a scientific or clinical paper to present individual case stories despite the opportunity and obligation of de-identification of the personal information of the client, because we believe that the experience of observing one's story told and interpreted by the third person language is a stressful one. On the other hand, we are obliged to spread every knowledge to our colleagues which can be helpful in diminishing human suffering. Moreover, the problem is not limited to the patient, it is also not easy for the therapist to be open in discussing a case material; both due to the interwovenness of the therapist's private life as well as possible tweakings in the method, the therapist may be too shy to share because of potential criticism (Sachs, 2013).

There are arguments about the relative lag of psychiatry's progress behind other medical disciplines for the last few decades in particular (Insel, 2013). For instance, taken as a common variable which is correlated with the destructive effects of all psychiatric disorders, the mental health sector has not been successful in reducing completed suicide rates, which remain one of the most common cause of death in several societies, ranking relatively high for young people in particular. Hence, psychiatry now faces a genuine challenge in terms of revisiting the adequacy of its strategies and tools.

Better integration of psychotraumatology and dissociation studies into mainstream psychiatry has been persistently proposed for a few decades. Success in this direction has been only limited. However, there has recently been an increased openness to this area globally and among researchers in particular (Şar, 2014a, 2014b). This positive trend should be supported by better clinical training because psychotraumatology and dissociative disorders require a greater than usual level of sensitivity on the side of the staff. An aim of better than ever average training points to the need for high quality teaching methods. In fact, the latter point seems to be valid in every area of science and practice and, hence, strategically important for the future of humanity. My experience of more than three decades in academic psychiatric institutions leads me to agree with the reports that teaching and learning in the mental health sector are faced with challenges (Kluft, 2013, 2014). For reasons easy to understand, this affects the teaching of psychotherapy in particular. Notwithstanding the importance of sensitive policies in recruitment of professionals and human resources in the mental health sector, it is time to think about possible pitfalls and their solutions.

References

Akyüz, G., Şar, V., Kuğu, N., & Doğan, O. (2005). Reported childhood trauma, attempted suicide and self-mutilative behavior among women in the general population. *European Psychiatry, 20*: 268–273.

American Psychiatric Association (1980). *Diagnostic and Statistical Manual of Mental Disorders* (3rd edn). Washington, DC: APA.

American Psychiatric Association (2013). *Diagnostic and Statistical Manual of Mental Disorders* (5th edn). Washington, DC: APA.

Bakim, B. (1998). *A Follow-up Study on Multiple Personality and Other Chronic Complex Dissociative Disorders.* Dissertation. Istanbul University Faculty of Medicine.

Barach, P. M. (1991). Multiple personality disorder as an attachment disorder. *Dissociation: Progress in the Dissociative Disorders, 4*(3): 117–123.

Battegay, R. (1987). Narzisstische Störungen im Lichte der modernen Psychoanalyse [Narcissistic disorders in the light of modern psychoanalysis]. *Schweizer Archiv für Neurologie und Psychiatrie, 138*: 45–59.

Beere, D. B. (2009a). Dissociative perceptual reactions: the perceptual theory of dissociation. In: P. F. Dell & J. A. O'Neil (Eds.), *Dissociation and Dissociative Disorders: DSM-V and Beyond* (pp. 209–222). New York: Routledge.

Beere, D. B. (2009b). The self-system as mechanism for the dissociative disorders: an extention of the perceptual theory of dissociation. In: P. F. Dell & J. A. O'Neil (Eds.), *Dissociation and Dissociative Disorders: DSM-V and Beyond* (pp. 277–285). New York: Routledge.

Belli, H., Ural, C., Kanarya-Vardar, M., Yesilyurt, S., & Oncu, F. (2012). Dissociative symptoms and dissociative disorder comorbidity in patients with obsessive-compulsive disorder. *Comprehensive Psychiatry, 53*(7): 975–980.

Berlin, H. A., Rolls, E. T., & Iversen, S. D. (2005). Borderline personality disorder, impulsivity, and the orbitofrontal cortex. *American Journal of Pychiatry, 162*: 2360–2373.

Bhuvaneswar, C., & Spiegel, D. (2013). An eye for an I: a 35-year-old woman with fluctuating oculomotor deficits and dissociative identity disorder. *International Journal of Clinical and Experimental Hypnosis, 61*(3): 351–370.

Brewin, C. R. (2001). A cognitive neuroscience account of post-traumatic stress disorder and its treatment. *Behavior Research and Therapy, 39*: 373–393.

Bowlby, J. (1973). *Attachment and Loss (Volume 2: Separation: Anxiety and Anger).* London: Hogarth.

Bülbül, F., Cakir, Ü., Ülkü, C., Üre, I., Karabatak, O., & Alpak, G. (2013). Childhood trauma in recurrent and first episode depression. *Anatolian Journal of Psychiatry, 14*: 93–99.

Burnham, D. L., Gladstone, A. I., & Gibson, R. W. (1969). *Schizophrenia and the Need-Fear Dilemma.* New York: International Universities.

Chodoff, P. (1997). Turkish dissociative identity disorder. *American Journal of Psychiatry, 154*(8): 1179.

Cronin, E., Brand, B. L., & Mattanah, J. F. (2014). The impact of the therapeutic alliance on treatment outcome in patients with dissociative disorders. *European Journal of Psychotraumatology, 5*: 22676. Available at: http:// dx.doi.org/10.3402/ejpt.v5.22676 [last accessed 17 November 2015].

Ellason, J. W., Ross, C. A., & Fuchs, D. L. (1996). Lifetime axis I and II comorbidity and childhood trauma history in dissociative identity disorder. *Psychiatry, 59*: 255–261.

Evren, C., Şar, V., Karadag, F., Tamar-Gurol, D., & Karagoz, M. (2007). Dissociative disorders among alcohol-dependent inpatients. *Psychiatry Research, 152*: 233–241.

Fertuck, E. A., Jekal, A., Song, I., Wyman, B., Morris, M. C., Wilson, S. T., Brodsky, B. S., & Stanley, B. (2009). Enhanced "Reading the Mind in the Eyes" in borderline personality disorder compared to healthy controls. *Psychological Medicine, 39*(12): 1979–1988.

Fischer, G., & Riedesser, P. (1999). *Lehrbuch der Psychotraumatologie [Textbook of Psychotraumathology].* Munich: Ernst Reinhardt.

Ford, J. (2009). Dissociation in complex posttraumatic stress disorder or disorders of extreme stress not otherwise specified. In: P. F. Dell & J. A. O'Neil. (Eds.), *Dissociation and Dissociative Disorders. DSM-V and Beyond* (pp. 471–483). New York: Routledge.

Forrest, K. (2001). Toward an etiology of dissociative identity disorder: a neurodevelopmental approach. *Consciousness Cognition, 10*: 259–263.

Freyd, J. J. (1994). Betrayal trauma: traumatic amnesia as an adaptive response to childhood abuse. *Ethics & Behavior, 4*(4): 307–329.

Howell, E. F. (2003). Narcissism, a relational aspect of dissociation. *Journal of Trauma and Dissociation, 4*(3): 51–71.

Insel, T. (2013). *Toward a new understanding of mental illness.* TED talk. Available at: www.ted.com/talks/thomas_insel_toward_a_new_ understanding_of_mental_illness [last accessed 17 November 2015].

Jaspers, K. (1913). *Allgemeine Psychopathologie [General Psychopathology].* Berlin: Springer.

Kaehler, L. A., & Freyd, J. J. (2009). Borderline personality disorder: a betrayal trauma approach. *Psychological Trauma: Theory, Research, Practice, and Policy, 1*(4): 261–268.

Karadağ, F., Şar, V., Tamar-Gürol, D., Evren, C., Karagöz, M., & Erkiran, M. (2005). Dissociative disorders among inpatients with drug or alcohol dependency. *Journal of Clinical Psychiatry, 66*: 1247–1253.

Karpman, S. B. (1968). Fairy tales and script drama analysis. *Transactional Analysis Bulletin, 7*(26): 39–43.

Kierkegaard, S. (1849). *Sickness Unto Death*. Princeton, NJ: Princeton University Press, 1983.

Kiliç, Ö., Şar, V., Taycan, O., Aksoy-Poyraz, C., Erol, T. C., Tecer, Ö., Emül, H. M., & Özmen, M. (2014). Dissociative depression among women with fibromyalgia or rheumatoid arthritis. *Journal of Trauma and Dissociation, 15*(3): 285–302.

Kiziltan, E., Şar, V., Kundakçi, T., Targic, I. L., & Tutkun, H. (1998). *Comorbidity in Dissociative Identity Disorder: a study using SCID-I, SCID-II and SCID-D*. Paper presented at the 15th Conference of the International Society for the Study of Trauma and Dissociation; Seattle, WA. Kluft, R. P. (1985). The natural history of multiple personality disorder. In: R. P. Kluft (Ed.), *Childhood Antecedents of Multiple Personality* (pp. 197–238). Washington, DC: APA.

Kluft, R. P. (1988). The dissociative disorders. In: J. Talbott, R. Hales, & S. Yudofsky (Eds.), *The American Psychiatric Press Textbook of Psychiatry* (pp. 557–585). Washington, DC: APA.

Kluft, R. P. (1991). Clinical presentations of multiple personality disorder. *Psychiatric Clinics of North America, 14*: 605–609.

Kluft, R. P. (1995). Six completed suicides in dissociative identity disorder patients: clinical observations. *Dissociation, 8*: 104–111.

Kluft, R. P. (2013). *Shelter from the Storm: Processing the Traumatic Memories of DID/DDNOS Patients with The Fractionated Abreaction Technique (A Vademecum for the Treatment of DID/DDNOS) (Volume 1)*. Seattle, WA: Createspace.

Kluft, R. P. (2014). *Good Shrink Bad Shrink*. London: Karnac.

Kogan, I. (2007). *Escape from Selfhood. Breaking Boundaries and Craving for Oneness*. London: International Psychoanalytical Association.

Kohut, H. (1971). *The Analysis of the Self: A Systematic Approach to the Psychoanalytic Treatment of Narcissistic Personality Disorders*. New York: International Universities.

Kuşkonmaz, E., Şar, V., & Kundakçi, T. (2000). Treatment of a case with dissociative identity disorder presenting as vaginismus. *Anatolian Journal of Psychiatry, 1*: 48–57.

Latalova, K., Prasko, J., Pastucha, P., Grambal, A., Kamaradova, D., Diveky, T., Jelenova, D., Mainerova, B., & Vrbova, K. (2011). Bipolar affective disorder and dissociation—comparison with healthy controls.

Biomedical Papers of the Medical Faculty of the University Palacky Olomouc Czech Republic, 155(2): 181–186.

Lewis-Fernandez, R., Martínez-Taboas, A., Şar, V., Patel, S., & Boatin, A. (2007). The cross-cultural assessment of dissociation. In: J. P. Wilson & C. C. So-Kum Tang (Eds.), *Cross-Cultural Assessment of Trauma and PTSD* (pp. 289–318). New York: Springer.

Liotti, G. (2006). A model of dissociation based on attachment theory and research. *Journal of Trauma and Dissociation, 7*(4): 55–73.

Lochner, C., Seedat, S., Hemmings, S. M., Kinnear, C. J., Corfield, V. A., Niehaus, D. J., Moolman-Smook, J. C., Stein, D. J. (2004). Dissociative experiences in obsessive-compulsive disorder and trichotillomania: clinical and genetic findings. *Comprehensive Psychiatry, 45*(5): 384–391.

Marino, G. (2009). *Kierkegaard on the couch.* The Opinion Pages, New York Times, 28 October. Available at: http://opinionator.blogs.nytimes.com/2009/10/28/kierkegaard-on-the-couch/ [last accessed 17 November 2015].

Martínez-Taboas, A., Lewis-Fernandez, R., Şar, V., & Agrawal, A. L. (2010). Cultural aspects of psychogenic non-epileptic seizures. In: S. C. Schachter & C. La France (Eds.), *Gates & Rowan's Non-Epileptic Seizures* (3rd edn) (pp. 127–137). New York: Cambridge University.

Moskowitz, A. K., & Corstens, D. (2007). Auditory hallucinations: psychotic symptom or dissociative experience? *Journal of Psychological Trauma, 6*(2/3): 35–63.

Nijenhuis, E. R. S. (2014). Ten reasons for conceiving and classifying posttraumatic stress disorder as a dissociative disorder. *Psichiatria e Psicoterapia, 33*(1): 74–106.

Nijenhuis, E. R. S., Spinhoven, P., Van Dyck, R., Van der Hart, O., & Vanderlinden, J. (1998). Degree of somatoform and psychological dissociation in dissociative disorder is correlated with reported trauma. *Journal of Traumatic Stress, 11*: 711–730.

Ogawa, J. R., Sroufe, L. A., Weinfield, N. S., Carlson, E. A., & Egeland, B. (1997). Development and the fragmented self: longitudinal study of dissociative symptomatology in a nonclinical sample. *Development and Psychopathology, 4*: 855–879.

Öztürk, E., & Şar, V. (2005). "Apparently normal" family: a contemporary agent of transgenerational trauma and dissociation. *Journal of Trauma Practice, 4*(3–4): 287–303.

Raymond, E. S. (1996): *The New Hacker's Dictionary* (3rd edn). Cambridge: MIT.

Ross, C. A. (1997). *Dissociative Identity Disorder. Diagnosis, Clinical Features, and Treatment of Multiple Personality.* New York: Wiley.

Ross, C. A. (2004). *Schizophrenia. Innovations in Diagnosis and Treatment.* Birmingham, NY: Haworth.

Ross, C. A. (2008). Paraphilia from a dissociative perspective. *Psychiatric Clinics of North America, 31*: 613–622.

Ross, C. A., Ferrell, L., & Schroeder, E. (2014). Co-occurrence of dissociative identity disorder and borderline personality disorder. *Journal of Trauma & Dissociation, 15*(1): 79–90.

Sachs, A. (2013). Boundary modifications in the treatment of people with dissociative disorders: A pilot study. *Journal of Trauma and Dissociation, 14*(2): 159–169.

Sakarya, D., Güneş, C., Öztürk, E., & Şar, V. (2012). "Vampirism" in a case of dissociative identity disorder and posttraumatic stress disorder. *Psychotherapy & Psychosomatics, 81*(5): 322–323.

Şar, V. (2006). The scope of dissociative disorders: an international perspective. *Psychiatric Clinics of North America, 29*: 227–244.

Şar, V. (2011). Dissociative depression: a common cause of treatment resistance. In: W. Renner (Ed.), *Female Turkish Migrants with Recurrent Depression* (pp. 112–124). Innsbruck: Studia.

Şar, V. (2014a). The many faces of dissociation: opportunities for innovative research in psychiatry. *Clinical Psychopharmacology and Neuroscience, 12*(3): 171–179. Available at: www.ncbi.nlm.nih.gov/pmc/articles/PMC4293161/ [last accessed 17 November 2015].

Şar, V. (2014b). Psychotraumatology and dissociative disorders. An avenue of innovation in studies on mental health. *Journal of Psychology and Clinical Psychiatry, 1*: 1–2.

Şar, V., Akyüz, G., Doğan, O., & Öztürk, E. (2009). The prevalence of conversion symptoms in women from a general Turkish population. *Psychosomatics, 50*(1): 50–58.

Şar, V., Akyüz, G., Kuğu, N., Öztürk, E., & Ertem-Vehid, H. (2006). Axis-I dissociative disorder comorbidity of borderline personality disorder and childhood trauma reports. *Journal of Clinical Psychiatry, 67*(10): 1583–1590.

Şar, V., Akyüz, G., Kundakçi, T., Kiziltan, E., & Doğan, O. (2004). Childhood trauma, dissociation and psychiatric comorbidity in patients with conversion disorder. *American Journal of Psychiatry, 161*: 2271–2276.

Şar, V., Akyüz, G., Öztürk, E., & Alioğlu, F. (2013). Dissociative depression among women in the community. *Journal of Trauma and Dissociation, 14*(4): 423–438.

Şar, V., Alioğlu, F., & Akyüz, G. (2014). Experiences of possession and paranormal phenomena among women in the general population: are they related to traumatic stress and dissociation? *Journal of Trauma and Dissociation, 15*(3): 303–318.

Şar, V., İslam, S., & Öztürk, E. (2010). *Childhood Trauma, Attachment Styles, Alexithymia and Suicidality in Dissociative Disorders: a Comparison with Major Depression.* Paper presented at the 27th Annual Conference of the International Society for the Study of Trauma and Dissociation, Atlanta, GA.

Şar, V., Koyuncu, A., Öztürk, E., Yargic, L. I., Kundakçi, T., & Yazici, A. (2007). Dissociative disorders in the psychiatric emergency ward. *General Hospital Psychiatry, 29*: 45–50.

Şar, V., Krüger, C., Martínez-Taboas, A., Middleton, W., & Dorahy, M. J. (2013). Sociocognitive and posttraumatic models are not opposed. *Journal of Nervous and Mental Disease, 201*(5): 439–440.

Şar, V., Kundakçi, T., Kiziltan, E., Bakim, B., & Bozkurt, O. (2000). Differentiating dissociative disorders from other diagnostic groups through somatoform dissociation in Turkey. *Journal of Trauma and Dissociation, 1*(4): 67–80.

Şar, V., Kundakçi, T., Kiziltan, E., Yargic, I. L., Tutkun, H., Bakim, B., Bozkurt, O., Özpulat, T., Keser, V., & Özdemir, O. (2003). Axis I dissociative disorder comorbidity of borderline personality disorder among psychiatric outpatients. *Journal of Trauma and Dissociation, 4*(1): 119–136.

Şar, V., Önder C., Kilinçaslan A., Zoroglu S. S., & Alyanak B. (2014). Dissociative identity disorder among adolescents: Prevalence in a university psychiatric outpatient unit. *Journal of Trauma and Dissociation, 15*(4): 402–419.

Şar, V., & Öztürk, E. (2007). Functional dissociation of the self: A sociocognitive approach to dissociation. *Journal of Trauma and Dissociation, 8*(4): 69–89.

Şar, V., & Öztürk, E. (2008). Psychotic symptoms in complex dissociative disorders. In: A. Moskowitz, I. Schaefer, & M. Dorahy (Eds.), *Psychosis, Trauma and Dissociation: Emerging Perspectives on Severe Psychopathology* (pp. 165–175). New York: Wiley.

Şar, V., & Öztürk, E. (2009). Psychotic presentations of dissociative identity disorder. In: P. F. Dell & J. A. O'Neil (Eds.), *Dissociation and Dissociative Disorders: DSM-V and Beyond* (pp. 535–545). New York: Routledge.

Şar, V., & Öztürk, E. (2013). Stimulus deprivation and overstimulation as dissociogenic agents in postmodern oppressive societies. *Journal of Trauma and Dissociation, 14*(2): 198–212.

Şar, V., Öztürk, E., & Kundakçi, T. (2002). Psychotherapy of an adolescent with dissociative identity disorder: change in Rorschach patterns. *Journal of Trauma and Dissociation, 3*(2): 81–95.

Şar, V., & Ross, C. A. (2006). Dissociative disorders as a confounding factor in psychiatric research. *Psychiatric Clinics of North America, 29*: 129–144.

Şar, V., Taycan, O., Bolat, N., Özmen, M., Duran, A., Öztürk, E., & Ertem-Vehid, H. (2010). Childhood trauma and dissociation in schizophrenia. *Psychopathology, 43*: 33–40.

Şar, V., Ünal, S. N., Kiziltan, E., Kundakçi, T., & Öztürk, E. (2001). HMPAO SPECT study of cerebral perfusion in dissociative identity disorder. *Journal of Trauma & Dissociation, 2*(2): 5–25.

Şar, V., Ünal, S. N., & Öztürk, E. (2007). Frontal and occipital perfusion changes in dissociative identity disorder. *Psychiatry Research-Neuroimaging, 156*: 217–223.

Şar, V., Yargic, L. I., & Tutkun, H. (1996). Structured interview data on 35 cases of dissociative identity disorder in Turkey. *American Journal of Psychiatry, 153*: 1329–1333.

Schore, A. N. (2003). The experience-dependent maturation of a regulatory system in the orbital-prefrontal cortex and the origin of developmental psychopathology. In: A. N. Schore (Ed.), *Affect Dysregulation and Disorders of the Self* (pp. 5–35). New York: Norton.

Steele, K., van der Hart, O., Nijenhuis, E. R. S. (2001). Dependency in the treatment of complex posttraumatic stress disorder and dissociative disorders. *Journal of Trauma & Dissociation, 2*(4): 79–116.

Steinberg, M. (1994). *Structured Clinical Interview for DSM-IV Dissociative Disorders—Revised (SCID-D-R)*. Washington, DC: APA.

Tagliavini, G. (2014). *Dissociation and Traumatization from Pierre Janet to Gianni Liotti and Beyond: Connecting some Dots in European Psychotraumatology*. Paper presented in the symposium on European perspectives on trauma: finding the common ground. Annual conference of the German-speaking Society of Psychotraumatology (DeGPT), Hamburg.

Tamar-Gürol, D., Şar, V., Karadag, F., Evren, C., & Karagoz, M. (2008). Childhood emotional abuse, dissociation and suicidality among patients with drug dependency in Turkey. *Psychiatry and Clinical Neurosciences, 62*(5): 540–547.

Tezcan, E., Atmaca, M., Kuloglu, M., Gecici, O., Buyukbayram, A., & Tutkun, H. (2003). Dissociative disorders in Turkish inpatients with conversion disorder. *Comprehensive Psychiatry, 44*(4): 324–330.

Tutkun, H., Yargic, L. I., & Şar, V. (1996). Dissociative identity disorder presenting as hysterical psychosis. *Dissociation, 9*: 241–249.

Tutkun, H., Yargiç, L. I., Şar, V., Türkoğlu, R., Alev, L., & İdrisoğlu, H. A. (1996). *Prevalence of Dissociative Disorders among Patients who Suffer from Chronic Headache*. Unpublished study.

Twombly, J. H. (2000). Incorporating EMDR and EMDR adaptations into the treatment of clients with dissociative identity disorder. *Journal of Trauma and Dissociation, 1*(2): 61–81.

Van der Hart, O., Witztum, E., & Friedman, B. (1993). From hysterical psychosis to reactive dissociative psychosis. *Journal of Traumatic Stress, 6*: 43–64.

Waldvogel, B., Ulrich, A., & Strasburger, H. (2007). Sighted and blind in one person. *Nervenarzt, 78*: 1303–1309.

Winkelman, M. (2011). A paradigm for understanding altered consciousness: the integrative mode of consciousness. In: E. Cardeña & M. Winkelman (Eds.), *Altering Consciousness: Multidisciplinary Perspectives (Volume 1)* (pp. 23–41). Santa Barbara, CA: Praeger.

World Health Organization. (1992). *International Classification of Diseases (ICD-10)* (10th edn). Geneva: WHO.

Yücel, B., Kiziltan, E., & Aktan, M. (2000). Dissociative identity disorder presenting with psychogenic purpura. *Psychosomatics, 41*(3): 279–281.

Zoroglu, S. S., Tüzün, Ü., Şar, V., Tutkun, H., Savaş, H. A., Öztürk, M., Alyanak, B., & Kora, M. E. (2003). Suicide attempt and self-mutilation among Turkish high-school students in relation with abuse, neglect and dissociation. *Psychiatry and Clinical Neurosciences, 57*: 119–126.

CHAPTER NINE

Dissociative identity disorder and its saturation with shame

Phil Mollon

It was over twenty years ago when I first knowingly encountered one or two psychotherapy clients with dissociative identity disorder (DID). I had scarcely heard of the concept, and had very little idea what it meant or what might cause such a condition. The nature of DID was forcefully brought to my awareness by the vivid clinical phenomena presented by these several patients, all severely disturbed and with long psychiatric histories. Radical shifts of consciousness and behaviour were interwoven with deeply shocking and disconcerting narratives of severe abuse, torture, murder, and bizarre quasi-religious rituals.

I have not seen large numbers of such patients. Indeed, 1 learned that I could not personally cope with the confusion and anxiety that they generated. In a clinical practice covering more than forty years, I have worked with a total of nine patients with clear DID, although I have seen somewhat more than this for assessment. On the other hand, I would estimate that I have seen hundreds of patients who show some degree of dissociation deriving from severe childhood trauma.

Autistic spectrum DID

There are, I suggest, two broad causes of DID. The first, the one most commonly cited, is severe and repeated childhood trauma, occurring in a context such that the child cannot escape and has no caring and trustworthy adult with whom to share the trauma. The second caus-ative factor is an autistic spectrum temperament. I do not mean that all, or even most, of those whose temperaments are on the autistic spec-trum, will develop DID. However, autistic sensitivity means that some people experience features of relatively ordinary life as traumatic. For people on the autistic spectrum, ordinary life tends to be overwhelming and traumatic—leading to a turning away from external reality and an investment in an alternative inner world populated by guardian entities which operate like intimidating mafia gangs (Rosenfeld, 1971) and do not take kindly to being spoken of.

The latter development is not unlike that found in some cases of people diagnosed with schizophrenia—a condition that sometimes is the result when a person on the autistic spectrum is subject to pro-longed stress (Mollon, 2015). I described an example of this in an ear-lier contribution (Mollon, 2001, pp. 167–178)—the case of Jo and the "outside people". Jo was a very sensitive woman, her boundaries very porous, easily invaded by external stimuli. Since childhood she had been dominated by hidden figures who controlled and denigrated her, functioning (as she put it) like "exoskeletons", providing strength like that provided by a tyrannical dictator in charge of a military junta. She pictured them as positioned around the back of her head. They strongly objected to her speaking of them and would threaten punishments, including making her self-harm. Jo had not been abused as a child. She had, however, always felt highly sensitive, and deeply ashamed of this. Her experience corresponds to what I have called the "porous per-sonality" (Mollon, 2015). Through the "prey-predator dynamic", such people turn against their own sensitive and vulnerable "prey" self, often creating a false "apparently normal" self which is presented to the outside world. The sensitive and shame-laden "prey" self is attacked because in that moment (of causing injury to the self) there is the relief of shift from prey to predator. This is the motivation for many forms of self-harm.

Jo's "outside people" operated like the alter parts of a person with DID in every respect other than coming out to talk to me. They listened, observed, controlled, spoke internally, and made their presence felt more strongly at certain times than others.

Although DID and schizophrenia are usually considered distinct, examples such as that of Jo call this clear diagnostic boundary into question. Another point to consider is that people with DID often have at least one part that might well be considered schizophrenic. For example, one person who, in most of her personality states, was not remotely schizophrenic, described an experience in which she believed her family had been taken over by aliens and sought help from health services and police in killing the aliens. Fortunately this episode did not last long and no harm was done.

A core feature of the experience of the people I describe here is that they felt profound and pervasive shame (Mollon, 2002)—about self, childhood family, and their dissociative patterns. They would try to hide all these and attempt to present as normal and cheerful.

Trauma-derived DID

Some develop DID not as a result of their autistic spectrum temperament but because of prolonged, repeated, and extreme childhood interpersonal trauma, abuse, and even torture. Those with more complex and severe DID sometimes give the impression of having endured deliberate childhood torture with the intention of creating DID which can function for the benefit of the abusers and their group. It is not difficult to imagine the potential advantages of DID to a group or network. For example, a person may function particularly well within certain roles and identity states because the more normal conflicts and uncertainties that characterise a more integrated, or non-dissociated, personality are absent. DID also allows more plausible secrecy and boundaries for certain activities, since the different parts of the person quite literally do not know what each other are up to. This would enable a person to function competently in a conventional role, in work, in society, and even within the family, whilst functioning in a quite clandestine way in another personality state. In this way, the role of "spy" or "secret agent" would suit a well-functioning person with DID. It seems entirely plausible that there are well-functioning people with DID who do not come to the notice of mental health services—and that it is only the ones whose DID is breaking down, or whose programming is beginning to lose its coherence, whom we see as patients for psychotherapy.

For a person to admit that her mind is divided, that they might hold a responsible and high status professional role but suddenly have the experience of feeling like a frightened and confused small child whilst in the boardroom, or that they cannot remember what they have been doing for the last twenty-four hours, or the last month, or even several years—these things are shameful. It is quite natural that the first reaction is to try to conceal these lacunae in adult functioning, out of shame as well as whatever internal prohibitions there might be upon disclosing the existence of hidden parts.

Moreover, the experience of being a "victim" of severe childhood abuse and trauma is shameful. There is great hatred of the abused victim self. The childhood assumption is he or she deserves the abuse—and thus the more severe the abuse, the more severe the shame. Shame and abuse can be eroticised, thereby further intensifying the shame. In this way, shame begets shame.

The psychotherapist who receives and suffers the communication of trauma and dissociation is also subject to shame. I have certainly found this to be the case. Often my patients would tell me things, or would behave in certain ways, that I found I could not easily discuss with colleagues. I became familiar with a particular look on people's faces that would seem to combine bewilderment, alarm, and scepticism—with perhaps a worry that I had become as mad as my patients. Family and friends outside my professional work appeared even less inclined to give any credence to my accounts of the kind of thing I was hearing (not that I ever disclosed any details).

As my experience accumulated, and as I explored and read widely in the developing literature on trauma and dissociation, I wrote the first British book on clinical work with people with "multiple personality", as it was called then. The book was *Multiple Selves, Multiple Voices* (Mollon, 1996). It was my second book—and my feelings about it were a mixture of pride and shame. I tended not to speak about it—and if I carried the book anywhere, I would hide the front cover with its title. I learned to downplay any interest in DID.

The book itself contained references to shame. For example, I wrote:

> Shame is inherent in sexual abuse. Indeed, sexual abuse is the ultimate shame, and probably that is its purpose—to transfer projectively shame from the abuser to the victim ... The affect of shame tends to block empathy. Therapists do not want to feel this most

toxic of emotions. I notice certain defensive reactions in myself if I present work with a particular shame-prone, and perhaps abused, patient in a seminar to colleagues. I feel afraid of being regarded as a fool if I believe the patient has been abused. I fear the scornful reaction if I describe empathy with the patient's experience. This leads me to emphasise the patient's aggression, her efforts to control me, and my scepticism and uncertainty regarding the question of whether she was sexually abused. I find that if I emphasise her aggression, my colleagues will seem more at ease than when I emphasise her position as a possibly "shame-ridden" victim of abuse. I too can then feel tough-minded, not a fool, not taken in, but vigilantly rooting out destructiveness wherever it may be hidden ... To accept the patient's perception is to risk shame in analytic circles. We may be seen as no more than an empathy-ridden counsellor. Unless we are decoding and revealing a hidden text, at odds with the patient's conscious account, we perceive ourselves as analytically impotent. (Mollon, 1996, pp. 54–55)

The book had mixed reviews. Some were extremely favourable—one reviewer saying it was the only book he had ever bought two copies of (one for himself and one for his department)—others less so, with one reviewer criticising my lack of attention to transference and countertransference and suggesting I was in a "beleaguered position" in relation to the British Psychoanalytic Society. It was true that transference and countertransference could appear less prominent in my account than might be the case in much psychoanalytic literature. Although these phenomena (of transference) occur with DID, just as with other participants in psychotherapy, the reality of severe trauma means that there is also a vulnerable human being trying to tell another human being about experiences that may be (literally) near unspeakable. Becoming able to speak of the unspeakable is a major achievement of a therapeutic process with some people.

This then provokes the transferences of interpersonal trauma. These are the client's terrors that (a) the therapist will not be able to tolerate hearing and knowing the unspeakable; (b) the therapist will disbelieve the narrative (confirming the long-held fears); (c) the therapist will go mad on hearing of what happened; (d) the therapist is somehow in league with the abusers; and (e) the therapist will become sexually excited on hearing of sexual abuse. One core dilemma is that the more the client begins to trust the therapist, the more distrust and anxiety is engendered. This is because of a fundamental belief, based on experience, that it is not safe to trust. Moreover, if the therapist seems to know too much about the kind of experience the client describes, the suspicion arises that he or she is part of the network of abuse. One common result of the activation of the transferences of interpersonal trauma is that the patient appears to deteriorate and become more disturbed as a result of therapy—a further source of shame for the therapist. There may even develop a transference psychosis, in which the client comes to believe the therapist really is an abuser. Through the relentless inevitability of transference logic, the therapist may at some point be perceived as a replica of the worst aspects of the abusers.

Another transference danger is that the therapist ultimately becomes the client's "victim", or "prey", to the "predator" parts of the client that are built on identification with the original abusers. This potential can be enhanced when parts of the client retain some loyalty to the original abusers, and thus view the therapist as an enemy. A highly undesirable situation may arise, in which both therapist and client deeply mistrust each other, and become wary of each other. In such a position, the therapist understandably becomes defensive, continually monitoring how his or her utterances might be viewed by the client. As a result of this, the client views the therapist as inauthentic. In such a position of psychological dishonesty, the therapist knows that he is not functioning optimally, and feels (consciously or unconsciously) both guilt and shame.

Transference is a dangerous thing. Talking about it tends to encourage it—particularly if this is done in a way that fails to make clear (a) it is not reality, and (b) it is an intrusion from the past that is distorting perception of the present. It can be explored relatively safely with "neurotic" patients, whose grasp of reality remains relatively sound. With more traumatised and disturbed clients, no such assumption of safety can be made. Transference is essentially a piece of madness—a distortion of perception. With neurotic patients this distortion co-exists with a more or less accurate perception of the "real relationship". It is only the existence of the "real relationship" of trust that allows transference to be examined. Without that safe, real relationship of trust, there is only transference—and therein lies madness. In such circumstances, "transference interpretations" by the therapist will be perceived by the client as paranoid attempts to control and impose the therapist's version of reality. Imposition of this kind of control is experienced as dangerous for victims of abuse, and may evoke shame (since helplessness and control by the other are closely associated with shame). Although psychoanalysis has developed a fashion for relentless focus upon negative transference in the "here and now", we would do well to heed Freud's warning that the task is to release the patient from the "menacing illusion" of transference as quickly as possible (Freud, 1940a). Transference is not the therapeutic vehicle—it is the enemy of sanity and therapy (Mollon, 2011).

Part of the difficulty for a therapist trained in conventional psychoanalytic methods, of strict boundaries, restricting the analyst's utterances to transference interpretations, use of free-associations and dreams, use of the couch, and so forth, is that DID tends to blow all these conventions away. The client does not behave like a psychoanalytic analysand! Instead of functioning on the basis of a unitary conscious mind, free-associating and dreaming, and thereby gradually revealing the contents of an unconscious mind, the person with DID presents not a topographic (horizontal split) unconscious, but a series of parallel dissociated consciousnesses with varying degrees of amnesic barriers between them. Some consciousnesses will think, feel, and behave like profoundly traumatised children. Suppose a child part of a woman client with DID feels she wants to sit next to the male therapist and hold his arm for reassurance and safety? Is it best for the therapist to refuse this—a response that the child would only experience as rejection, and perhaps hatred? If the child is allowed to do this, what is the position a few minutes later when the client switches and she is then a bewildered and possibly shamed adult woman who finds herself holding her male therapist's arm? There are many such dilemmas that do not permit easy or obvious solutions.

These factors leave the practitioner somewhat bereft of the comfortable shelter of the psychotherapeutic "establishment"—the established set of beliefs, assumptions, and cultural practice within one's professional home. The therapist is torn between following the client's developmental and healing agenda, on the one hand, and conforming to the prevailing professional paradigms on the other. In recognising a client as suffering from DID, we engage with a diagnosis which is still regarded with great suspicion by many colleagues in the mental health professions, give possible credence to narratives of events which are generally not believed to take place, and explore adaptations of psychotherapeutic technique which place us outside the familiar and safe ground of our original training. All this places the psychotherapist working with DID in the position of shame—the deviant speaking of the unspeakable.

Another context that is relevant for those practitioners who have trained in psychoanalytic approaches is that we tend to be in mid-life or older during our training. The long analyses, and necessary deference to training analysts, teachers, and seminar leaders, all tend towards an infantilising effect. Our analysts and analytic teachers do have real power over our professional and personal lives—thereby adding to the pressures for conformity to the "establishment" and the anxieties created by deviance from this. Since DID, as a concept and as a pattern or clinical phenomena, cannot be accommodated by most psychoanalytic theories, its recognition by the practitioner is itself potentially viewed as a deviant act!

Back in the early 1990s, another intimidating context was the emergence of the intense controversy over recovered memories and "false memories". This was fierce and alarming, combining scientific and political dispute, with considerable media interest. A number of us comprised the British Psychological Society working party on recovered memories—several memory scientists, and a couple of us with some clinical experience. We all found the task of exploring this area—the science, the clinical phenomena, the "false memory" lobby groups, and the media interest—profoundly disconcerting, confusing, and at times frightening. Needless to say, we worked hard and with integrity to try to formulate some scientifically valid and clinically useful guidelines—but found ourselves in a maelstrom of controversy. I think we were all, to an extent, traumatised by this experience.

A personal experience

Writing this reminds me, free-associatively, of another disturbing episode. Around this time, in the mid-1990s, I was still completing my lengthy training as a psychoanalyst (although I had already trained first as a clinical psychologist and then as a psychotherapist). The psychoanalytic training was particularly prolonged because of my geographical location and difficulty in finding appropriate training patients. When I started the training some years previously, a regional psychotherapy trust fund had given me a small loan to assist, on the understanding that it would be repaid on completion of the training. One day I received a telephone call from a senior psychoanalyst within my society. He informed me he had taken up a position on the board of this trust and had been horrified to hear that I had an outstanding loan. Appearing unwilling to listen to my explanation, he stated a grossly inflated sum that he believed I owed, and declared that I must pay this back immediately or "there would be trouble". Shouting down my attempts to speak, he sounded most threatening, and I felt distinctly shocked and frightened. I had fantasies that he was going to send round some kind of heavy mob to beat me up. This was all the more shocking to me because previously I believed we were on cordial terms. No doubt he believed mistakenly that I was in breach of the agreement, and trying to avoid repaying an overdue debt, and he felt embarrassed because I belonged to his society. The effect on me was to trigger cardiac symptoms leading to specialist investigations. This senior figure died some years ago. It is a matter of regret to me that I did not take up this matter with the ethics committee, since I am quite sure that my colleagues would have considered his bullying behaviour inappropriate and abusive. I did not, of course, do so because I felt intimidated and shamed—and, like the victims of abuse, tended to assume that the situation was my fault and that I would be blamed and the "authorities" would side with the abuser.

I mention this episode because, although trivial by comparison with the serious and extreme abuse suffered by some of our patients, it illustrates how psychotherapists too can be intimidated, shamed, and silenced. The "establishment", and its representatives, whether these are parents or senior colleagues, tends to turn nasty when its mores, assumptions, and self-image are challenged.

People with DID, and those who try to work therapeutically with them, are doomed to suffer shame because:

- DID is still generally regarded as not really existing.
- Experiences that give rise to DID are generally considered not to exist—claiming that they may exist is a challenge to the social (and professional) establishment.
- As a concept and clinical phenomenon, DID challenges the assumptions within much of psychoanalysis and clinical psychology—and thus colleagues cannot "hear" or understand what is communicated because they have no conceptual framework for it.
- DID challenges conventional modes of psychotherapy, pushing the clinician to adapt and explore—and thus leaving the comfortable shelter of the familiar and established.
- The "establishment" may tend to become abusively intimidating in trying to silence expression of challenge.

- Sexual abuse involves shame—the shame of powerlessness, vulnerability, and violation.
- The dynamics of abuse involve the projective transmission of shame down the line—and the therapist is at the end of the line.

For these reasons, I have for some years declared that although I do know something about DID, I choose not to work with this condition. Others are able to—but I know my own limit.

References

Freud, S. (1940a). *An Outline of Psycho-Analysis. S. E., 23:* 141. London: Hogarth.

Mollon, P. (1996). *Multiple Selves, Multiple Voices: Working with Trauma, Violation and Dissociation.* Chichester: Wiley.

Mollon, P. (2001). *Releasing the Self. The Healing Legacy of Heinz Kohut.* London: Whurr.

Mollon, P. (2002). *Shame and Jealousy. The Hidden Turmoils.* London: Karnac.

Mollon, P. (2011). A Kohutian perspective on the foreclosure of the Freudian transference in modern British technique. *Psychoanalytic Inquiry, 31*(1): 28–41.

Mollon, P. (2015). *The Disintegrating Self.* London: Karnac.

Rosenfeld, H. (1971). A clinical approach to the psychoanalytic theory of the life and death instincts: an investigation of the aggressive aspects of narcissism. *International Journal of Psychoanalysis, 52:* 169–178.

CHAPTER TEN

What's different about ritual abuse and mind control

Alison Miller

Someone recently told me that I needed a break from "studying evil". That phrase, *studying evil*, stuck with me, and as I thought about it, I realised that it is indeed what I have been doing. The people I have treated for the past twenty-five years, survivors of mind control and ritual abuse, whom I study and learn from and write about and hopefully help heal, have been harmed by more than just traumatised perpetrators passing on their own abuse and dysfunction to the next generation. They have, as children, been traumatised by highly organised evil. We know of highly organised evil from what the Nazis did in the Holocaust, and we know of the Nazi doctors who experimented in heinous ways on children, in the concentration camps, a place where there were no ethical guidelines for research on human beings. What is not generally known is that these same Nazi doctors, along with experts of other nationalities eager to learn from them, continued their experiments after the war, guiding international political and criminal groups who wanted to learn how to train children to participate in illegal activities their whole lives without their conscious knowledge of this participation. The key was to create dissociative disorders in those children through severe, life-threatening trauma.

Many groups, particularly religious ones, had already been doing this, but not in a scientific manner. According to Randy Noblitt,

> Linda Blood wrote a book, *The New Satanists* in which she gives a remote history of "satanism", possibly extending to the era of Gnostics before the Inquisition. The "left hand path" includes transgressive spirituality associated with many mainstream religions. In Judaism there were heresies (Sabbateans, Frankists) who used transgressive sexual rituals and provided their own version of the Qabala (rather than the authentic Jewish Kabbalah) to the contemporary magical brotherhoods. There are violent "red sects" in vodun, but other followers of vodun claim to "do no harm", like European and American Wiccans. Even in Buddhism there are Tantrics who either follow or at least explore the left hand path. The left hand path may be historically old—who can say for sure? There may be a variety of cults which have pursued dark spirituality throughout history. (ibid., 2015, p. n)

The "possession" by evil spirits, which these cults believe in, involves intense suffering that causes dissociative splitting of the mind or brain. It is my belief that the supposed evil spirits manifested in cult members are dissociated alter personalities who believe what their perpetrators taught them. This is not to discount the possibility of genuine spiritual entities, only to make it clear that dissociative disorders have always been the result of violent ritualistic abuse. It was not until the twentieth century, when science married evil spirituality, that the leaders of such groups realised they were creating dissociative disorders. Perhaps they were surprised, but they quickly took advantage of this knowledge to expand their repertoire.

Wendy Hoffman's memoirs, *The Enslaved Queen: A Memoir about Electricity and Mind Control* (2014) and *White Witch in a Black Robe: A True Story about Criminal Mind Control* (2016), use her personal experience over seventy years to trace some of the early connections between the Nazi doctors, US and international political groups, secret societies (in her case the Illuminati and a hidden group within the Freemasons), magical religions which connected worship with sexual violence, and traditional organised crime involving child prostitution and pornography, human trafficking, and drug smuggling. She remembers her grandfather, a top-level Illuminati programmer of human minds, and his assistant swapping methods with the Nazi doctor Josef Mengele, and American and international politicians taking advantage of both these sources of mind control knowledge. She shows how these, her primary owners, sold her services when she was still a child and an adolescent, for prostitution and breeding, to organised criminal groups which traded in child sexual victims and babies for various kinds of misuse.

Secrecy is the prime directive for all individual victims and for all such groups. The occult religions that worship evil entities, as well as those which believe in the balance of good and evil, have survived for centuries through secrecy. Just as traditional organised crime like the Italian Mafia was able to hide its existence for many years, so have the organised criminal groups that abuse children in these ways. In the twentieth and twenty-first centuries we have seen this secrecy maintained in two primary ways: through the security and alarm systems implanted in the hidden alter personalities of victims by their abusers, and through the highly planned stories placed in the media and the helping professions about what is going on when a survivor remembers and begins to disclose abuse.

Creation of complex dissociative disorders in victims

Mind controlling perpetrator groups, whether religious, political, or merely criminal, create highly organised, structured personality systems in their victims. The typical media portrayal of mind control is of an adult volunteer whose mind is split through hypnosis and conditioning so that she can switch into different personalities with different skills. I wish this were all there is to it, but this is not at all what I have encountered in my clinical work. Minds are indeed split, but for mind control to be effective it has to begin in infancy and to involve life-threatening torture on top of a base of insecure or no attachment. My mind-controlled clients have been trained from birth, or (if it occurs outside the home) from a very young age (around three), through drugs, torture, and life-threatening trauma to become many "people". Movies, music, stories, pictures, and virtual reality technology were all used when the children were so young that they could not distinguish fantasy or story from reality. This was done to make these children believe the things the abusers wanted them to believe. These internal child parts were then re-traumatised recurrently to stop them from growing older, and were carefully stored in designated internal locations so that they could be accessed later in life to do their "jobs" as brainwashed children and adolescents in adult bodies. Parts (inner people) containing emotions and bodily sensations were stored separately from narratives and from those alter personalities who were designated to commit evil acts such as ritual murder, assassination, torture, and other crimes. The separation of all these parts imprisoned these inner "people" in their traumatic situations and original ages, located in designated internal places to be available for calling up by the abuser group through pre-assigned signals when wanted to perform an assigned task. Survivors are often aware of internal "worlds" or "structures" in which their parts live. Strong barricades or walls, reinforced by torture, are constructed in these internal worlds to prevent communication between parts. Many other therapists with whom I communicate have observed the same phenomena.

I imagine the physiology of dissociative splitting to be as follows: each alter personality is a specific brain circuit, either very tiny (a single neuron) or more complex, if it has more life experience. This circuit can only hold a certain amount of information; when it is about to become overloaded, it is automatically closed off and the brain opens a new circuit. Life-threatening trauma and extreme emotional or physical pain can overload a circuit quite quickly, so new circuits—potential alter personalities—are formed, sometimes many of them, in such situations. Sophisticated abuser groups deliberately create these newly opened circuits, capture them with names and assigned signals, and make use of them.

This separation of alters (parts, circuits) makes the task of reconstituting the memories of the original training very difficult for survivors and their therapists. This is not like simple dissociative identity disorder, in which a person traumatised, for example, by incest, has four or five distinct parts, each of whom carries a set of memories. Every human experience or memory consists of several different kinds of input: impressions from each of the senses, a variety of emotions, and cognitions that make all of these aspects of the experience into a story line. An overwhelming experience in childhood is not fully processed and put together at the time of the experience; rather, it remains separated into channels of input that made up the experience. These different aspects of experience can become alter personalities, especially in the hands of sophisticated mind controllers who treat them as such. In mind-controlled personality systems, there are hundreds of alter personalities, representing all aspects of the person's experiences. Some contain only emotions, some bodily sensations such as pain or sexual feelings, some sounds or words, some visual images, others tastes or smells, representing all the channels of information in the original experience during which those alters were split off.

In order to reconstitute a traumatic memory for healing purposes, all those parts of the person involved in that memory need to come together. This is possible in many but not all mind-controlled personality systems. If the person was mind-controlled throughout childhood, there are often parts who have been trained to locate all the other parts who are involved in a particular memory. However, if the person only experienced such trauma for a brief period, say through a daycare for young children, the personality system is much less organised and the memories more difficult to access and work through. Mind controllers want the personality systems they control to be well organised so that they can call up specific alter personalities to perform their tasks, such as various kinds of sexual skills, assassination, or theft. Fortunately for therapists, it is possible to access this internal organisation to help clients work through their memories. In my experience, when a survivor client, including not just the "front person" (what therapists used to mistakenly call the "host"), but also the designated leaders of the internal personality system, is determined to recover and trusts me as her therapist, I can trust those internal leaders to bring forward the different sections of the system for healing in the right order.

Deliberate recruitment of victims as perpetrator group members

Michael Salter (2012), in his qualitative study of sixteen adult survivors of ritual child sexual abuse, comments that "Children and adults subject to ritual abuse may actively collude in their own victimisation, complicating efforts at detection, intervention and treatment" (ibid., p. 440).

> Within traumatic ordeals in which they were forced into contact with death and blood and human waste, participants' views of themselves ultimately came to accord with the view expressed by their abusers. Regardless of the specific ideological content of the *mythos* of abusive groups, the practice of ritual abuse served to constitute the victimised child and/or woman as polluted and undeserving of love or care. The resulting internal sense of *anomie* then bound the child to the abusive group, since he/she had lost his/her sense of

communion or belonging to a wider social order ... By following a process of sustained dehumanisation with the promise of redemption, ritual abuse was an effective strategy in legitimising sexual exploitation to victims and enjoining their active participation in their abuse and the abuse of others. (ibid., p. 447)

Salter has described a phenomenon that is mystifying to many outsiders who have contact with survivors. It is mystifying because outsiders are unaware of the extent of the deliberate mind control techniques used by the abuser groups. One of the groups' important goals is isolation of victims and survivors from the outside world. Yes, they use the degradation that Salter describes, but there is much more, specifically forced perpetration. In my experience, every survivor who grows up as part of such a group is forced to perpetrate in some way. With an adult man's hand over her hand, a little child is made to stab or sexually abuse an animal or a vulnerable human being. After this is done, the child is told that she is evil, and only the group and its deity can now accept her. Although the "front person" of the survivor is usually not aware of these experiences (or she would go insane), the resulting shame can maintain the survivor's isolation and continued connection to the group. It appears that the victims Salter interviewed had not consciously remembered forced perpetration.

Abuser groups tell children that the group is their family, and the children are their property, to do with what they want. There is programming to keep victims isolated from people who are not part of the abuser group. If anyone in these children's lives sickens or dies, the children are told it is their fault, that they are poisonous to others because they are so evil. Satanic and Luciferian groups pair each child with a "disposable" child, usually one whose existence is not known in the outside world. After the children form a friendship bond, often the only bond the child has ever had, the chosen child's hand is used to kill the "disposable" child, and the living child is told that anyone he or she loves will die. The group members tell such children that the acts that they have committed are so evil that no one but the group will ever accept them. Unfortunately, this can sometimes be true. Some therapists as well as some potential friends of survivors find their reality so difficult to bear that they cannot listen to it. Survivors are acutely attuned to what a listener can take, and will not disclose to those who cannot handle it. They have spent their childhoods, and often much of their adult lives, taking care of other people, and it does not help them if they have to take care of those to whom they disclose. It is important for survivors to know, however, that there are genuine people who will be their friends or their therapists, who see them as human beings who have suffered and who will extend respect and compassion to them.

There is also specific programming to make victims afraid of therapists, physicians, clergy, and law enforcement officers, all of whom abuse the children while in their professional role. Sometimes it is just a group member in uniform; other times it is an actual physician or priest or pastor or therapist or police officer who belongs to the group. Needless to say, the groups assign these roles and professions to members according to their abilities.

Groups also impersonate actual therapists, creating scenarios for abducted and drugged survivors which range from sexual abuse and torture by the supposed therapist, to the therapist's apparent presence and leadership at rituals, to the therapist just doing "bad therapy", yelling at and blaming the client. I was frequently impersonated by members of a particular satanic cult when I first worked with survivors in the early 1990s, and I devised with my clients a way for them to tell the difference between me and the impersonator. I noticed that these clients frequently didn't look directly at my face. I discovered that in childhood each of these people had experienced a scenario when a "therapist" told him or her not to look at him, then told the child to look, and when the child looked he had put on a devil mask and horns, and raped them. I had one crooked finger, and I told my clients to look at my hands and see whether the person purporting to be me had this crooked finger. They learned to distinguish between us. Ironically, however, although these clients who were actually abused by my impersonator did not quit therapy with me, another client (from a different abuser group) did stop seeing me when someone pretending to be me yelled at her in a supposed therapy session. She was an artist, and had told me a few weeks earlier that she was compulsively drawing the interior of my office, no doubt for the purpose of the abuser group replicating it elsewhere.

"Access training" of alter personalities

All child abusers, of course, tell the children they abuse not to tell anyone else what they have experienced. The words they say to children range from, "It's our little secret", to "You don't want me to go to prison, do you?" to "I'll kill your mother if you talk to anyone about this". However, the training used by mind controllers is much more systematic, and relies on the dissociative personality system for its effectiveness. Organised abuser groups, including those associated with government agencies and the military, place the highest priority on their abuse of children not being discovered. Therefore, they train the inner parts of their victims' personality systems to be loyal, silent, and obedient, and to report any disclosures the person may have made or memories the person is beginning to have. These trainings override all other training.

Punishment for disobedience or disloyalty is swift and cruel. Beatings, imprisonment, torture, rape, electroshock, being left overnight in a coffin filled with rotting flesh or biting insects ... abuser groups do not hesitate to hurt children severely in order to get across their instructions to never disobey. There are also "object lessons" in which someone purported to be a traitor is killed painfully, for example, by being skinned alive, while other children watch. The usual consequence threatened for disobedience or disloyalty is death to the victim or her loved ones.

Each victim's personality system is usually set up as a hierarchy or a set of interrelated hierarchies. Those in charge, usually adolescent alters, give orders to those under their command. Under them are punishers or enforcers who administer punishments to disobedient alters. These punishments include the use of parts of traumatic memories to retraumatise—for example, flooding of feelings of despair, memories of being forced to perpetrate, the pain of a rape, or hallucinating the presence of the perpetrators in the therapy room. There are alters trained to attempt suicide and to harm the body in the case of disloyalty; the dangerously suicidal ones believe they do not belong to the body and will not die with it. The person hears frightening voices, imitating the voices of the abusers, telling them not to talk, and if they do talk about the abuse, the trained alters will administer these partial memories as punishments. The person's dysfunction increases the longer she is disloyal. Terrified inner children are doing their assigned "jobs" of punishing, to make the person obey the rules, in the belief that any punishment given by the actual abusers, who know everything, will be worse. If this persists for long, the punishments grow more intense, and there are alters trained to physically return to the group so that the perpetrators can put it right. If they don't return to the abusers, they may well exhibit such serious psychiatric symptoms that they are hospitalised. And in my experience, psychiatric hospitals often have perpetrator group members on staff to deal with recalcitrant survivors. In addition, many alters are trained to "come when called", that is, to respond to access triggers such as beeps over the phone or hand signals from across the street, so that perpetrator group members can abduct them and torture them into submission and forgetting.

All the childhood training relies on what I call the "big lie". The powerful adult abusers emphasise to their child (and later adult) victims that they know everything their victims do or say and, in some cases, even everything they think. Trickery is used when the victims are children to make them believe this lie. There are many versions of the big lie, for example: "The invisible all-seeing eye always sees you"; "Satan (or God) is always watching you and will let us know about you"; "Your stuffed animals (or the crows, or microchips, we put in your body) report on you to us"; "We have magical abilities to know what you do, say, and think". Young children believe such lies and do not understand the concept of deception. The abuser groups rely on survivors having child parts who are young enough to continue to believe such things even after the person has reached adulthood. The use of child and adolescent parts is basic to mind control. The youngest children are taught magical versions of the big lie; adolescents and adults are taught technological versions.

The abuser group often does know what the person is doing or saying, especially if she has remembered or disclosed forbidden material. When the person is still a child and her family is involved in the abuser group, it is easy for her to be observed. When the person has grown up and moved away, the group knows through young reporter alter personalities reporting to them. Reporter alters, believing the big lie, have the job of contacting a designated group member if there has been disloyalty, having been taught that they had better tell the group or the all-knowing group will punish them severely. The reporters are not put under the authority of the internal leaders, but may see themselves as spies, spying on the rest of the person on behalf of the abusers. The existence of reporter alters is hidden from the main person and from those alters in charge of the personality system. The individual feels a strong urge to "phone home", contacts their designated person, usually by telephone, switches into a reporter alter, and gives the information, then switches back. The main person has no idea that reporting has occurred. Neither do the alters who are in charge of the personality system. When the group punishes them for disloyalty, it reinforces their belief in the big lie, because they have no idea that it was someone inside their own body who reported.

When a reporter alter reports that a victim has made disclosures, the group goes into action immediately. In my experience, such groups are quite bold in calling survivors back and re-traumatising them to close down their memories and terrify them about the consequences of remembering and telling. If you are a therapist or a friend of a survivor, it may take a long time for you to establish trust with your survivor client or friend. As soon as she begins disclosing to you, reporting is likely to occur and the perpetrator group may take action to close down the client's memories or make her quit therapy.

Public discrediting of survivors and therapists

People still speak in whispers in the hallways at the conferences of the International Society for the Study of Trauma and Dissociation (ISST-D), when they talk about ritual abuse or mind control. The society was nearly destroyed by the false memory advocates' attacks of the 1990s, including a highly organised media campaign to discredit those working with recovered memories and dissociative disorders, culminating in lawsuits against respected professionals. The persons and cases attacked were almost exclusively those dealing with organised criminal abuse, in particular what has been called "ritual abuse", that is, sadistic child abuse with at least the trappings of satanism.

In order to survive, the ISST-D had to broaden its scope to focus on trauma in general, as a result reducing the emphasis on the severe dissociative disorders. When I gave a basic workshop at the 2014 conference about specific clinical skills for working with dissociative clients, an attendee, whose own presentation on attachment I had attended, admitted to me that he knew nothing about dissociative disorders. Although many of the leaders in the field are indeed experts in treatment of complex dissociative disorders, very few of the presentations address those disorders directly, and almost none deal directly with organised abuse. Discussion of these matters does, at least, go on in the relative privacy of an online special interest group, which has over a hundred members, but it took many years before the society became brave enough to allow this.

Organised abuser groups have deliberate strategies to make survivors' memories appear false. I had two cases in which a child at age five or six was led to believe she was witnessing the murder of someone she knew, who had actually moved to live somewhere else. In one of these cases the police investigated, only to find the alleged victim alive. The group had staged a ritual murder and my client as a child was instructed to remember this person being killed. In the second case, as I was now wise to this strategy, I asked whether any other parts of the survivor (alter personalities) had seen the murdered person later in life, and sure enough, the girl who had been "killed" had made a visit to her home town in her teens.

Groups also deliberately simulate impossible events such as alien abductions, which alters are taught to bring to memory if the person begins to make disclosures. When I worked through an alien abduction memory with a client, the "spaceship" was kept in the courtyard of the cult training centre.

There are many other scenarios to make a survivor look psychotic, such as telling drugged alters that they are rock stars or politicians or dead celebrities, or that they are to take on the identities of whoever is around them. Rapid switching between alters can create a schizophrenic "word salad". Organised abuser groups can simulate any known mental disorder in their victims. One advantage of making people display symptoms of recognised mental illnesses is to get survivors whose memories are "leaking" to be admitted to mental hospitals where abuser group members on staff can access them.

When disclosures began in the 1980s, while genuine professionals were being attacked, so-called ritual abuse experts sprang up to provide consultation to therapists, see their clients, and teach others techniques to assist in recovery. Some were sincere; others appear to have been planted ahead of time by the organised criminal groups in order to "close down" survivors who were beginning to remember and disclose their abuse. *The Enslaved Queen* (Hoffman, 2014) has a chapter entitled "Trapped in therapy" in which the author describes having been sent to no fewer than four such "experts", the last of whom closed her down effectively for thirteen years.

The important thing to know about present-day organised child abuse, including that perpetrated by satanic and other "left-hand" religious cults, is that it is very psychologically sophisticated organised crime. As well as all the methods of torture we know of from newscasts, it uses well-thought-out and practised psychological techniques—on children. We now know that psychologists had a large hand in directing the use of torture in the Guantanamo Bay prison. Similarly, since the

Second World War, the training of children to be used for sexual, political, and occult religious purposes has been overseen by specialists in child development. Perpetrators within organised networks learn methods of child abuse which rely on the deliberate creation of dissociative disorders in children, and take advantage of children's developmental stages to create inner mental structures and beliefs which will prevent the children from making clear disclosures, both at the time of the abuse and in the future when they are grown up or away from the original abusers. Each survivor's complex personality system includes very elaborate security mechanisms that ensure that the perpetrator group and handlers are notified and can take action if the child or adult begins to remember and/or disclose the abuse. The dissociative disorder, and the activities of the alter personalities, are hidden from the view of other people and of the "front person" who lives the child's or survivor's everyday life.

Despite all this, it is possible to help survivors heal and achieve safety. Therapists and supportive friends need to pursue a strategy of establishing rapport with the dominant alter personalities, those in charge of the internal hierarchies, and showing them how they have been deceived. With such help, these internal leaders can help the other parts work through their traumatic memories and achieve personal freedom. Law enforcement specialists need to recognise the existence and complexity of this kind of abuser group, and not just write off those persons who tell what appear to be tall tales while making suicide attempts and harming their bodies. Society needs to become aware. What we don't know *can* hurt us all.

References

Blood, L. (1994). *The New Satanists*. New York: Grand Central/Warner.

Hoffman, W. (2014). *The Enslaved Queen: A Memoir about Electricity and Mind Control*. London: Karnac.

Hoffman, W. (2016). *White Witch in a Black Robe: A True Story about Criminal Mind Control*. London: Karnac.

Noblitt, R. (2015). Post to the Ritual Abuse and Mind Control special interest group discussion list (private listserv), January 10.

Salter, M. (2012). The role of ritual in the organised abuse of children. *Child Abuse Review*, 21: 440–451.

CHAPTER ELEVEN

Reflections on the treatment of dissociative identity disorder and dissociative disorder not otherwise specified—a closer look at selected issues

Richard P. Kluft

oons (1986) followed up the work of twenty clinicians, each treating one patient with dissociative identity disorder (DID), then called multiple personality disorder (MPD), for an average of thirty-nine months. Nineteen had not treated DID before. Twenty-five per cent of their patients achieved and sustained complete integration as defined by five of the six criteria used in Kluft's studies (Kluft, 1984a, 1986). Others had achieved partial integrations, or complete integrations that proved unstable. Two-thirds were reported much improved. Psychodynamic psychotherapy and hypnosis were the primary therapeutic modalities. Treatments averaged only one session per week, half the intensity currently recommended (International Society for the Study of Trauma and Dissociation, 2011). No other study offers comparable insight into therapeutic encounters between non-specialist therapists and stringently diagnosed DID patients. Coons' patients resembled the early cohorts reported by Kluft (Kluft, 1984a, 1986), an experienced therapist employing similar therapeutic techniques.

By 1986 the dissociative disorders field had evidence, quite striking by the standards of the day, that psychodynamic psychotherapy plus hypnosis resulted in outcomes that appear astonishingly brief and puzzlingly effective by today's standards. The time was ripe both to replicate and expand Coons' study in other settings and to study factors in the work of therapists achieving unusually good results. However, these opportunities were squandered. Coons' research was and remains rarely cited. Undocumented and unstudied by others, the work of master therapists became relegated to the realm of the anecdotal and legendary, often treated dismissively by contemporary scholars.

Precious and irreplaceable knowledge was lost. For example, few actually know how Cornelia Wilbur treated DID patients. *Sybil* (Schreiber, 1973) describes Cornelia Wilbur's work as a neophyte, treating her first DID patient. The psychotherapy of "Sybil" bears scant resemblance to Wilbur's practices at the peak of her prowess. Her legend survives, but her hard-won wisdom and burnished expertise is largely forgotten.

Cornelia Wilbur never stopped growing as a clinician. Critics said she fostered dependency, but Wilbur was ahead of her time. She anticipated the emphasis modern clinicians accord to attachment, regarding dependency as a developmental matter to be revisited in therapy in order to create a foundation of secure connectedness from which healthy autonomy could grow. Far from being overly indulgent, Wilbur was demanding of herself, her patients, and others. After she achieved rapid successful outcomes with two patients I referred after failing to help, she chided me none too gently for having misunderstood and mismanaged their transferences.

Cornelia Wilbur was pragmatic, no slave to theory. In 1978 I told her about the hypnotic techniques I was developing (Kluft, 1982). Unbeknownst to me, she thought them over, and adopted some. Years later, in 1986, she paid me an astonishing compliment: "Well, Rick," she said, "if I had known these techniques when I was treating Sybil, I think her treatment (which lasted over eleven years) would have been over in about four years!" Always eager to enhance and expand her skill sets, Wilbur had mastered my methods and achieved faster results.

Wilbur improved her skills without discarding her analytic identity. Now we witness model after model arise in the dissociative disorders field, each promoting itself as an improvement and presenting rationales for its being adopted in place of earlier approaches. Their claims remain largely undocumented.

Ironically, while it still can be argued that the techniques of the mid-1980s were equal or superior to those being promoted almost thirty years thereafter, both psychodynamic psychotherapy and hypnosis have fallen into disfavour. Student clinicians are generally trained in cognitive-behavioural models, often graduating with a primitive knowledge of psychodynamics. Since the "memory wars" of the 1990s, many in the dissociation field have taken pains to proclaim their avoidance of hypnosis, oblivious to the fact that such an assertion is inherently self-deceptive, as discussed below.

Core dissociative phenomena

What must we address when we treat DID? Many attempts have been made to define, constrict, and circumscribe the realm of dissociative phenomena. Space precludes discussion of these efforts and the considerations that motivated them. In the process of the formulation of almost every such effort, much of substance has been put aside, a scientific expression of dissociation and denial.

Some attempts have redefined dissociation to make selected aspects more amenable to psychological or neuropsychophysiological research. Some privilege their preferred paradigm so indiscriminately that many phenomena long considered classic dissociative manifestations are severed from the dissociative fold. Such elective tunnel vision permits the elaboration of preferred paradigms without the inconvenience of addressing phenomena and observations inconsistent with them. Whatever is not encompassed within that paradigm's focus is dismissed *a priori*.

Rather than follow such Procrustean traditions, I ask, "What is the range of dissociative phenomena which we encounter in our work with DID?" Experience has taught me that inclusive views promote both intellectual honesty and effectiveness in treatment. They offer some degree of prophylaxis against constructing views of DID based on considerations remote from clinical realities. Perspectives taking dismissive stances toward the dissociative phenomena they do not encompass in effect declare those phenomena non-dissociative by fiat rather than acceptable standards of proof. Models that grant tacit or overt permission to disregard phenomena and findings on the basis of rationales that promote intellectual expediency and convenience simply are not scientific.

A few years ago the participants in a panel at a professional meeting suddenly went off topic and began to discuss DID. Statements completely incongruent with the clinical realities of the condition were expressed with strong conviction. When I raised a question, both chair and panelists replied that I did not understand dissociation.

Scholarly battles surrounding the definition of hypnosis demonstrate that celebrated scientists are capable of privileging their ideas above actual data when that data is offered by supporters of alternative conceptualisations. In a 1994 (Kluft, 1994) editorial I questioned whether dissociation was best understood as a unitary concept, or whether it consisted of diverse phenomena that would require multiple paradigms in order to embrace them.

I have observed and described thirteen occasionally overlapping categories of dissociative phenomena in clinical DID populations (Kluft, 2009):

1. Alters, or personalities, personality states, identities, dissociated selves, sub-personalities, personifications, and so on.
2. Identity confusion, which might present as befuddlement or apparent good function in the absence of knowing who one is.
3. Amnesia, with the full range of removals from owned autobiographical experience, from complete unavailability of memory of an event/s through awareness without ownership or endorsement of the reality of the event/s.
4. Compartmentalisation/modularity phenomena: for example, alters and/or ego states (Watkins & Watkins, 1997); segregation of some subsets of information from other subsets of information in a relatively rule-bound manner (Spiegel, 1986); the BASK (Behaviour, Affect, Sensation, Knowledge) dimensions of Braun (1988a, 1988b).
5. Detachment, as in depersonalisation and derealisation in the perception of self and/or others; and also in concerns over whether memories are real or unreal; also seen in alters' lacking senses of ownership or responsibility for the actions of other alters (Kluft, 1991).
6. Absorption.
7. Altered states of consciousness: for example, hypnotic/autohypnotic/ spontaneous trance phenomena.
8. Failures of compartmentalisation such as intrusion phenomena, including both alters, memories, phenomena usually associated with psychosis (Kluft, 1987b), and the intrusive expression of the BASK (Braun, 1988a) dimensions.
9. Simultaneous operation of separate self-aware processes or states of mind, including parallel distributed processing, elsewhere thought known phenomena (Kluft, 1995), unconscious thought (Dijksterhuis,

Bos, Nordgren, & van Baaren, 2006), inner world activities (Kluft, 1988), and creativity by alters not in apparent executive control.

10. Simultaneous executive activity by separate self-aware processes or states of mind—copresence phenomena (Kluft, 1984b).

11. Inner world and third reality phenomena: events within that inner world that are accorded historical reality and which sometimes intrude into ongoing experiences, and/or affect ongoing experiences from behind the scenes (Kluft, 1998).

12. Switching and shifting.

13. Multiple reality disorder (Kluft, 1991), for which dissociative identity disorder (formerly called multiple personality disorder) is the delivery and maintenance system.

A theoretical model or approach to treatment that fails to address the full spectrum of what the patient's psychopathology entails resembles a map with blank spots marked "terra incognita". It falls short of depicting the actual terrain that the therapy may be forced to traverse.

In 2013 (Kluft, 2013a), I presented an analysis of twenty-two contemporary theories of dissociation, most of which were associated with particular paradigms of treatment. Using the most liberal of inclusion criteria, the average theory encompassed 4.9 of these thirteen core phenomena. For example, although the study of actual DID patients demonstrates that they are characterised by high hypnotisability (Frischholz, Lipman, Braun, & Sachs, 1992), absorption, a key aspect of hypnosis, was addressed by only three of the twenty-two models (14%), and altered states by six (30%). While fifteen (68%) addressed compartmentalisation, only six (27%) addressed failures of compartmentalisation, which are associated with some of DID's most distressing symptoms. Indices of the complexity of the DID patient's functioning, such as simultaneous alter functioning and attention to activities of their inner world, ranged from 22% to 39%.

It seems difficult to avoid the conclusion that clinicians are being presented with models that failed to encompass the range of phenomena with which they must contend in treating DID. Some exclusions are remarkably ironic. The study of hypnotic phenomena is often marginalised or omitted from the study of a patient population characterised by high hypnotisability, a population noted earlier to respond well to treatments that embrace the use of hypnosis! Since hypnotisability is largely driven by genetic endowment (Raz, Fan, & Posner, 2006), it will be difficult to attempt exploration of the biological underpinnings of DID unless this startling omission is redressed.

A second logical conclusion to be drawn is that schools of therapy which omit attention to core dissociative phenomena, no matter how glittering their promises, brochures, websites and endorsements, are incomplete, and that if optimal results are sought, their use must be augmented with contributions from other schools of thought, often schools of thought they purport to surpass or replace.

A third conclusion is that politics and fashion intrude into what passes for objective scholarship. Negative uproar foments motivated scepticism while the buzz-words *du jour* elicit confirmatory bias, independent of the demonstration of their worth.

A fourth and overarching conclusion is that all but two of those twenty-two models have been extended toward DID from foundations in other areas of clinical experience, theoretical orientations, and schools of treatment. It might be helpful to understand them as instances of intellectual imperialism and colonialism which never accorded sufficient value to the ideas and phenomena indigenous to territories to which they lay claim, DID and/or dissociation. Small wonder that they arrive at partial and incomplete conceptualisations and understandings of the intellectual and clinical territory they attempted to claim. Brenner (2001, 2004) builds multiple bridges toward DID from various models and toward various models from DID, managing to encompass the vast majority of relevant considerations. Braun's BASK model (Braun, 1988a, 1988b) was generated from the phenomena of DID. Fine's (1991, 1993) approaches are DID-derived. Kluft's (2013a) conceptualisations reflect a bringing together of interventions found to be useful, and is therapy-derived.

Paradigms and secondary loss

Kuhn (1996) observed that science tends to advance by jumps rather than via the systematic building of new knowledge upon prior foundational information. Such jumps, or "paradigm shifts" (ibid., 1996), occur when one model of understanding supplants another. The adherents of the new paradigm see the world and even the same facts and phenomena from a different perspective than that embraced by the adherents of other paradigms. What is "scientific" in one paradigm may be dismissed as "unscientific" in another. Therefore, notwithstanding what may be gained or newly illuminated by a new paradigm, its ascendency may lead to a secondary loss, the disregard of legitimate data and understanding acquired under the aegis of a previous paradigm now being devalued (Kluft, 2013b; Laor, 1985).

Two otherwise outstanding recent contributions demonstrate these phenomena. The authors of *The Haunted Self* (Van der Hart, Nijenhuis, & Steele, 2006), the foundational text of structural dissociation theory, are unquestionably skilled clinicians who know hypnosis well. However, in elaborating their model, hypnosis is mentioned only once, in a list. The author of *Intensive Psychotherapy for Persistent Dissociative Processes: The Fear of Feeling Real* (Chefetz, 2014), a relational perspective on the treatment of dissociative processes, becomes so immersed in his exploration of that particular model which he overlooks discussing the goals of dissociative disorder treatment and exploring the fate of the alters or the concepts of integration and resolution, and stumbles in commenting about hypnosis. The privileging of the relational model effectually omits what does not nest well within it.

The flight from hypnosis

The flight from hypnosis in the contemporary study and treatment of DID has been dramatic and irrational. DID patients have strong hypnotic talent. When assessed with standard instruments, they prove to be the most highly hypnotisable cohort of psychiatric patients (Frischholz, Lipman, Braun, & Sachs, 1992). Hypnotisability as a talent is driven largely by genetic factors (Raz, Fan, & Posner, 2006). The majority of reported successful treatments have been knowingly facilitated by hypnosis. Given that hypnotisability resides in the patient, patients' hypnotic talents may become manifest in any therapy whether or not therapists attempt to mobilise them.

I have modified Spiegel and Spiegel's (2004) definition of hypnosis to clarify its importance for this chapter: Hypnosis is a state of alert concentrated attention such that while certain objects of attention receive the vast majority of the attention, the rest of the stimuli the world has to offer and the remainder of one's mental contents do not receive much attention. It involves elements of absorption (the capacity to give something one's largely undivided and rapt attention), dissociation (the capacity to disconnect the links that usually bind some mental processes or materials to others), and suggestibility.

It follows that hypnotic phenomena may occur in subjects or patients as a result of a type of suggestion made by the hypnotist, called an induction (heterohypnosis); by subjects or patients inducing these phenomena themselves (self-hypnosis or auto-hypnosis); or by subjects or patients experiencing them without an attempt being made to do so in response to inner or external stimuli (spontaneous trance). Therapists control neither self-hypnosis nor spontaneous hypnosis except in their theories and/or imaginations. Assertions that a therapist or experimenter neither utilised nor encountered hypnosis in work with a DID individual are simply inaccurate.

Many who argue against the use of hypnosis and insist they avoid its use make the conceptual error of confusing performing a ritual of induction with the core of what constitutes hypnosis. Since neither self-hypnosis nor spontaneous trance requires a therapist's formal induction, this argument is not compelling.

Misunderstanding hypnosis may deprive patients of the optimal benefit of certain hypnotic interventions associated with successful treatment. Further, believing that hypnosis occurs only after formal inductions may cause the believer to not appreciate that anything said to a DID patient may be received by a person in an unrecognised eyes-open waking trance, and may carry the power and impact of a hypnotic or posthypnotic suggestion. Unwanted responses to unwitting suggestions by those left in a residual trance state after inadequate dehypnosis are well-documented phenomena (e.g., Gruzelier, 2000; Kluft, 2012a, 2012b, 2013b; MacHovec, 1986).

Failure to attend to certain characteristics of the highly hypnotisable individual may contribute to both misdiagnoses and unwanted complications in therapy. High hypnotisables may develop strong transference responses rapidly, access powerful emotions and primary process materials more readily, may develop imagery as vivid as actual reality, and experience what they envision as if it were actually being relived.

The individual in trance is likely to focus intensely upon some aspects of what is being experienced while attention to other aspects fades away. Critical judgement and observational capacities are compromised by the failure to take all rather than some information into account, leading to a reduction in the patient's GRO, or generalised reality orientation (Shor, 1959). The GRO is the background of awareness, the frame of reference, or the context in which we interpret our thoughts, feelings, perceptions, and experience. It is the foundation of rational thought, of secondary process. One illustration of the consequences of its diminution in hypnosis is the problem of trance logic (Orne, 1965), the capacity to entertain two incompatible perceptions without being aware of or troubled by their incompatibility, a cognitive failure that can generate significant difficulties. This capacity for trance logic is at the basis of the DID patient's ability to accept being different people, being different ages, being in different places simultaneously, and entertaining similar simultaneous incompatible perceptions of and attitudes toward others.

Many crises in treatment and endless rumination about the problems posed by so-called psychotic personalities are directly related to clinicians' failures to take hypnosis and the characteristics of the highly hypnotisable patient into account. On dozens of occasions I have used hypnosis to halt, explore, and resolve "psychotic regressions" in DID patients presented to me for consultation. The recent work of Vedat Şar and his colleagues (Akyüz, Dogân, Şar, Yargic, & Tutkun, 1999) should remind us that episodes of "hysterical psychosis" are common in DID patients. Şar's group discovered the existence of DID in Turkey by studying instances of "hysterical psychosis", a common diagnosis in Istanbul psychiatric emergency services.

The unfamiliarity of many clinicians and scholars with hypnosis, the alleged difficulty in incorporating hypnosis into experimental designs, and the political uproar which has surrounded hypnosis in the context of the false memory controversies have rendered the study of hypnosis in the dissociative disorders difficult to fund and/or to pursue. Many distanced themselves from hypnosis and matters often deemed related to hypnosis, such as accessing and working directly with alters, abreaction, and facilitating integration. With little or no data, but with profound fear of litigation and chastened by the caustic disapproval of many vocal and well-positioned authorities world-wide, the dissociative disorders field largely abandoned approaches which were effecting rather successful outcomes as noted above, had demonstrated the capacity to render the treatment of DID more safe and contained, and were less likely to be fraught with crises and emergencies (Fine, 1991; Kluft, 1983).

The adroit use of hypnosis remains the most effective approach to controlling and containing abreactions, to restabilising unsettled alter systems, to intervening in crises of many varieties, and to reorienting, restabilising, and realerting a dissociative patient after painful and/or emotionally intense therapeutic work (Kluft, 2013b).

The flight from integration

Antoine Despine had accomplished the successful integration of DID patients prior to 1840 (Ellenberger, 1970; Fine, 1988; McKeown & Fine, 2008). Anecdotal accounts (Schreiber, 1974; Sizemore, & Pitillo, 1977) and reports of series of integrated patients (Kluft, 1984a, 1986) have long been in the literature. Yet many modern authorities appear to avoid the subject of integration, or speak of it dismissively. At one recent scientific meeting a plenary speaker remarked that integration was no longer a serious subject of discussion. Some modern texts actually fail to address it.

Integration was a major concern in the early modern era of the study of DID. Since then, however, the application to DID of models derived from areas remote from DID have often overlooked or dismissed matters which are central to DID, especially the phenomena of alters and the process of integration. Commenting on the work of the expert clinicians in her research series, who used a variety of therapeutic approaches, Brand (2013) reported a rate of integration in series that was significantly lower than the rate of integration reported in those treated by Coons' neophytes or by Kluft. This is a rather thought-provoking observation! While the differences may reside in the characteristics of the patient populations, we must consider as well whether differences in treatment approaches and treatment goals played a significant role in eventual therapeutic outcomes. Hypnosis and hypnotic techniques play many useful roles in accessing alters and promoting their integration. When their use is drastically reduced, small wonder that integration is less discussed, and less frequently achieved.

In the past it was assumed that with extensive experience might come a degree of knowledge and wisdom. Now, such contributions are often dismissed a priori as anecdotal, unconfirmed by external observers and undocumented by objective measures. Those taking such dismissive stances almost always are advocates of an alternative model of research or practice, which makes it reasonable to wonder whether their pronouncements are tainted by confirmatory bias and/or motivated scepticism.

Here is what I have observed: while integration is possible in many circumstances, it should not be pursued to the detriment of other concerns. Beginning in the early 1970s, I enjoyed a unique opportunity to study, see in consultation, treat and follow up an increasingly large cohort of DID patients (Kluft, 1982, 1984a, 1985, 1986, 1993, unpublished data). Here I discuss only patients whom I treated as their primary therapist in long-term psychotherapy.

Eighty-nine per cent of the individual psychotherapy patients from my long-term follow-up series achieved stable total integration by criteria utilised in my research studies (Kluft, 1984a). Even though I continue to grow in experience and skill, I will be unable to replicate such results with the cohorts of patients referred to me in recent years. My current patients are usually veterans of failed DID treatments, sophisticated and opinionated about aspects of their treatment. Most are quite geographically mobile due to the nature of modern career trajectories. Few can continue an intense treatment without running afoul of logistic and financial constraints, which were less dominant considerations several decades ago.

I am preparing a twenty- to thirty-year follow-up study comparing eighteen DID patients who achieved and sustained a complete integration for twenty years or more, eight treatment failures, and five persons still struggling in treatment. It is clear that integration can be achieved and maintained by many DID patients. Further, the integrated patients, after initial periods of readjustment, demonstrated sustained success in their lives.

That said, it remains destructive to insist upon pursuing integration as the ideal outcome or "holy grail" of all DID treatments. Many patients are not good candidates for definitive treatment by virtue of the nature of their difficulties or logistic constraints. They require either 1) supportive treatment directed primarily toward symptom amelioration, safety, improved functioning, and an enhanced quality of life, or 2) a slow and gradual treatment that makes optimal use of what opportunities are presented to process trauma and pursue integration. Such efforts are interim rather than final steps for those en route to a more definitive treatment, but they leave patients better situated to live comfortably. It is not generally helpful to inform a suffering patient, directly or indirectly, that he or she is not a candidate for a theoretically optimal outcome unless the patient's pressures and efforts to proceed in that manner (regardless of its inadvisability) are causing difficulties. The perfect can become the enemy of the good.

However, on the basis of the sustained superior adjustment of those patients who have achieved and sustained complete integration, I would suggest that when a therapy does not include the option of working toward integration, it implicitly restricts the scope of what may be achieved on that patient's behalf, and may preclude the patient's attaining the enhanced quality of life which achieving integration may bring. Clinical experience suggests that therapist and patient do best by ameliorating the patient's function and inner state of mind and seeing where that process takes the treatment.

A few years ago several other colleagues and I sat on a panel. A person in the audience asked, "Can DID really be integrated? Can it really be cured?" One panelist took the microphone and remarked, "Sometimes, but it can be a long and difficult process." A second agreed, observing that "the temptations DID patients face to quit or to compromise can be very, very strong". I thought it best not to speak. The two commentators were former DID patients of mine, now long integrated and making meaningful contributions to the field.

It is foolish to start the treatment of a DID patient either focusing on integration or taking a dismissive stance toward that possibility. If integration is idealised to the patient, those for whom it may not be possible will suffer a sense of inadequacy and an ongoing series of narcissistic wounds and humiliations, and/or hurt and rage about not being able to receive the optimal care that might bring about an optimal outcome. When patients ask about integration I am more attuned to respond to the "First, do no harm" aspects of the situation than toward making cognitive/psychoeducational responses. I must choose my words carefully, because almost anything I say may be turned to the purpose of critical self-attack. I inform my patients, "My crystal ball is still at the shop and the damn technicians can't seem to fix it. So," I continue, "we'll have to wait and see what develops and what course of treatment seems wisest as we both do our best on your behalf." With some exceptions, I do not push patients toward integration. Apart from being insistent on matters of safety, I reserve my exhortations for effecting the best possible therapeutic alliance. One common exception relates to the patient's age. If a therapist has the opportunity to help a child or younger patient build a firm foundation for entering adult life from an integrated stance, knowing what we know about the adult lives of DID patients, I doubt it is ethical to promote incomplete therapeutic goals.

Many patients who begin treatment determined to integrate ultimately decide that they are unwilling to do some of the work that seems necessary to make integration possible. As one patient said to me recently, "If I go there, I lose whatever I have left of my family. I'll come back after my father has passed away." Conversely, I have had many patients who spent years railing against integration suddenly realise that more and more of their alters have integrated or faded or come closer together without giving any signs that they were doing so.

The natural state of the well-functioning mind is not a solid impenetrable monolithic mental apparatus with an adamantine and unified self. I think of it as a situation in which the patient's mental functions are flying in a tight and functional formation, achieving effective executive functioning in a manner that generates sufficient mastery and resilience for life to be lived relatively seamlessly and without discontinuities. The ego states of an integrated DID patient are not recapitulations of former alters, remaining invested in autonomy and a sense of being separate. They play their parts in a well-orchestrated manner that does not generate unwanted disruptive misadventures.

It has been my experience that such an outcome is best achieved by complete integration in the sense of the cessation of dysfunctional dividedness. In contrast, resolutions (better functioning, stable adaptations with or without partial integration) have proven more prone to decompensation and regression under stress. A mind accustoming itself to resolution is not practicing and working to perfect the smoother more confluent manner of function seen with integration. When alters' autonomous identities and senses of self are retained, under stress the threshold for a return to dysfunctional dividedness is lowered. This impression, while based on a considerable body of experience, cannot be represented as a proven clinical fact.

Addressing alters

At the beginning of the modern era of the treatment of DID, ingenuity in accessing alters and bringing them into the therapeutic dialogue was a skill to be admired. Hypnosis was helpful in facilitating such access and promoting integration. However, voices from outside the field fretted that efforts to access other alters might in fact create them. Cautions were offered, advising against trying to contact alters not in evidence. Those who worked with DID were often accused, rather contemptuously, of creating and/or worsening a condition they could enrich themselves by treating in intense and often prolonged sessions.

Martin Orne (Orne, Dinges, & Orne, 1984) claimed to have frustrated the efforts of notorious serial killer the "Hillside Strangler" to malinger, feigning DID. His work was lionised in the press and literature, and celebrated in a documentary film allegedly produced by a relative of one of Orne's associates (Barnes, 1984). Orne's encouraging the suspect to produce another alter in response to his suggestions that an alter of a particular type should be present was perceived as a brilliant master-stoke.

The battles over this case generated more heat than light. Those who took positions "stuck to their guns," with the exception of John Watkins, who was able to reflect objectively and even-handedly. Shortly thereafter a paper (Kluft, 1987a) demonstrated that the four assumptions and tests Orne had used to argue that the Hillside Strangler was a malingerer were not grounded in indisputable fact. Further, the type of personality Orne believed had been created in response to his suggestions, a child alter, is an almost universal finding in legitimate cases of DID. Therefore Orne's demonstration, however dramatic, was virtually meaningless as a proof of malingering (Kluft, 1987c). Orne never published a reply or rebuttal to this article.

Yet in the context of the false memory controversy, accusations of the iatrogenesis of false memories went hand in hand with accusations of the iatrogenesis of DID. Approaches to the treatment of DID which circumvented dealing directly with alters and eliciting autobiographical information were advocated and promoted. Further, at that very point in time papers linking dissociation with problematic attachment issues were published (Barach, 1991; Liotti, 1992).

By 1994/5 many authorities were favouring reconceptualising DID as a condition based primarily on disorganised or type D attachment. They made statements in workshops and articles which indicated that they favoured using circumlocutions which avoided accessing or working directly with alters, and some claimed that trauma was not an essential aspect of the etiology of DID. Some colleagues continue to express these perspectives.

Limitations of space preclude an exhaustive review of these matters, but it is possible to make sense of this morass, and offer a reasonable synthesis to the contemporary clinician.

First, no evidence documented beyond the level of vehement opinion has been presented to demonstrate that DID can be created in an otherwise normal individual by the types of interventions used in studies purporting to demonstrate the creation of iatrogenic DID. Such studies have yet to produce anything resembling the naturalistic condition.

However, if an authority begins with the assumption that the condition does not exist as a naturalistically occurring phenomenon, and demonstrates that his subjects can be induced to enact DID-like behaviours, that authority may deem it proper within his paradigm to state that the creation of DID has been demonstrated.

Long ago, as a young actor on stage, I was coached and directed to behave and speak like Cary Grant, who had played the same role in a motion picture. If we assume there was no such person as Cary Grant, I might have been put forward as a genuine Cary Grant. But there was a real Cary Grant, and let me assure you that while I was a reasonably competent actor, not a single young woman attending the play's performances mistook me for a genuine Hollywood matinee idol and behaved accordingly.

Second, it is clear that given established DID, suggestions both direct and indirect, social pressures, and other forms of stress and influence can lead to the creation of alters which are directly attributable to those inputs.

DID patients often will continue to create alters to handle life's intercurrent stressors, and the perceived trauma of therapy itself. It is not difficult to understand that a coping strategy which has been in place and reasonably successful for decades might come in to play during treatment. Patients of mine have developed alters to "do the therapy" or handle a hospital stay while the others remain untouched. Alters based on me have been created to preclude being alone between sessions. Some have been created expressly to divert me in one way or another.

Over the years, many colleagues have believed that certain types of personalities are inevitably present in DID. They have explored their patients vigorously for such alters, and frequently found them. Their followers believed that finding the predicted types of parts confirmed their theories about what causes or what is the true nature of DID. Those who did not share their beliefs considered such alters iatrogenic artifacts.

Problematic situations may occur when the particular type of alter which is suggested entails a risk of unwanted consequences. I will illustrate this with three examples well known to me:

1) A psychotherapist came to believe quite strongly that DID was almost always the consequence of satanic ritual abuse in childhood and explored every patient for evidence of "satanic" alters, both with and without the induction of formal trance. Soon many of her patients reported being flooded with horrible memories of terrible experiences, the reality of which could not be assessed. The alters, based on her understanding of satanic cults, involved the patient in disgusting and unnecessarily destructive behaviours. One of her patients, whom I saw in consultation, had destroyed her pet cats in the course of a bizarre ritual she devised.

2) Many therapists either unaware of the nuances of human development or under the sway of religious or philosophical beliefs unrelated to clinical realities became convinced, and convinced others, that each person has a central core, a basic unitary identity. In DID, they argued, it was important to identify the central core personality, which was the essence of the DID patient, the "real person". This permitted them and their adherents a degree of comfort in their work, but was never demonstrated to be either accurate or helpful to their patients. In fact, it imposed upon their therapeutic endeavours and their patients an unproven belief system inconsistent with what is known about the development of human identity.

3) A colleague known to be a particularly kind and good individual became convinced that there was an entity in each DID patient who was good, kind, and honourable, an entity that could be counted upon to be wise, loving, and helpful. The more I learned about this notion, the more it became clear to me that my colleague was projecting aspects of herself into her patients and seeing what she wanted to see. However, since identification with this sort of person was often creating hope in her patients, who never could have believed that they shared the good qualities of their beloved therapist in any way, and promoted their self esteem, the discovery/iatrogenic creation of such entities did not appear to be causing any problems at first glance. However, I do wonder whether such an approach might block the expression and the treatment of negative elements in the transference as treatment proceeds.

From a common sense perspective, most impasses in the treatment of DID prove related to the presence of alters, either known or previously unidentified, which do not or will not enter the treatment. One of the big risks in DID treatment involves the sudden intrusion into the ongoing work of previously undiscovered alters/traumatic memories. That is why many expert therapists make efforts to map and explore the alter system (Fine, 1991, 1993; Kluft, 2000, 2013b).

Furthermore, it is well known that alters feeling neglected or bypassed may experience painful rejection and narcissistic injuries, even if they have caused their dilemmas by hiding away or declining to participate, and frequently interrupt or sabotage the therapy. Is it preposterous to wonder whether an entity with a sense of self, who comes to feel unrecognised or uncared about, might feel hurt by such rejection and cause unwanted difficulties? These matters are addressed at length in Kluft (2006).

At this point in the history of the treatment of DID, therapists should become aware of the many benefits to treatment which are associated with accessing and working directly with the alters, and strongly consider engaging with them rather than finding ways to side-step such involvements. However, their efforts should be tempered by an awareness that since many naturalistic alters have been formed in response to pressures and suggestions from powerful others, their efforts should be gentle and circumspect to minimise such outcomes.

The unfortunate marginalisation of self-psychology in the treatment of the dissociative disorders

My own psychodynamic work with DID relies heavily on several ideas developed by Heinz Kohut (1971, 1977; Kohut & Wolf, 1978; also see Lessem, 2005), the founder of self-psychology. Kohut's concept of self as a centre of initiative and experience comes closer to grasping the essence of alters as active mental elements than terms like personality or identity, which denote more stable and comprehensive patterns of adaptation. Self captures more fully the DID patient's diverse ways of being. It is the qualities of self-hood that distinguish the quintessence of alters from the baseline definition of ego states (Kluft, 1988, 1991; Watkins & Watkins, 1997). Self-psychology anticipated relationalists' appreciation of the simultaneous existence and operation of multiple selves, a circumstance that Freud could not conceive as possible (Freud, 1912g).

Basic Kohutian concepts abound, unrecognised, in dissociative disorders treatment. The impact of parental failure upon a child's subsequent safety and stability is appreciated, as is the need for such failures to be repaired by transmuting internalisation. The importance of reflecting back to patients an empathic understanding of their feelings, of providing a model of caring, integrity, and strength which can be idealised and with which identification can occur, and the usefulness of interpretations which provide insight into experience in the moment as well as to a link to the past is well understood. It is accepted as common wisdom that incessant unfolding of incident after incident in which perceived empathic failures are followed by the restitution of empathic attunement may dominate therapeutic discourse in the treatment of DID. Empathic interventions often permit the patient to be brought back from the brink of fragmentation to stability.

That notwithstanding, with the exception of the work of Ullman and Brothers (1988) and a few others, Kohut's ideas have been marginalised, bypassed, or coopted without due credit. Why? First, Kohut's language is rather difficult and his arguments are burdened by the psychoanalytic politics of his era. Second, Kohut's rise to prominence was rapidly followed and eclipsed by the emergence of the relational school of psychoanalysis, which addressed many shared concerns in a more accessible manner. Third, the dissociative disorders field became infatuated with attachment theory and intrigued by relational theory in the 1990s. Fourth, for many younger therapists trained in the cognitive-behavioural tradition, their notion of development and dynamics begins and ends with attachment theory. Fifth, models of trauma treatment with little interest in the intrapsychic and psychodynamic have proliferated.

This is one more instance in which the emergence of new paradigms has pushed aside contributions of considerable worth. Space restrictions preclude my offering more than a few brief observations.

Kohut appreciated that children generally have two parents. He discussed the role of the father in contributing to the growth of the child, both in normal circumstances and in the face of maternal failings. It would be fair to say that the preferred paradigms and models that dominate many discourses in the trauma field have been grotesquely neglectful of the importance of the father in human development, except when the father is portrayed as absent or as a perpetrator. One consequence of this is the implicit if not explicit devaluing of males in the treatment of traumatised female patients by omission of attention to what good fathers/males have to offer. It is not an accident that many traumatised women who were treated badly, betrayed, and neglected by significant women in their lives are nonetheless strongly opposed to working with male therapists. The recent literature has not been kind, objective, or rational in its discussions of the male of the species.

Kohut understood that notwithstanding the importance of empathic attunement and repairing the hurt occasioned by countertransference errors (wonderfully explicated by Dalenberg, 2000), insight was essential to anchor the impact of empathic interaction and to facilitate the transmuting internalisations that brought new strength and structure to the mind. While his insights on empathy were considered among his most important contributions, I am most impressed by his emphasis upon the synthesis of empathy and insight. Kohut described leading edge interpretations, addressing the empathic issues, and trailing edge interpretations, underscoring intellectual insight and dynamics. This balance of empathy and insight was carried forward into the work of some but not all relationalists. Further, Kohut's conceptualisations of aggression and libido are very helpful in work with the traumatised. While much is made of angry and abusive personalities, and those who attribute borderline features to DID patients may bring Kernberg's (1975) theories about aggression in that condition to their work with DID, Kohut regarded such strong emotions in raw form as the deterioration products of failures in relatedness. I find this perspective very helpful in avoiding a blaming/critical attitude toward difficult alters in my DID patients. Finally, I find Kohut's concept of the self-state dream a useful concept to bear in mind when working with DID. Some very complex dreams prove to be a perceptive overview of the patient's sense of herself and her alter system.

Lessem's (2005) recent book is clear and thoughtful. It has made Kohut's concepts and approaches much more accessible to mental health professionals. Self-psychologist Michael Franz Basch (1980) and affect theorist Donald Nathanson (1992) often discussed the interplay of self-psychology and shame theory. Sadly, their dialogues were private conversations, but in our conversations over the years, Nathanson shared many insights into the bridges they built in during their dialogues. In my own practice, I sense the strong connection of self-psychology and the treatment of shame responses.

Shame

When my good friend Donald Nathanson asked me to provide a review of his upcoming book, *Shame and Pride* (1992), I read it over a weekend and walked into my office on Monday a much-improved clinician. It is only in the last few years that the importance of shame in understanding and treating the traumatised has finally moved into the mainstream of traumatology. Nathanson's work, especially his delineation of the "compass of shame", permits a far more sensitive and nuanced approach to much of what is most demoralising to the DID patient. Often it is shame, the most painful and socially isolating affect, that drives DID patients to initiate and maintain dissociative defences, to work to maintain a disconnect between and among alters, and to withhold material which is within their awareness, but they decline to share lest their shame be known to others. Often what DID patients are most reluctant to share is what they were forced to do to others, what they chose to do rather than to face some horrible mistreatment, and what they did after childhood, retrospectively confronting themselves with accusations that they now were old enough to defy or escape their abusers. My work with the affect of shame and the related affects of disgust and dissmell early in treatment paves the way for revelations without intrusive inquiries, and less torment during the processing of traumatic experiences. Since shame involves the severing of connections and a profoundly depreciated view of the self, shame work is always an attack, usually indirect, against dissociative defences, and against the DID patient's sense (either globally or in a few alters) that she is completely disgusting and unlovable.

Not surprisingly, shame work follows naturally from an appreciation of the emotional burden borne by the traumatised individual, and both psychoeducational and dynamic work with shame meshes quite well with the interventional patterns of self-psychology and dissociative disorders treatment (Kluft, 2007).

Completing the circle

Many readers have already surmised that in pointing out some conceptual problems in the dissociative disorders field, and in recommending the inclusion of what is often overlooked, omitted, and de-emphasised, I have backed into presenting my own empirically derived approach to the psychotherapy of DID.

I continue to use psychodynamic psychotherapy and hypnosis, augmented but not supplanted by the additional modalities I am always learning. I utilise my patients' hypnotic potential, mindful of both appropriate cautions and the sensitivities of the highly hypnotisable patient. Although hypnotisability is an attribute of the patient, my use of overt hypnotic interventions with any given patient depends on the history and dynamics of that patient, and the interpersonal process that develops between us. Sometimes heterohypnotic interventions are declined or contraindicated.

In my work, formal hypnosis serves mostly to access and work with alters, to manage the processing of trauma, to effect stabilisation, to extricate patients from trance, and to facilitate integration. I map the system, usually without hypnosis, utilising the approach of Fine (1991, 1993), sometimes with modifications (Kluft, 2013b). I use shame reduction to pave the way for the sharing of painful material and trauma processing. Shame reduction works best if shame-related withdrawal and isolation is countered by welcoming the humiliated person or alter very directly (one of the twenty rationales offered elsewhere (Kluft, 2006) for working directly with alters). Such outreaches effectively strengthen the therapeutic alliance with those previously less engaged alters.

With the patient as a whole and/or an alter I employ Kohutian approaches to empathy and interpretation to facilitate structure building. Such efforts help strengthen the patient before therapy proceeds to process trauma, and continue side by side with trauma work once that has begun. Using hypnotic and other techniques, most alters are shielded from the impact of the processing of trauma until an appropriate time, minimising the intrusion of trauma work into the remainder of the patient's life (Fine, 1991, 1993; Kluft, 1982, 2013b). Patients who have become confident that trauma processing can be contained and function safeguarded, or at least somewhat protected, are less hesitant to proceed. The process of integration that follows trauma work is described elsewhere (Kluft, 1993).

Conclusion

Far from being a pessimist or cynic about the psychotherapy of the dissociative disorders, I am profoundly optimistic about what can be achieved on behalf of this group of patients if therapists diligently pursue clarity of understanding and decline to succumb to the often seductive allure of models and practices that all too often promise more than they can deliver, and distract them from mastering and practicing other potentially helpful approaches. No single model has proven adequate to embrace and explicate the dissociative disorders and their treatment. That is why I am constantly learning new approaches. Carrying through a treatment which follows the path of a particular model with confidence and an aesthetic sense that the right thing has been done risks becoming an exercise in hermeneutics which succeeds more in illustrating the alleged elegance of the model than in providing optimally effective care to the patient (see Goldberg, 2014). In the absence of perfect models and practices, we must do our best to discern what works best in a given situation, and to proceed to apply what seems to work best, rather than exhort ourselves to abide by what looks best in the light of a particular paradigm, what is promoted most by one authority or another, or what makes us feel best or most comfortable as we make use of it. We must be there for the patient. Unless we are dealing with a patient in danger of doing imminent harm to another, privileging third parties over the primacy of patient care, whether those third parties are schools of thought, colleagues, authorities, companies, agencies, or institutions is always a countertransference enactment (Hirsch, 2008), and is best avoided.

References

Akyüz, G., Dogån, O., Şar, V., Yargic, L., & Tutkun, H. (1999). Frequency of dissociative identity disorder in the general population in Turkey. *Comprehensive Psychiatry*, 40: 151–159.

Barach, P. (1991). Multiple personality as an attachment disorder. *Dissociation*, 4: 117–123.

Barnes, M. (1984). *The Mind of a Murderer* (documentary videotape). Washington, DC: Public Broadcasting Service.

Basch, M. F. (1980). *Doing Psychotherapy*. New York: Basic.

Brand, B. (2013). *The Findings and Treatment Implications of the Treatment of Patients with Dissociative Disorders (TOP DD) Study*. Presented at Reflections on clinical practice and clinical research in traumatic stress, Sheppard Pratt Hospital, Baltimore, MD, 27 April.

Braun, B. G. (1988a). The BASK model of dissociation: Part I. *Dissociation*, 1(1): 4–23.

Braun, B. G. (1988b). The BASK model of dissociation: Part II. Treatment. *Dissociation*, 1(2): 16–23.

Brenner, I. (2001). *Dissociation of Trauma: Theory, Phenomenology, and Technique.* Madison, CT: International Universities.

Brenner, I. (2004). *Psychic Trauma: Dynamics, Symptoms, and Treatment.* Lanham, MD: Aronson.

Chefetz, R. (2014). *Intensive Psychotherapy for Persistent Dissociative Processes: The Fear of Feeling Real.* New York: Norton.

Coons, P. (1986). Treatment progress in 20 patients with multiple personality disorder. *Journal of Nervous and Mental Disease, 174:* 715–720.

Dalenberg, C. (2000). *Countertransference and the Treatment of Trauma.* Washington, DC: APA.

Dijksterhuis, A., Bos, M, Nordgren, L., & van Baaren, L. (2006). On making the right choice: the deliberation-without-attention-effect. *Science, 311:* 1005–1007.

Ellenberger, H. (1970). *The Discovery of the Unconscious.* New York: Basic.

Fine, C. G. (1988). The work of Antoine Despine: the first scientific report on the diagnosis and treatment of multiple personality disorder. *American Journal of Clinical Hypnosis, 31:* 33–39.

Fine, C. G. (1991). Treatment stabilization and crisis prevention: pacing the therapy of multiple personality disorder patients. *Psychiatric Clinics of North America, 14:* 661–675.

Fine, C. G. (1993). A tactical integrationalist perspective on the treatment of multiple personality disorder. In: R. P. Kluft & C. G. Fine (Eds.), *Clinical Perspectives on Multiple Personality Disorder* (pp. 135–153). Washington, DC: APA.

Freud, S. (1912g). A Note on the Unconscious in Psycho-Analysis. *S. E., 12:* 257. London: Hogarth.

Frischholz, E., Lipman, L., Braun, B., & Sachs, R. (1992). Psychopathology, hypnotizability, and dissociation. *American Journal of Psychiatry, 149:* 1521–1525.

Goldberg, A. (2014). On understanding understanding: how we understand the meaning of the word "understanding". *Journal of the American Psychoanalytic Association, 62:* 677–691.

Gruzelier, J. (2000). Unwanted effects of hypnosis: a review of the evidence and its implications. *Contemporary Hypnosis, 17:* 163–193.

Hirsch, I. (2008). *Coasting in the Countertransference: Conflicts of Self Interest between Analyst and Patient.* New York: Routledge.

International Society for the Study of Trauma and Dissociation. (2011). Guidelines for treating dissociative identity disorder in adults (3rd revision). *Journal of Trauma & Dissociation, 12:* 115–187.

Kernberg, O. (1975). *Borderline Conditions and Pathological Narcissism.* Lanham, MD: Aronson.

Kluft, R. P. (1982). Varieties of hypnotic interventions in the treatment of multiple personality. *American Journal of Clinical Hypnosis, 24:* 230–240.

Kluft, R. P. (1983). Hypnotherapeutic crisis intervention in multiple personality. *American Journal of Clinical Hypnosis, 26*: 73–83.

Kluft, R. P. (1984a). Treatment of multiple personality. *Psychiatric Clinics of North America, 7*: 9–29.

Kluft, R. P. (1984b). An introduction to multiple personality. *Psychiatric Annals, 14*: 19–24.

Kluft, R. P. (l985). The natural history of multiple personality disorder. In: R. P. Kluft (Ed.), *Childhood Antecedents of Multiple Personality* (pp. 197–238). Washington, DC: APA.

Kluft, R. P. (1986). Personality unification in multiple personality disorder. In: B. G. Braun (Ed.), *Treatment of Multiple Personality Disorder* (pp. 29–60). Washington, DC: APA.

Kluft, R. P. (1987a). The simulation and dissimulation of multiple personality disorder. *American Journal of Clinical Hypnosis, 30*: 104–118.

Kluft, R. P. (1987b). First-rank symptoms as a diagnostic clue to multiple personality disorder. *American Journal of Psychiatry, 144*: 293–298.

Kluft, R. P. (1987c). The simulation and dissimulation of multiple personality disorder. *American Journal of Psychiatry, 30*: 104–118.

Kluft, R. P. (1988). The phenomenology and treatment of extremely complex multiple personality disorder. *Dissociation, 1*(4): 47–58.

Kluft, R. P. (1991). Multiple personality disorder. In: A. Tasman & S. Goldfinger (Eds.), *Annual Review of Psychiatry (Volume 10)* (pp. 161–188). Washington, DC: APA.

Kluft, R. P. (1993). Treatment of dissociative disorder patients: an overview of discoveries, successes, and failures. *Dissociation, 6*: 87–101.

Kluft, R. P. (1994). Dissociation or dissociations? Multiple personality disorder or multiple personality disorders? *Dissociation, 7*: 1.

Kluft, R. P. (1995). The confirmation and discontinuation of memories of abuse in dissociative identity disorder patients: a naturalistic clinical study. *Dissociation, 8*: 253–258.

Kluft, R. P. (1998). Reflections on the traumatic memories of dissociative identity disorder patients. In: S. Lynn & K. McConkey (Eds.), *Truth in Memory* (pp. 304–322). New York: Guilford.

Kluft, R. P. (2000). The psychoanalytic psychotherapy of dissociative identity disorder in the context of trauma therapy. *Psychoanalytic Inquiry, 20*: 259–286.

Kluft, R. P. (2006). Dealing with alters: a pragmatic clinical perspective. *Psychiatric Clinics of North America, 29*: 291–304.

Kluft, R. P. (2007). Applications of innate affect theory to the understanding and treatment of dissociative identity disorder. In: E. Vermetten, M. Dorahy, & D. Spiegel (Eds.), *Traumatic Dissociation: Neurobiology and Treatment* (pp. 301–316). Washington, DC: APA.

Kluft, R. P. (2009). A clinician's understanding of dissociation: fragments of an acquaintance. In: P. Dell & J. O'Neill (Eds.), *Dissociation and the Dissociative Disorders: DSM-V and Beyond* (pp. 599–623). New York: Taylor & Francis.

Kluft, R. P. (2012a). Hypnosis in the treatment of dissociative identity disorder and allied states: an overview and case study. *South African Journal of Psychology, 42*: 146–155.

Kluft, R. P. (2012b). Issues in the detection of those suffering adverse effects in hypnosis training workshops. *American Journal of Clinical Hypnosis, 54*: 213–232.

Kluft, R. P. (2013a). *"That's the reason they're called lessons," said the Gryphon, "because they lesson from day to day".* Reflections on the Treatment of DID, 1970–2012. Presented at Reflections on clinical practice and clinical research in traumatic stress, Sheppard Pratt Hospital, Baltimore, MD; 27 April.

Kluft, R. P. (2013b). *Shelter from the Storm.* North Charleston, SC: CreateSpace.

Kohut, H. (1971). *The Analysis of the Self.* New York: International Universities.

Kohut, H. (1977). *The Restoration of the Self.* New York: International Universities.

Kohut, H., & Wolf, E. S. (1978). The disorders of the self and their treatment: an outline. *International Journal of Psycho-Analysis. 59*: 413–425.

Kuhn, T. (1996). *The Structure of Scientific Revolution* (3rd edn). Chicago: University of Chicago.

Laor, N. (1985). Prometheus the impostor. *British Medical Journal (Clinical Research Edition), 290*: 681–684.

Lessem, P. (2005). *Self Psychology: An Introduction.* Lanham, MD: Aronson.

Liotti, D. (1992). Disorganized/disoriented attachment in the etiology of the dissociative disorders. *Dissociation, 5*: 196–204.

MacHovec, F. (1986). *Hypnosis Complications: Prevention and Risk Management.* Springfield, IL: Thomas.

McKeown, J. M., & Fine, C. G. (Eds. & Trans.) (2008). *Despine and the Evolution of Psychology: Historical and Medical Perspectives on Dissociative Disorders.* New York: Palgrave MacMillan.

Nathanson, D. (1992). *Shame and Pride.* New York: Norton.

Orne, M. T. (1965). Undesirable effects of hypnosis: their determinants and management. *International Journal of Clinical and Experimental Hypnosis, 13*: 226–237.

Orne, M., Dinges, D., & Orne, E. (1984). On the differential diagnosis of multiple personality in the forensic context. *International Journal of Clinical and Experimental Hypnosis, 32*: 118–169.

Raz, A., Fan, J., & Posner, M. (2006). Neuroimaging and genetic association in attentional and hypnotic processes. *Journal of Physiology*, *99*: 483–491.

Schreiber, F. R. (1974). *Sybil*. New York: Warner.

Shor, R. (1959). Hypnosis and the concept of the generalized reality orientation. *American Journal of Psychotherapy*, *13*: 582–602.

Sizemore, C., & Pitillo, E. (1977). *I'm Eve*. Garden City, NY: Doubleday.

Spiegel, D. (1986). Dissociating damage. *American Journal of Clinical Hypnosis*, *29*: 123–131.

Spiegel, H., & Spiegel, D. (2004). *Trance and Treatment* (2nd edn). Washington, DC: APA.

Ullman, R., & Brothers, D. (1988). *The Shattered Self: A Psychoanalytic Study of Trauma*. New York: Analytic.

Van der Hart, O., Nijenhuis, E., & Steele, E. (2006). *The Haunted Self: Structural Dissociation and the Treatment of Chronic Traumatization*. New York: Norton.

Watkins, J. G., & Watkins, H. H. (1997). *Ego States: Theory and Therapy*. New York: Norton.

EPILOGUE

Amelia van der Merwe

Chaos narratives, which do not constitute a "proper" story, where there is a lack of coherent sequence, a lack of control, are difficult to hear (Frank, 1995). This is often the case in life writing, in stories of survival of trauma. Orange, Atwood, and Stolorow (1997, p. 42) call this "the dread of structureless chaos". They are difficult to hear because they are personally threatening (Frank, 1995). This is because what the listener hears becomes a possibility or a reality in the life of the listener; the listener often has to distance himself from the narrative to make it bearable (ibid., 1995). Frank (ibid., p. 101) reflects on how interviewers directed Holocaust survivors towards alternative narratives which demonstrate "the resilience of the human spirit", failing to bear witness to the real stories the survivors have to tell because of their own fears; their own emotional inadequacies. Interviewers who cannot bear their potential likeness to their traumatised interviewees tend to steer their interviewees away from their chaos narratives towards a restitution narrative of progress, for example, by encouraging them to focus on happy endings, in the case of the Holocaust, towards the liberation, when survivors, unlike their interviewers, did not experience liberation as the great dividing line which ordered and gave meaning to their experience (ibid., 1995). Shapiro (2011, p. 69) calls believing in the inevitability and greater authenticity of these restitution narratives and quest narratives (where you are better off at the end of the story than the beginning), "comic", in reference to the "comic plot" as opposed to the "tragic plot" in literary theory. In fact, for people about whom Frank (1995) writes, with liberation "the real trouble begins: the trouble of remaking a sense of purpose as the world demands" (ibid., p. 107). This calls to mind the horseman in Kluger's (2001) tale, who feared crossing a lake covered by a thin layer of ice; once he made it to the other side, he looked back, and instead of feeling relief or joy, realising what he had survived, he died of fright.

Chaos narratives are always embodied and always somewhat beyond speech (Frank, 1995). Like Frank, one of Scarry's (1985) main points is that pain resists, if not destroys, objectification in language. Scarry argues that pain destroys or negates the contents of consciousness; that it obliterates all psychological content, and so renders the subject silent. This means that the self, which would be expressed and projected through language, disintegrates (ibid.). This is why pain is so often embodied, and in the case of DID, that embodiment may be perplexingly multiplicitous.

In conclusion to this book, I would like to talk briefly about the construction of identity under traumatic circumstances. It is clear from survivors' voices in this book, particularly Annalise, that they so often feel not only guilt and responsibility, but also shame. Foucault's theory of self-surveillance (Foucault, 1977), which is symbolically based on the design of the Panopticon, a circular building with an observation tower in the middle of an open space surrounded by an outer wall, and which beautifully illustrates the power differential which metaphorically plays out so often between those in power and those they oppress, significantly contributes to the construction of identity. In this theory, the outer wall of the Panopticon includes cells (for occupants like prisoners or mental patients for instance; any form of victim). The cells are flooded with light, so inhabitants are easily discernible and visible to an official invisibly positioned in the central tower/office. However, the concrete walls dividing the cells make the occupants invisible to each other. The ever-visible occupant, Foucault (1977) argues, is always "the object of information, never a subject in communication" (ibid., p. 202). He goes on to suggest that,

> He who is subjected to a field of visibility, and who knows it, assumes responsibility for the constraints of power; he makes them

play spontaneously upon himself; he inscribes in himself the power relation in which he simultaneously plays both roles; he becomes the principle of his own subjection. (ibid., pp. 202–203)

By constantly observing the occupants and positioning them in a state of constant visibility, the efficiency of the institution is optimised. Those who are constantly watched, adopt the identity that is thrust upon them by those who observe them, so it guarantees the continued function of power, even when there is no one actually asserting it. It is in this respect that the Panopticon functions routinely, automatically.

What this theory tells us is that we become what our often revered and admired, even loved enemies—our oppressors—who in the case of the dysfunctional or abusive family system are disguised as "caregivers", unconsciously want us to become, in order to maintain the status quo: their position of power, and our position of subservience and dependence. This feeds into a shame-based identity. Shame-based identities often develop in people who have been traumatised by others. How traumatised people often continue to be treated constitutes secondary traumatisation and amplifies their shame, which feeds into perpetrator defined identities.

At this point, I would like to emphasise the theoretical postulations of Fairbairn (1943) to explain the development of perpetrator-defined identities. Feelings of "badness" constitute a common defence among people who have been abused. Abuse survivors identify with and internalise intolerably bad objects and carry the burden of "badness" and shame because it is more tolerable to believe that the self is bad, and so in control, than to accept that the loved perpetrator, whose abuse is random and unpredictable, is bad. According to Fairbairn, internalisation is an attempt to control these bad objects that have wielded power over them in the external world; however, "these objects retain their prestige for power over him (the survivor) in the inner world. In a word, s/he is 'possessed' by them, as if by evil spirits." (ibid., p. 67)

Fairbairn argues that the ego seeks relationships with these internal objects; and that repression is primarily directed against these internalised objects. Once internalised and repressed, these objects are both unsatisfying and frustrating, and tempting and alluring; retaining both contradictory qualities simultaneously. This causes a great deal of ambivalence. The individual deals with this in the following way: 1) by splitting the individual into two objects, one good and one bad;

2) by internalising the bad object in an attempt to control it; 3) by splitting the internalised bad object in turn into two objects, a) the exciting or needed object, and b) the rejecting object; 4) by repressing both these objects and using aggression in the process; and 5) by using further aggressing in splitting off from her central ego and repressing two subsidiary egos (the libidinal ego and the saboteur ego, so challenging Freud's tripartite structure of the psyche) which remain attached to these internalised objects. This gives rise to the multiplicity of ego (identity) that we associate with trauma-related dissociation. It is also important to note that this attachment to bad internalised objects is additionally a means of avoiding being objectless and abandoned. This is why individuals who have been abused tend to cling to painful experiences because it enables them to continue relating to relationships with bad internal objects (ibid.).

These three points bring us to the twin experiences of survivor "guilt", and the politics of anonymity. Whether conscious or unconscious, the acceptance of a perpetrator-defined identity usually, in torture situations, involves impossible situations in which the survivor is made complicit in the harming of others. This does not lead to guilt; it leads to shame. Shame is a far more intense and pathological emotional experience in which the whole self, not simply a behaviour, is considered inferior, defective, flawed, contaminated and deserving of traumatic events. Lynd (1958) captures shame's pervasiveness and effect on the whole self by explaining that:

> An experience of shame of the sort I am attempting to describe cannot be modified by addition, or wiped out by subtraction, or exorcised by expiation. It is not an isolated act that can be detached from the self. It carries the weight of "I cannot have done this. But I have done it and I cannot undo it, because this is I." (ibid., p. 50)

Shame silences. The literature emphasises the speechlessness associated with shame, and the difficulty of expressing shame inducing experiences concisely in language (Lewis, 1971; Lewis, 1992). It is not only medico-legal reasons that kept Anna from publishing this memoir, it is also a continuing, deep-seated shame associated with her complicity in the pain of others. In holding onto a perpetrator defined, shameful identity, she has become "the principle of his (her) own subjection" (Foucault, 1977, p. 202–203), she lugs the burden of "badness" and shame because it is more bearable to believe that she is bad, and so in control, than to accept that her loved perpetrators, whose abuse was arbitrary and unpredictable, are bad. Through internalising them, she also avoids abandonment from them, which is frightening because traumatic bonding results in emotionally intense relationships. Some of these processes are pathological, yet protective in the short term. She tells us that there are massive disadvantages to allowing her shame to continue to silence her into withholding her name and her story. She feels that once again she is making herself complicit with the perpetrators, that she is facilitating the continued power differential between them. That she is sending a message that what she says in this memoir should perhaps not be believed, that it has little credibility, and therefore she should, among other reasons, be ashamed. At the very thought, she says, I feel myself imploding, and the need to say, scream, shriek my name and my story curls from under my very fingertips. My time will come, she says. A time when I will feel no ambivalence; when I have kicked the perpetrators off my back, spat them out of my system once and for all, and consistently believe in their, rather than my own, badness. When I can face being abandoned by them, and believe in an alternative identity not defined by complicity and shame. In this dreadful spirit, I conclude this epilogue with a quote from Primo Levi (1975) chosen by Anna to describe the futility of words, contradicted by the perpetual drive to express, a man so closely acquainted with survivor "guilt" (shame)—so much so that he himself could not survive his own survival:

> It is possible to demonstrate that this completely arbitrary story is nevertheless true. I could tell innumerable other stories, and they would all be true: all literally true, in the nature of the transitions, in their order and data. The number of atoms is so great that one could always be found whose story coincides with any capriciously invented story. I could recount an endless number of stories about carbon atoms that become colors or perfumes in flowers; of others which, from tiny algae to small crustaceans to fish, gradually return as carbon dioxide to the waters of the sea, in a perpetual, frightening round-dance of life and death, in which every devourer is immediately devoured; of others which instead attain a decorous semi-eternity in the yellowed pages of some archival document, or the canvas of a famous painter; or those to which fell the privilege

of forming part of a grain of pollen and left their fossil imprint in the rocks for our curiosity; of others still that descended to become part of the mysterious shape-messengers of the human seed, and participated in the subtle process of division, duplication, and fusion from which each of us is born. Instead, *I will tell just one more story, the most secret, and I will tell it with the humility and restraint of him who knows from the start that his theme is desperate, his means feeble, and the trade of clothing facts in words is bound by its very nature to fail* [emphasis added].

It is again among us, in a glass of milk. It is inserted in a very complex, long chain, yet such that almost all of its links are acceptable to the human body. It is swallowed; and since every living structure harbors a savage distrust toward every contribution of any material of living origin, the chain is meticulously broken apart and the fragments, one by one, are accepted or rejected. One, the one that concerns us, crosses the intestinal threshold and enters the bloodstream: it migrates, knocks at the door of a nerve cell, enters, and supplants the carbon which was part of it. This cell belongs to a brain, and it is my brain, the brain of the me who is writing; and the cell in question, and within it the atom in question, is in charge of my writing, in a gigantic miniscule game which nobody has yet described. It is that which at this instant, issuing out of a labyrinthine tangle of yeses and nos, makes my hand run along a certain path on the paper, mark it with these volutes that are signs: a double snap, up and down, between two levels of energy, guides this hand of mine to impress on the paper this dot, here, this one. (ibid., p. 232)

References

Fairbairn, W. R. D. (1943). The repression and return of bad objects. In: D. E. Scharff & E. F. Birtles (Eds.), *Psychoanalytic Studies of the Personality* (pp. 59–82). London: Tavistock, 1952.

Foucault, M. (1977). *Discipline and Punish: The Birth of the Prison.* A. Sheridan (Trans.). London: Penguin.

Frank, A. (1995). *The Wounded Storyteller: Body, Illness and Ethics.* Chicago, IL: University of Chicago.

Kluger, R. (2001). *Landscapes of Memory: A Holocaust Girlhood Remembered.* New York: Bloomsbury.

Levi, P. (1975). *The Periodic Table*. New York: Knopf.

Lewis, H. B. (1971). *Shame and Guilt in Neurosis*. New York: International Universities.

Lewis, M. (1992). *Shame: The Exposed Self*. New York: Free.

Lynd, H. M. (1958). *On Shame and the Search for Identity*. New York: Harcourt, Brace.

Orange, D. M., Atwood, G. E., & Stolorow, R. D. (1997). *Working Intersubjectively: Contextualism in Psychoanalytic Practice*. New York: Analytic.

Scarry, E. (1985). *The Body in Pain: The Making and Unmaking of the World*. New York: Oxford University.

Shapiro, J. (2011). Illness narratives: reliability, authenticity and the empathic witness. *Medical Humanities, 37*(2): 68–71.

INDEX

abuse *see also* child sexual abuse,
    organised abusers, ritual
    abuse, ritual abuse and mind
    control, satanic ritual abuse
  believing abuse incident, 114–115
  exposing abuser, 28
  organised abusers, 25
  survivor condition, 163
access training of alter personalities,
    227–230
acute dissociative reaction to stress,
    195–196
aggression, 251, 262
aggressor, 9
Aglan, A., 173
Agrawal, A. L., 193
Aksoy-Poyraz, C., 188, 193
Aktan, M., 194
Akyüz, G., 90, 95, 128, 135, 184,
    187–188, 191, 193, 200, 241
Aldridge-Morris, R., 164
Alev, L., 95
Alexander, K. W., 173

Alexander, P. J., 98
Alioğlu, F., 135, 187–188, 200
Allison, R. B., 18, 112
Alpak, G., 187
alterations in consciousness, 73
altered states of consciousness, 236
alters, 245–249 *see also* dissociative
    identity disorder (DID)
  clash of, 5
  cooperative personality alter, 92
  final alter, 49–50
  first alter, 29–30
  personalities, 224–225
  personality training, 227–230
  separation of, 224
Alyanak, B., 186, 191, 196–198, 201
American Psychiatric Association
    (APA), 96, 134, 181
amnesia, 63, 75, 92–94, 97, 102,
    113, 117, 122, 126, 133, 236
  dissociative, 122, 184–185,
    189, 195–196
  infantile, 173

Anna, xix, xxii, xxiv, xxviii, 45, 48,
    57–58, 164, 262–263
Anna (Korean immigrant to USA),
    99–100
Annalise, 11–12, 23–24, 29–30, 35–37,
    45–46, 49–53, 260 see also Kali,
    Precious, Triumph
anxiety and substance use disorders,
    197–198
apparently normal part of personality
    (ANP), xxii, 70, 76, 119–120,
    126
Arnold, M. M., 173
artificial somnambulism, 63–64
Atmaca, M., 193
attachment, 53, 119, 183–185, 190, 192,
    223, 230, 234, 250, 262
    disorder, DID as, 75, 197, 246
    disorganised, 75, 124
    entangled, 23–24
    figure, xxviii
    pattern, xxii, xxvi, 23
    -related dissociation, 183
attention deficit hyperactivity disorder
    (ADHD), 198
Atwood, G. E., 259
autistic spectrum DID, 212–213
autobiographical memory, 21
Avis, J. M., 175
Azam, E., 62, 64, 93

Bach-Loreaux, Mary, 30–35
Bakim, B., 191, 193, 195–196, 201
Barach, P., 75, 183, 246
Barnes, M., 246
Basch, Michael Franz, 251
Bates, B. L., 164
Battegay, R., 190
Baubet, T., 135
Beck, M., 41
    accusation on, 43–44
    Leaving the Saints, 43
    in support of, 45
Beck Anxiety Inventory (BAI), 138
Beck Depression Inventory (BDI), 138
Becoming Yourself, 17, 26

Beere, D. B., 184–185
Benedetta Carlini, tale of, 92
Bennett, E. S., 112
Bennett, Paula, 37–41
Berkowitz, A. S., 77
Berlin, H. A., 198
Bernstein, E. M., 72
Berry, J., 95
Bhugra, D., 98
Bhuvaneswar, C., 194
Bianchi, I., 75
Binet, A., 65
bipolar mood disorder, 126–127, 189, 198
Birt, A. R., 174
Bleuler, E., 69
Bliss, E. L., 72
Block, S. D., 173
Blood, L., 222
Blume, E. Sue, 14, 24–25
    Secret Survivors, 24–25
Boals, A., 173
Boatin, A., 182
Boe, T., 95
Boon, S., 95, 118
Boor, M., 112
borderline personality disorder (BPD),
    184–185, 191–193, 196, 198
Bos, M., 236
Bourguignon, E., 96
Bouri, M., 98
Bourneville, D., 61, 63
Bourru, H., 62, 64
Bowers, M., 71
Bowlby, J., 183
Boysen, G. A., 104
Bozkurt, O., 191, 193, 196, 201
Brand, B. L., 77–79, 121, 200, 242
Braun, B. G., 72, 113, 142, 236–239
Brecher-Marer, S., 71
Breeman, L., 77
Bremner, J. D., 118, 120–121, 173, 238
Breuer, J., 64, 66
Brewin, C. R., 122, 186
Brockman, R., 98
Brodsky, B. S., 185
Bromberg, P., 74

Brothers, D., 250
Brown, D., 73, 92, 117, 122
Brown, P., 66
Bryant, R. A., 175
Bülbül, F., 187
Burnham, D. L., 190
Burot, P., 62, 64
Butler, J., 95, 172
Buyukbayram, A., 193

Cakir, Ü., 187
Campbell, R. A., 135
Campion, J., 98
Camuset, L., 64, 93
Canetti, L., 120–121
Cardeña, E., 73, 78, 134–135
Carlson, E. B., 64, 72, 75, 78, 193,
        120, 124
case of
    Eve, 71
    Louis Vivet, 64–65
Castillo, R., 98
Chalavi, S., 76, 78
Chan, Y. H., 100
Chande, A., 127
chaos narratives, 259–260
Charcot, J. M., 94
Charney, D. S., 118, 120
Chaturvedi, S. K., 95
Chaves, J. F., 78, 112, 125
Chefetz, R., 74, 195, 239
Chen, J., 95
child sexual abuse (CSA), 74, 117, 166,
        173–174, 225
Chodoff, P., 185
Chu, J. A., 113–115, 173
Clancy, S. A., 173–175
Clark, C. R., 142
Classen, C., 77, 120–121
Cleckley, H. M., 71, 112, 165
clinical psychopathology, 181
cognitive distortions, 5–6
compartmentalisation, 236
confidentiality, 4–5
conflict, 5
Connolly, D. A., 172

consciousness, 69
    alterations in, 73
    altered states of, 236
contextualisation, 164
controversies on DID, 111–113
conversion disorder, 73
Coons, P., 112, 233
Coons' study, 233–234
cooperative personality alter, 92
Cordon, I. M., 173
core dissociative phenomena,
        235–238
Corfield, V. A., 199
Corstens, D., 196
Courage, M. L., 173
Crabtree, A., 69
Craik, F. I. M., 119
Crapanzano, V., 101
creating dissociative disorders, 221,
        223–225
Creswell, J. W., 134–136, 142–143
Cronin, E., 200
cross-cultural perspectives DID,
        95, 104
    culture-bound disorders
        of identity, 91
    non-me entities, 96
    pathological possession, 97
cross-temporal perspectives DID,
        89, 91–95, 104
    belief in Satan, 91
    cooperative personality alter, 92
    exorcism, 92
    tale of Benedetta Carlini, 92
cult-created hand signals, 26
culture-bound disorders of identity, 91
curative factors in psychotherapy, 175

Dai, Y., 95
Dalenberg, C. J., 78
Das, J. A., 98
Davies, J. M., 74
Davis, W., 99
De Jong, 77, 97, 135
Dell, P. F., 76–77, 90, 136
Delport, C. S. L., 136

den Boer, J. A., 76, 78, 119, 125
de Rivera, J., 113
Desai, G., 95
Despine, C. A., 64, 93
detachment, 236
De Vos, A. S., 142
diagnostic challenge in DID,
        181–182, 184
difficulty in time concept, 6–7
Dijksterhuis, A., 236
Dikobe, A. M., 103
Dinges, D., 246
Ding, Q., 99
discrediting of survivors, 230–232
disorganised attachment
        (D-attachment), 75
dissociating dissociation *see also*
        dissociative identity disorder
        (DID)
    belief in severity of abuse, 114–115
    controversies on DID, 111–113
    false memory syndrome, 115–118
    in favour of, 113–114
    longitudinal studies, 124
    memory recovery, 128
    socio-cognitive model, 124–126
    trauma and dissociation, 120–122
    trauma and memory, 122–124
dissociation, 68, 183
    aggression, 9
    amnesia and DID, 184–185
    cases of, 64–65, 71
    in children and adolescents, 74
    clash of alters, 5
    cognitive distortions and
        misunderstandings, 5–6
    conceptualisation, 76–77
    confidentiality of study, 4–5
    conflict, 5
    consciousness, 69
    difficulty in time concept, 6–7
    dissociation, 68
    and dissociative disorders, 76
    dynamic state of, 183
    by external factors, 126
    across globe, 89

    handbook of, 74
    healing power of first
        person account, 9
    illustrative descriptions of, 92–95
    impact of going public, 9
    informed consent in clinical
        practice, 5
    integrative failure, 65–67
    issue in trust, 8–9
    lack of evidence, 127
    neurobiological basis of, 118–120
    in non-clinical populations, 95
    patients of, 211
    possession trance in, 134
    post-traumatic model of, 90
    and schizophrenia, 70
    shame, 7
    socio-cognitive model of, 90, 96
    and sociocultural influences, 78–79
    transferential contaminants to
        informed consent, 6
    transformations in, 8
    and trauma, 120–122
    trauma-dissociation theory, 165–166
    validity of, 96
dissociative amnesia and DID, 184–185
dissociative complexity, 70–71
dissociative depression, 187–189
dissociative disorder not otherwise
        specified (DDNOS), 133, 195,
        197
DSM-IV-TR, 96–97
Dissociative Disorders Interview
        Schedule (DDIS), 72
Dissociative Experiences Scale (DES),
        72, 136–137, 189
dissociative identity disorder (DID),
        4, 71, 74, 97–99, 128, 164, 233
        see also alters dissociating
dissociative phenomena, overlapping
        categories of, 236
dissociative prose style, 57
dissociative psychosis, 62–63
dissociative splitting physiology, 224
dissociative subtype of PTSD, 77
dissociative trance disorder (DTD), 95

Dissociative Trance Disorder Interview
Schedule (DTDIS), 138
Diveky, T., 189
Doğan, O., 78, 90, 95, 128, 193, 200,
241
Dorahy, M. J., 63, 71, 76, 78, 90, 104,
135, 186
double conscience, 63–64, 66
double personality, 70
Draijer, N., 95, 118
DSM-IV dissociative disorders, 72
During, E. H., 135
Dutra, L., 75

Easton, S., 114
Edelstein, R. S., 173
Egeland, B., 75, 124, 193
Eisen, M. L., 173
Elahi, F. M., 135
Ellason, J. W., 95, 186–187, 189–191,
194–195, 197, 199
Ellenberger, H. F., 64, 71, 93, 242
Elliott, D. M., 137
emotional part of personality (EP), 70,
76, 119
Emrich, H. M., 95
Emül, H. M., 188, 193
Ensink, K., 103
Enslaved Queen, The, 12, 18–19,
21, 23, 25, 222, 231
Erkiran, M., 197
Erol, T. C., 188, 193
Ertem-Vehid, H., 184, 191, 193
Eshun, S., 135
Espí Forcén, C., 135
ethical considerations, 143
evil spirit possession, 261
Evren, C., 197
exorcism, 92
experiences of DID patient, 133
analysis, 142–143
data collection, 139–142
discussion, 155–157
ethical considerations, 143
possession of unknown external
origin, 143–147

possession trance as diagnostic
criterion, 134
research methodology, 136–139
shifts in identity between
singularity and multiplicity,
147–155
eye movement desensitisation
reprocessing (EMDR), 77, 187

Fairbairn, W. R. D., 261
Fairbank, J. A., 77
false memory, 172–174
syndrome, 115–118
False Memory Syndrome Foundation
(FMSF), 115, 172
Fan, Q., 237, 239
Farrants, J., 172
Faure, H., 64
Feast of the Beast, 14
feelings of badness, 261
Feigon, E. A., 113
Félida X., 64
Ferenczi, S., 67
Ferracuti, S., 135
Ferrell, L., 192
Fertuck, E. A., 185
Fine, C. G., 64, 74, 77, 238, 241–242,
249, 253
Fischer, G., 75, 190
Flournoy, T., 93
Ford, J., 190
Forrest, K., 198
Foucault, M., 260, 262
theory of self-surveillance, 260–261
Fouché, C. B., 135–136, 142
Frank, A., 36, 259–260
Fraser, G. A., 74
Frawley, M. G., 74
French, C. C., 114
Freud, S., 64, 66–67, 217, 249
Frewen, P. A., 78
Frey, L. M., 114–115
Freyd, J. J., 113, 117, 122, 172–173,
185
Friedl, M. C., 95
Friedman, B., 72, 195

Frischholz, E., 237, 239
Fuchs, D. L., 186–187, 189–191, 194–195, 197, 199
functional neurological symptoms, 193–194

Gadit, A. A., 98
Gamze, A., 78
Ganaway, G. K., 78, 112, 125
Gangdev, P. S., 95
Ganzel, B. L., 113–115
Gardner, R. A., 115
Gast, U., 95
Gaw, A. C., 99
Gecici, O., 193
Geraerts, E., 173–174
Gergen, K., 165, 171
German-language dissociation organisation, 77
Gernaat, H. B. P. E., 77, 135
Ghetti, S., 173
Gibson, R. W., 190
Giesbrecht, T., 164
Ginzburg, K., 95
Gladstone, A. I., 190
Gleaves, D. H., 78, 90, 117
Glover, T. A., 173
Gmelin, E., 92
going public
    to help others, 3, 14, 29
    impact of, 9, 16
Gold, S. N., 117
Goldsmith, R. E., 111
Goldstein, E., 115
Gonzalez, A., 77
Good, B. J., 112
Good, M. I., 165
Goodhart, S. P., 69
Goodman, G. S., 173
Goodwin, J., 62, 92
Gordon, B., 172
Graafland, M., 122
Grambal, A., 189
Grant, C., 247
Greaves, D. H., 71, 172
Green, J. P., 90

Griffin, M. G., 122
Grisaru, N., 102
Grossman, L. R., 172
Gruzelier, J., 240
Güneş, C., 187
Gurung, D., 135

Hacking, I., 71, 165, 172
Hallibrun, M., 98
Halliburton, M., 135
Hammond, D. C., 73, 117
Handbook of Dissociation, 74
Harley, D., 135
Harris, L. S., 173
Hartocollis, L., 165–166
Harvey, A. G., 175
Haselrud, J., 95
Hauer, B. J. A., 173
Haunted Self, The, 76
healing factors, 176
healing power
    of first person account, 9
    of writing, 22–23
Healing the Unimaginable, 25
Hegeman, E., 135
Hemmings, S. M., 199
Henley, E. H., 135
Herman, J. L., 113, 164, 173
Hilgard, E. R., 71
Hill, J., 173
Hippocratic axiom, 4
Hirsch, I., 254
Hoffman, W., 12, 222, 231 see also Miller, Alison
    Becoming Yourself, 17
    difference in early memory, 21
    Enslaved Queen, The, 12, 18–19, 21, 23, 25, 222–231
    entangled attachments, 23–24
    explicit memory, 21
    exposing abuser group, 28
    Feast of the Beast, 14
    final alter, 49–50
    finding real-self, 20
    first alter of, 29–30
    life-changing decision, 17

link through family name, 20
mastermind controller, 19
mind control, 21–22
narration credibility, 27
nature of human spirit, 14
using own name, 12, 15–17, 19
perpetrators' names, 19
pseudonym, 17–20
publisher, 18
recovery, 26
ritual abuse, 13
safety concerns, 18
scary memoir, 12–23
somatoform memories, 21
straining to know truth, 14
writing for healing, 22–23
Hope, L., 114
Horst, R., 94
Horwitz, A. V., 164
Hough, R. L., 77
Howard, K. I., 112
Howe, M. L., 173
Howell, E. F., 67, 74, 190
Huber, M., 78
human experience inside diagnostic
    scheme, 200–202
Huntjens, R. J. C., 173
Huska, J. A., 137
hypnosis, 239–242
hypnotically induced division of
    personality, 63
hysteria, 66

iatrogenic DID, 172
identity
    confusion, 236
    construction under traumatic
        circumstances, 260
identity shift, 147–155
İdrisoğlu, H. A., 95
Illuminati, the, 15
image validity, 175
impulsivity and compulsivity, 198–199
infantile amnesia, 173
informed consent, 5
inner self-helper, 62

inner world and third reality
    phenomena, 237
Innis, R. B., 122
Insel, T., 201
integration of DID patients, 242–245
integrative failure, 65–67
internal working models (IWM), 183
International Society for the Study
    of Multiple Personality and
    Dissociation (ISSMP&D), 72
International Society for the Study
    of Trauma and Dissociation
    (ISST-D), 230
interpersonal nature of DID, 185
interpersonal phobia, 185
intimidation and shame, 218–220
Islam, F., 95, 135, 190
Itzkowitz, S., 67, 74
Iversen, S. D., 198

James, W., 68
Jäncke, L., 76, 78
Janet, P., 63–66, 69
Jaspers, K., 181
Jekal, A., 185
Jelenova, D., 189
Jelicic, M., 173–174
Joanna, 50–51
Jones, D. P. H., 173
Jordan, K., 77
Joseph, R., 122
Jung, C. G., 70
Juthani, N. V., 98

Kaehler, L. A., 185
Kaiz, M., 112
Kali, 49–50
Kamaradova, D., 189
Kapur, S., 119
Karabatak, O., 187
Karadag, F., 197
Karagoz, M., 197
Karpman, S. B., 183
Kenny, M. G., 164
Kernberg, O., 251
Kerner, J., 93

Kersten, J., 64
Keser, V., 191, 196, 201
Keyes, B. B., 95
Kianpoor, M., 101
Kienzler, H., 135
Kierkegaard, S., 188
Kihlstrom, 116, 172–173
Kiliç, Ö., 188, 193
Kilinçaslan, A., 186, 191–192,
        196–198, 201
Kim, U., 95
Kinnear, C. J., 199
Kirmayer, L., 135
Kirsch, I., 78, 112, 125
Kirshberg, A., 95
Kiziltan, E., 95, 186–187, 189–191,
        193–199, 201
Kleijn, W. I., 97, 135
Kleinman, A., 171
Kluft, R. P., 7, 64, 72–74, 77, 182, 184,
        187, 201, 233–234, 236–237,
        239–243, 246, 249, 252–253
Kluger, R., 260
Knudsen, H., 95
Kogan, I., 192
Kohut, H., 190, 249–251
Komproe, I. H., 78, 135
Koopman, C., 64, 120–121
Kora, M. E., 199
Kordackie, J., 113
Korf, J., 76, 78, 119
Kosslyn, S. M., 175
Koyuncu, A., 78, 194
Kramer, L., 95
Krüger, C., 90, 103–104, 186
Krystal, J., 118, 120
Kuğu, N., 184, 191, 193
Kuhn, T., 238
Kulka, R. A., 77
Kuloglu, M., 193
Kundakçi, T., 186–187, 189–191,
        193–199, 201
Kupperman, Kim Dana, 18

La Marca, R., 76, 78
Lanius, R. A., 77, 121
Lasko, N. B., 175

Latalova, K., 189
Lazzari, 135
Lehman, D. R., 174
Lensvelt-Mulders, G., 77
Lenzenweger, M. F., 174
Lessem, P., 251
Levack, B. P., 135
Levine, R. E., 99
Lewis, H. B., 262
Lewis-Fernandez, R., 182, 193
Lierens, 62, 92
Lilienfeld, S. O., 90, 78, 112, 125, 164
Lindsay, D. S., 112, 173
Liotti, D., 75, 183–184, 246
Lipman, L., 237, 239
Lochner, C., 199
Loewenstein, R. J., 73, 77–78, 121,
        164
Loftus, E. F., 172–173
Luechinger, R., 76, 78
Lundt, C., 104, 135
Lynd, H. M., 262
Lynn, S. J., 78, 90, 112, 125, 164
Lyons-Ruth, K., 75

MacHovec, F., 240
Macklin, M. L., 175
Mainerova, B., 189
Marino, G., 188
Marmar, C. R., 77, 120–121
Marquis de Puységur, 63
Martell, Y., 35
Martin, M. F., 164
Martínez-Taboas, A., 90, 95, 104, 135,
        182, 186, 193
Mataboge, C. K., 103
Matjave, M., 95
Mattanah, J. F., 200
Matthews, J. A., 113–115
Mayran, L. W., 95
Mazzoni, G., 112
McDermott, K. B., 172
McDougall, W., 70, 76
McHugh, P. R., 164
McKeown, J. M., 64, 242
McNally, R. J., 173–175
McNary, S., 77

Mechanic, M. B., 122
medial prefrontal cortex (MPFC), 118
Memon, A., 112
memory
    distortion, 174
    early, 21
    reconstitution, 225
    recovery, 128, 172–173
    wars, 172
memory and DID
    agreements, disagreements,
        166–172
    attention-seeking, 172
    contextualising, 164
    curative factors in psychotherapy,
        175
    false memories, 173–174
    healing factors, 176
    iatrogenesis, 172
    memory distortion, 174
    and trauma-dissociation theory,
        165–166
    validity of source of image in brain,
        175
Mercer, J., 135
Merckelbach, H., 164, 173–174
Merskey, H., 64, 78, 96, 111, 126–128,
        164
Metzler, R. J., 120–121
Michelson, L. K., 74
Mickes, L., 173
Middleton, W., 90, 95, 104, 186
Milchman, M. S., 173
Miller, A., 16, 17, 24 see also
        Hoffman, W.
    Becoming Yourself, 26
    credibility of Hoffman's narration,
        27
    Healing the Unimaginable, 25
    kind of writing, 58
mind control, 21–22, 222–224
mind controlling perpetrator
        groups, 223
Minton, K., 75
Mitchell, S. L., 64
Modestin, J., 95
Moffatt, J., 92

Mollon, P., 212–215, 217
Moolman-Smook, J. C., 199
Moore, S. A., 173
Moreau de Tours, J. J., 93
Morgan, D. Y., 173
Moro, M. R., 135
Moroz, T. M., 119
Morris, M. C., 185
Moscovitch, M., 119
Moskowitz, A., 69–70, 78, 196
Mosquera, D., 77
Motlana, L. M., 103
Mulhern, S., 111
Multidimensional Inventory of
        Dissociation (MID),
        77, 136–137
multiple personality disorder (MPD),
        62, 71, 73–75, 233
    clinical perspectives on, 74
multiple reality disorder, 237
Murphy, P. E., 95
Myers, C. S., 70, 93
Myers, F., 68
Myrick, A., 77

name significance, 20
Nathan, D., 172
Nathanson, D., 7, 251–252
National Institute of Mental Health
        (NIMH), 4
Nemiah, J. C., 72
Ness, L., 135
Neupane, D., 135
neutral identity system (NIS), 125
neutral personality state (NPS), 119
Newton, B. W., 71
Ng, B. Y., 100
Nibley, H., 43
Nickel, V., 95
Niehaus, D. J., 199
Nieuwenhuis, J., 135
Nijenhuis, E. R. S., 63, 73, 76–78, 119–120,
        125, 135, 185–186, 194, 239
Noble, Kim, 46–48
    All of Me, 48
Noblitt, R., 222
non-me entities, 96

Nordgren, L., 236
Norton, G. R., 114

Offer, D., 112
Ofshe, R., 172
Ogawa, J. R., 75, 124, 193
Ogden, P., 75
Ogle, C. M., 173
Önder, C., 186, 191–192, 196–198, 201
O'Neil, J. A., 76
Orange, D. M., 259
organised abuse, 25, 28, 228, 230–231
Orne, M. T., 164, 241, 246
Orr, S. P., 175
Ost, J., 114
other specified dissociative disorder
        (OSDD), 134–136, 138–139,
        141, 196
Özdemir, O., 191, 196, 201
Özmen, M., 188, 193
Özpulat, T., 191, 196, 201
Öztürk, E., 78, 184, 186–194, 196, 198–200
Öztürk, M., 199

Paans, A. M. J., 76, 78, 119
Pain, C., 75, 77
Paris, J., 90
Pastucha, P., 189
Patel, S., 182
pathological possession, 97
peace, chasing, 45–46
Peluso, J. P., 173
Peri, T., 120–121
peri-traumatic dissociation, 77, 120
perpetrator
        ambivalence towards, 11
        emotional enmeshment with, 23–24
        name of, 19
personality disorders, 189–191
personality dissociation, 61
Peter, B., 78
Petersen, B., 44
Pickles, A., 173
Pineda, A., 173
Piotrowski, Z., 71
Piper, A., 96, 111

Pitillo, E., 242
Pitman, R. K., 174–175
Plano Clark, V. L., 134, 136
Pope, K. S., 116
porous personality, 212
Porter, S., 174
Posner, M., 237, 239
possession
        literature on, 131
        trance as diagnostic criterion, 134
        of unknown external origin, 143–147
possession trance disorder (PTD), 97
        in the African syncretist context,
                102–104
        in a Confucian context, 99–100
        in a Hindu context, 98–99
        a Muslim context, 100–102
post-traumatic division of personality, 76
post-traumatic model (PTM), 124–125
post-traumatic Stress Checklist—
                Civilian (PCL-C), 137
post-traumatic stress disorder (PTSD),
                120, 186–187
Powell, R. A., 78, 112, 125
Prasko, J., 189
Pressley, M., 172
Prince, M., 68, 94
programming, 17, 25, 226–227
pseudonym, 17–20, 35–37
        Annalise, 41–43
        Bennett, P., 37–41
        British survivor, 50–51
        chasing peace, 45–46
        Kali, 49–50
        Triumph, 51–53
psychiatric comorbidity of DID, 181
        acute dissociative reaction to stress,
                195–196
        anxiety and substance use
                disorders, 197–198
        attachment-related dissociation, 183
        bipolar mood disorder, 189
        borderline personality disorder,
                191–193
        diagnostic and therapeutic
                considerations, 199–200

diagnostic challenge in DID,
    181–182, 184
dissociative amnesia and DID,
    184–185
dissociative depression, 187–189
dynamic state of dissociation, 183
functional neurological symptoms,
    193–194
human experience inside of
    diagnostic scheme, 200–202
impulsivity and compulsivity,
    198–199
interpersonal nature of DID, 185
interpersonal phobia, 185
personality disorders, 189–191
post-traumatic stress disorder,
    186–187
psychotic disorders, 195
schizo-dissociative disorder, 196–197
somatic symptom disorder, 194–195
psychoanalysis and dissociation, 75
psychotherapy of DID, 252–253
psychotic disorders, 195
Putnam, F. W., 4, 72, 74, 77, 90, 124, 127

Quas, J. A., 173

Ray, W. J., 74
Raymond, E. S., 186
Raz, A., 237, 239
Read, J. D., 112, 172
reading the mind in the eyes test
    (RMET), 185
real-self, 20
recovered memory, 172–173
    therapy, 43
Redlich, A. D., 173
reflections on treatment, 233, 253–254
    addressing alters, 245–249
    Coons' study, 233–234
    core dissociative phenomena,
        235–238
    empirically derived approach
        to psychotherapy of DID,
        252–253
    hypnosis, 239–242

integration of DID patients,
    242–245
knowledge lost, 234
marginalisation of self-psychology,
    249–251
overlapping categories of
    dissociative phenomena, 236
paradigms and secondary loss,
    238–239
shame, 252
treatment outcome, 233
Wilbur's practices, 234
Reinders, A. A. R. S., 76, 78, 119, 125
Reis, R., 102, 135
repression against internalised objects,
    261–262
Resick, P. A., 122
restitution narratives, 259–260
Rhodes, G. F., 95, 101
Rhue, J. W., 90
Rieber, R., 71
Riedesser, P., 190
ritual abuse, xxii, xxvii–xxviii, 13,
    23, 25, 28, 41, 89, 163 see also
    satanic ritual abuse
ritual abuse and mind control, 13, 15,
    18, 26, 221
    access training of alter
        personalities, 227–230
    alter personalities, 224–225
    creating dissociative disorders,
        221, 223
    deliberate recruitment of victims,
        225–227
    discrediting of survivors, 230–232
    mind control, 222–224
    mind controlling perpetrator
        groups, 223
    physiology of dissociative splitting,
        224
    by religious groups, 222
    secrecy, 223
    separation of alters, 224
    traumatic memory
        reconstitution, 225
    worship with sexual violence, 222

Rivers, W., 67, 115
Robertson, B., 103
Rodewald, F., 95
Roediger, H. L., 172
Rolls, E. T., 198
Ronfeldt, H. M., 120–121
Rosenfeld, H., 212
Rosik, C. H., 115
Ross, C. A., 69–70, 72, 74, 90, 95–96,
        114, 127, 135, 164, 182, 184,
        186–187, 189, 190–192,
        194–197, 199
Rosser-Hogan, R., 120
Rubin, D. C., 173

Saadon, M., 102, 104
Sacco, R., 135
Sachs, A., 113, 237, 239
Sachs, R. G., 201
Sainton, K., 95
Sakarya, D., 187
Salter, M., 225
Sapkota, R., 135
Şar, V., 78, 90, 95, 104, 128, 135, 182, 184,
        186–201, 241
Sarbin, T. R., 78, 112, 125
Satan, 91
satanic ritual abuse (SRA), 37–38, 41,
        74, 112, 248
Saywitz, K. J., 173
Scarry, E., 260
scary memoir, 12–23
Schacter, D. L., 173–174
Schäfer, I., 78
Schatzow, E., 113
Scheflin, A. W., 73, 117
schizo-dissociative disorder, 196–197
schizophrenia, 69–70
Schlenger, W. E., 77
Schlumpf, Y. R., 76, 78
Schmahl, C., 121
Schore, A. N., 198
Schreiber, F. R., 71, 120–121
Schreiber, S., 165, 234, 242
Schroeder, E., 75, 135, 192
Schurink, W., 135, 142
secrecy, 223

Seedat, S., 199
Sekine, Y., 95
self-psychology marginalisation, 249–251
Seligman, R., 135
separation of alters, 224
sexual violence and worship, 222
Shah, S. K., 135
Shahay, R. N., 98
Shalev, A. Y., 120–121
Shaligram, D., 95
shame, 7, 214–215, 252
    -based identities, 261
    intimidation and, 218–220
    speechlessness, 262–264
shame and DID, 211, 214
    autistic spectrum DID, 212–213
    case of intimidation and shame,
        218–220
    patients of DID, 211
    porous personality, 212
    transferences of interpersonal
        trauma, 215–216
    trauma-derived DID, 213–218
Shapiro, J., 259
Shawahday Bakri, R., 95
Shobe, K. K., 173
Shor, R., 240
Showalter, E., 164, 166
Sidis, B., 68–69
Siegel, D., 21
Silberg, J., 77
simultaneous executive activity, 237
Sinason, V., 74
Singer, J., 75, 176
singularity and multiplicity, 147–155
situationally accessible memory
        (SAM), 123
Sizemore, C., 242
Smeets, E., 173–174
Smith, S. M., 172
socio-cognitive model (SCM), 124–126
Sokudela, B. F., 103
somatic symptom disorder, 194–195
somatoform
    dissociative symptoms, 63
    manifestations of dissociation, 71–72
    memories, 21

Somatoform Dissociation
    Questionnaire (SDQ-20), 137
Somer, E., 91–92, 95, 101–102, 104
Song, I., 185
Southwick, S. M., 118, 120
Spanos, N. P., 90, 104, 112, 172
speechlessness, 262–264
Spiegel, D., 73, 75–78, 97, 120–121, 135,
    172, 194, 239
Spinhoven, P., 194
spirit, nature of human, 14
Spitzer, B., 175
Srivastava, D. K., 98
Sroufe, A., 75, 193, 124
Stanley, B., 185
Steele, K., 63, 76, 77, 119–120,
    185, 239
Stein, D. J., 199
Steinberg, M., 72–73, 138, 182
Stolorow, R. D., 259
Strasburger, H., 194
Structured Clinical Interview for
    DSM-IV Dissociative
    Disorders (SCID-D), 72
Structured Clinical Interview for
    DSM-IV Dissociative
    Disorders—Revised
    (SCID-D-R), 138
Stuss, D. T., 119
subgenual anterior cingulate cortex
    (sgACC), 124
survivor, British, 50–51
Swartz, L., 102, 135
Sybil, 71, 112, 127, 165, 172, 234
Symptom Checklist 90—Revised
    (SCL-90-R), 137

Tagliavini, G., 183
Taieb, O., 135
Tamar-Gürol, D., 197
Tamarkin, G., 95
Targic, I. L., 187, 191
Taves, A., 135
Taycan, O., 188, 193
Taylor, E., 68, 164
Taylor, W., 71
Tecer, Ö., 188, 193

Terhune, D. B., 134–135
Tezcan, E., 193
Theory of Structural Dissociation of the
    Personality (TSDP), 125
Thigpen, C. H., 71, 112, 165
Tichenor, V., 120
Timmer, S., 173
transferences of interpersonal trauma,
    215–216
transferential contaminants to
    informed consent, 6
Traub, C. M., 111–113, 119, 124
trauma
    -derived DID, 213–218
    and dissociation, 120–122
    -dissociation model, 165
    generated dissociation, 74
    and memory, 122–124
trauma identity system (TIS), 125
trauma-related dissociation of
    personality, 61, 79
    1980s work, 71–72
    1990s work, 72–75
    nineteenth century work, 63–68
    twentieth century work, 68–71
    twenty-first century work, 75–78
Trauma Symptom Inventory—2
    (TSI-2), 137
Traumatic Experiences Checklist
    (TEC), 137
traumatic memories with DID, 73–74
traumatic personality state (TPS), 119
Triumph, 51–53
trust issue, 8–9
truth, straining to know, 14
Tulving, E., 119
Türkoğlu, R., 95
Tutkun, H., 95, 182, 186–187, 189–191,
    193–197, 199, 201, 241
Twombly, J. H., 77, 187

Uchinuma, Y., 95
Ülkü, C., 187
Ullman, R., 250
Ulrich, A., 194
Ünal, S. N., 198
Ural, C., 198

Üre, I., 187
Urquiza, A., 173

validity of image source in brain, 175
Van Baaren, L., 236
Van der Hart, O., 62–64, 66, 71–72,
    76–77, 92, 94, 119–120, 122,
    185, 194–195, 239
Van der Kloet, D., 164
Van der Kolk, B. A., 66, 72
Van der Merwe, 3
Van Duijl, M., 78, 97, 134–135,
Van Dyck, R., 194
Van Heerden, J., 173–174
Van Minnen, A., 173
Van Ochten, J. M., 77
Van Osch, M. J. P., 76, 78
Van Son, M. J. M., 77
VanBergen, A., 104
Vanderlinden, J., 194
Varma, L. P., 98
ventral-medial prefrontal cortex
    (vmPFC), 124
verbally accessible memory (VAM), 122
Vermetten, E., 76, 121
victim recruitment, 225–227
Vos, H. P. J., 76, 78, 119, 125
Vrbova, K., 189

Wager, N., 173
Waldvogel, B., 194
Waller, N., 124
Wang, L., 95
Wang, Z., 95
Ward, C. H., 138
Watkins, J. G., 71, 113, 249
Weber, D. L., 122
Weder, E. V., 76, 78
Weiner, L. A., 134–135
Weinfield, N. S., 75, 124, 193
Weiss, D. S., 77, 120–121
Wessel, I., 173
Wieland, S., 77
Wiesel, E., 89
Wig, N. N., 98

Wilbur, C., 234
Willemsen, A. T. M., 76, 78, 119, 125
Williams, J. M. G., 173
Wilson, S. T., 185
Winfrey, O., 44
Winkelman, M., 191
Winocur, G., 119
Winograd, E., 173
Witztum, E., 102, 195
Wolcott, H. F., 136
Wolf, E. S., 249
Wood, M. E., 111
worship and sexual violence, 222
Wright, D. B., 114
writing
    Beck, M., 43–46
    for healing, 22–23
    Noble, K., 46–48
    with own name, 12, 15–17,
        19, 30–35
    under pseudonym, 12, 16, 17
Wyatt, 43, 44
Wyman, B., 185

Xiao, Z., 95
Xu, Y., 95

Yan, H., 95
Yanik, M., 95
Yargic, L. I., 95, 182, 186, 189–191,
    194–197, 199, 201, 241
Yazici, A., 194
Yongmi Yi, K., 99
Young, W. C., 111, 113
Yu, J., 95
Yücel, B., 194
Yuille, J. C., 174

Zemach, E., 67
Zhang, H., 95
Zimmermann, E., 76, 78
Zoellner, L. A., 173
Zoroglu S. S., 186, 201, 191–192,
    196–198
Zou, Z., 95